W9-BTO-909

Elizabethan England

Other Books in the Turning Points Series:

Turning | Points
IN WORLD HISTORY

Elizabethan England

Laura Marvel, *Book Editor*

Bonnie Szumski, *Editorial Director*
Scott Barbour, *Managing Editor*

Greenhaven Press, Inc., San Diego, California

Library of Congress Cataloging-in-Publication Data

Elizabethan England / Laura Marvel, editor.
    p. cm. — (Turning points)
   Includes bibliographical references and index.
   ISBN 0-7377-0483-7 (pbk. : alk. paper)
   ISBN 0-7377-0484-5 (lib. : alk. paper)
   1. Great Britain—History—Elizabeth, 1558–1603. 2. England—Civilization—16th century. I. Marvel, Laura. II. Turning points (Greenhaven Press)
DA355 .E59 2002
942.05'5—dc21
                                     2001033972
                                            CIP

Cover photo: The Bridgeman Art Library International Ltd.
Library of Congress, 35, 139

© 2002 by Greenhaven Press, Inc.
P.O. Box 289009, San Diego, CA 92198-9009

Printed in the U.S.A.

Contents

Chapter 3: Cultural Turning Points

able. At the same time significant advances in literacy contributed to a growing audience for printed literature.

Chapter 4: Conquests and Discoveries

Elizabeth's effort to maintain a balance of power in Europe, her use of her principal secretaries as chief officers of foreign affairs, and her creation of a corps of professional diplomats show clear evidence of a step toward creation of a distinctive foreign policy office.

Although the famous defeat of the Spanish Armada in 1588 inspired Spain to build up naval strength to continue its assault on England, the English achieved a different kind of victory during the eighteen-year war. English privateering (private assaults on enemy ships) during the war helped establish England's reputation as an enterprising maritime power.

Although Sir Walter Raleigh was not among the 107 men who established the first Virginia colony on Roanoke Island in 1585, Raleigh organized the exploratory expedition that claimed Virginia for Queen Elizabeth, and he convinced Elizabeth that colonization of America was in England's national interest.

Foreword

Certain past events stand out as pivotal, as having effects and outcomes that change the course of history. These events are often referred to as turning points. Historian Louis L. Snyder provides this useful definition:

> A turning point in history is an event, happening, or stage which thrusts the course of historical development into a different direction. By definition a turning point is a great event, but it is even more—a great event with the explosive impact of altering the trend of man's life on the planet.

History's turning points have taken many forms. Some were single, brief, and shattering events with immediate and obvious impact. The invasion of Britain by William the Conqueror in 1066, for example, swiftly transformed that land's political and social institutions and paved the way for the rise of the modern English nation. By contrast, other single events were deemed of minor significance when they occurred, only later recognized as turning points. The assassination of a little-known European nobleman, Archduke Franz Ferdinand, on June 28, 1914, in the Bosnian town of Sarajevo was such an event; only after it touched off a chain reaction of political-military crises that escalated into the global conflict known as World War I did the murder's true significance become evident.

Other crucial turning points occurred not in terms of a few hours, days, months, or even years, but instead as evolutionary developments spanning decades or even centuries. One of the most pivotal turning points in human history, for instance—the development of agriculture, which replaced nomadic hunter-gatherer societies with more permanent settlements—occurred over the course of many generations. Still other great turning points were neither events nor developments, but rather revolutionary new inventions and innovations that significantly altered social customs and ideas, military tactics, home life, the spread of knowledge, and the human condition in general. The developments of writing, gunpowder, the printing press, antibiotics, the electric light, atomic energy, television, and the computer, the last two of which have recently ushered in the world-altering information age, represent only some of these innovative turning points.

Each anthology in the Greenhaven Turning Points in World History series presents a group of essays chosen for their accessibility. The anthology's structure also enhances this accessibility. First, an introductory essay provides a general overview of the principal events and figures involved, placing the topic in its historical context. The essays that follow explore various aspects in more detail, some targeting political trends and consequences, others social, literary, cultural, and/or technological ramifications, and still others pivotal leaders and other influential figures. To aid the reader in choosing the material of immediate interest or need, each essay is introduced by a concise summary of the contributing writer's main themes and insights.

In addition, each volume contains extensive research tools, including a collection of excerpts from primary source documents pertaining to the historical events and figures under discussion. In the anthology on the French Revolution, for example, readers can examine the works of Rousseau, Voltaire, and other writers and thinkers whose championing of human rights helped fuel the French people's growing desire for liberty; the French *Declaration of the Rights of Man and Citizen*, presented to King Louis XVI by the French National Assembly on October 2, 1789; and eyewitness accounts of the attack on the royal palace and the horrors of the Reign of Terror. To guide students interested in pursuing further research on the subject, each volume features an extensive bibliography, which for easy access has been divided into separate sections by topic. Finally, a comprehensive index allows readers to scan and locate content efficiently. Each of the anthologies in the Greenhaven Turning Points in World History series provides students with a complete, detailed, and enlightening examination of a crucial historical watershed.

Introduction

Although England suffered poverty, plague, rebellion, and religious strife during Elizabeth's reign, the popular image of the period, which persists to the present day, is one of relative stability at home, energetic expeditions of discovery, and an unprecedented flowering of literary genius. Perhaps the common perception endures not only because Elizabeth herself cultivated an image that inspired confidence and a sense of national well-being but also because her earliest biographers (for political reasons of their own) repeated the official Elizabethan propaganda and, in the words of historian Christopher Haigh, "presented Elizabethan England as a golden age of wise rule and national achievement."[1] A growing number of historians have questioned the laudatory interpretation of Elizabeth and Elizabethan England; however, historian Lacey Baldwin Smith acknowledges the queen's expert manipulation of public opinion and credits Elizabeth with successfully courting popular acclaim and presenting herself as "the symbol of unity" that the people desired and to which "they could sacrifice their lives and give their hearts."[2] In Smith's opinion,

> Elizabeth's greatest accomplishment was her success in infusing her government and her realm with the confidence, pride, and energy that sent [Sir Francis] Drake around the globe, led [Sir Walter] Raleigh to plant nations in the wilderness of the New World, and inspired [William] Shakespeare to eulogize [England in his play *Richard II* as] "This royal throne of kings, this scepter'd isle/ . . . This precious stone set in the silver sea/ . . . This blessed plot, this earth, this realm, this England."[3]

Despite the common perception of Elizabethan England as a golden age, it was actually a time of contradictions. It was certainly an age of splendid achievement, but it was also an age of squalor. It was an age dominated by the queen and her court, and an age when England remained predominantly rural. It was an age of rapidly developing commerce and an age of deplorable poverty.

During Elizabeth's reign the population of England grew from under 3 million to over 4 million people, and about 90 percent of the population lived in the countryside. Rising population kept wages low and increased unemployment, yet overall production increased. Historian John Guy explains the situation:

> Agricultural improvement promoted economic growth at the cost of peasant distress; increased production generated prosperity for landlords and impoverishment for wage-earners. The main dynamic of change was growth, but the effect was to polarize society. . . . While the diet of the upper strata improved, their houses were bigger and more comfortable than before, and their furniture and tableware rose to new levels of sophistication, the diet of the poor deteriorated, and they lived in bare cottages or rural hovels.[4]

The upper strata included the hereditary aristocracy, the rapidly growing class of gentry (those who possessed property and therefore qualified for a coat of arms), and the yeoman freeholders of land. This group, perhaps 60,000 yeoman, nearly 15,000 gentry, and about 550 knights by 1603, prospered, but, according to Guy, "perhaps two-fifths of the population were on the margin of subsistence."[5]

London, England's largest city, grew astronomically during Elizabeth's reign. A city of perhaps 90,000 in 1550, London reached a population over 215,000 by 1603. Enterprising merchants and tradesmen in the cloth, leather, agricultural-implements, and household-goods businesses came to London and prospered. The indigent, underemployed, and unemployed also swelled the London population, living in poverty and misery in the overcrowded slums. As historians Frederic A. Youngs Jr., Roger B. Manning, Henry L. Snyder, and E.A. Reitan explain, for the upper ranks of society, London was, "a glittering Renaissance city . . . , the home of the Court and the hub of the legal world [as well as] the center of a social season with plays and amusements."[6] For the less fortunate, London was dangerous. They clarify that "crime was endemic, fire was a constant danger . . . , filth was everywhere because the crush of people placed impossible demands on the manifestly inadequate sanitary facilities, and sickness and the plague spread rapidly through the teeming population."[7]

Elizabethan England was certainly an age of splendid national achievement, but it was also an age of increasing economic and social inequality. That Queen Elizabeth was able to inspire her government and her people with the loyalty, confidence, and energy necessary for national achievement at sea and in the arts during times of economic and social distress is testimony to the effectiveness of the image she was able to cultivate and sustain.

Early Challenges for the Virgin Queen

Elizabeth was twenty-five when she ascended the throne of England. The daughter of Henry VIII and Anne Boleyn, Elizabeth was the third of Henry VIII's offspring to rule England. Elizabeth's half brother, Edward, became king at the age of nine when Henry VIII died in 1547. Elizabeth's half sister, Mary, became queen when Edward died in 1553. When Mary died in 1558, Elizabeth became queen and ruled for nearly half a century (1558–1603). The short reigns of Edward and Mary had bred confusion and suspicion in England. During Henry VIII's reign, the English church had retained the doctrine and liturgy of the Roman Catholic Church (even though it existed under royal rather than papal authority). During Edward's reign, the boy king's lord protector, John Dudley, duke of Northumberland, had imposed reformed Protestantism on the country. Mary was determined to reimpose Catholicism on England. She married Philip of Spain, a staunch Catholic, and persecuted Protestants on such a scale that she was remembered as "Bloody Mary." In addition, economic distress caused by an increasing population, a decreasing wool production and export, and a spiraling inflation produced unemployment, hunger, and rebellion. Elizabeth inherited a country suspicious of female rule and, in the words of Lacey Baldwin Smith, "floundering in spiritual and financial bankruptcy."[8]

To dispel the gloom that had settled on the country, Elizabeth held a coronation that projected an image of wealth, confidence, and strength. To alleviate her subjects' anxiety at the prospect of a second female ruler, she created an image of herself as both male and female. She artfully dramatized the masculine attributes she shared with her father, Henry VIII (intelligence and bravery), and she even appeared "in breastplate and helmet, mounted on a charger"[9] to address her troops at Tilbury, according to historians Sara Mendelson and Patricia Crawford. She also capitalized on the feminine characteristics that could move her subjects' love and loyalty by creating, in the words of Mendelson and Crawford, "a stage setting in which her subjects' obedience was translated into the romantic language of chivalry."[10] By presenting herself as the unattainable mistress, the Fairy Queen, the chaste goddess Diana, she encouraged her courtiers to woo and worship her. By presenting herself as the Virgin Mother, she reached out to the destitute and offered understanding and hope. As both male and female, Elizabeth proclaimed her self-sufficiency and established both her authority and benignity.

Although Elizabeth was urged to marry by her privy council, by Parliament, and by countless influential individuals in order to form a beneficial political alliance and to produce an heir, she remained single throughout her long reign. Some historians contend that she invited and rejected foreign suitors as part of her foreign policy negotiations. Other historians consider her decision to rule alone a means to mediate political rivalries at home. Historian Susan Doran believes that Elizabeth did in fact wish to marry, twice, but was too cautious and too politically adept to insist on her personal preference when any of her leading councilors opposed the match. "She listened to counsel, rejected controversial matches and in the event remained single."[11]

Religious Settlement and Fiscal Reform

To counter the suspicion and fear that the rapid religious reversals of the previous two reigns had bred, Elizabeth promoted nationalism over religious factionalism. Although she was hailed as the Protestant savior, she refused to align herself with Protestant radicals and instead attempted a compromise between Catholicism and Protestantism based on a broad consensus. In 1559 Elizabeth assumed the title of supreme governor of the Church of England, with Parliament's approval; a slightly amended form of the 1552 Protestant Prayer Book was also approved by Parliament in 1559. The Church of England resembled the Catholic Church in retaining bishops and parishes, but the liturgy prescribed by the Prayer Book was Protestant. Although the religious compromise offended extreme Protestants and extreme Catholics, it did relieve fear and suspicion among the masses, and the Church of England was generally popular. Since the religious settlement also reestablished the power of the monarch over the government of the church, the queen was able to promote the compromise as unifying and national. The church experienced periodic pressure from radical Protestants to further reform what Lacey Baldwin Smith calls its "rags of popery,"[12] but Elizabeth remained firmly committed to the Church of England as originally conceived, and by the 1580s Anglicanism had developed its unique form and liturgy as the middle way between unreformed Catholicism and radical Protestantism.

To rebuild the failing economy, the queen's government took several decisive steps during the early years of her reign. It withdrew debased coinage and issued a new currency that, according to Smith, "improved the foreign rate of exchange and netted the government a profit of forty-five thousand pounds." Elizabeth then paid off the debt she had inherited from the reign of her half sister, Mary. As Smith explains, "By 1562 the crown, for the first time since the days of Henry VII, lived on its own historic sources of income—about £250,000 in all—with only minimal help from Parliament."[13]

The Spanish Threat and Fear of Catholicism

Philip of Spain had been the husband of Elizabeth's half sister, Mary. In 1556, while married to Mary, he became King Philip II of Spain, but he was never crowned king of England. When Mary died in 1558, Elizabeth ascended the English throne unchallenged, and Philip II married Elizabeth Valois, the daughter of Henry II of France. During the first decade of Elizabeth's rule, Philip II of Spain, champion of and crusader for Catholicism, and Elizabeth, who resisted popular pressure to become the champion of Protestantism, were able to maintain diplomatic relations. However, popular hostility toward Spain and Elizabeth's decision to allow commercial and colonial ventures that antagonized Spanish shipping nearly led to war in 1568. Tension between the countries increased during the second decade of Elizabeth's reign. Sir Francis Drake's circumnavigation of the globe (1577–1580), which made Drake a national hero and netted his investors (who included the queen) huge profits primarily at Spain's expense, incensed Philip. According to historian Kenneth R. Andrews, Elizabeth's decisions to send aid to the rebellious Dutch, whom Philip was attempting to subdue, and to send Drake on a mission to "interrupt the flow of treasure to Philip's war machine"[14] in 1585 were designed to limit Philip's aggression and to sustain a European balance of power. However, Philip construed Elizabeth's actions as convincing evidence of the need for a direct assault on England. In 1585 Philip began to prepare his armada campaign.

Philip's mission was to destroy the meddling, middle-aged female whose birth and thus claim to the throne were illegitimate in the eyes of the Catholic world. (Pope Clement VII had resisted Henry VIII's demand for a divorce from his first wife, Katherine of Aragon, Mary's mother. When Henry married Anne Boleyn, Elizabeth's mother, the pope excommunicated Henry. Elizabeth's father was therefore a heretic in Philip's view; Boleyn was a whore; and Elizabeth was a bastard.) According to military historian Geoffrey Parker, Philip's plan was to gather an imposing armada of over a hundred vessels. The Spanish Armada was to sail to the Netherlands and escort the duke of Parma's army of experienced veterans to Kent. The army would then march through Kent and take London. Philip expected an English Catholic uprising to aid the invaders and had negotiated with Elizabeth's cousin, Mary Stuart, Queen of Scots, to effect the unseating of Queen Elizabeth.

Mary Stuart had been forced to abdicate the throne of Scotland in favor of her thirteen-month-old son, James, in 1567 and had fled to England at that time. She was staunchly Catholic and was considered by Philip and by some Catholics in England the legitimate heir to the English throne. She was the great-granddaughter of King Henry VII and the granddaughter of Henry VIII's sister, Margaret Tudor. Although Mary Stuart was allegedly involved in countless treasonous intrigues and ill-advised plots against Elizabeth's life through the nineteen years she spent in England, Elizabeth was reluctant to execute her cousin. Mary's presence in England and her plotting had heightened popular suspicion of Catholics, and Elizabeth had been forced to change her policy of moderation and toleration as a result of the increasingly strong anti-Catholic feeling in the country. Pressure from Nationalists and Protestants who insisted that the queen exterminate the "monstrous and huge dragon"[15] finally moved Elizabeth to sign the warrant for Mary's execution in 1587.

In 1588, when Philip had amassed his armada of 130 vessels, including huge Portuguese galleons and large, slow Spanish merchant ships, Mary was dead; nevertheless, Philip expected to execute the rest of his plan. The English met his armada with about 140 ships, of which around 60 were effective fighting ships. This fleet of fast, efficient English warships and private ships, armed with superior artillery, prevented the rendezvous of the Spanish Armada with the duke of Parma's forces in the Netherlands by outsailing and outgunning the Spanish. The Spanish Armada was forced to head north "to brave the storms of the North Atlantic and the inhospitable shores of Ireland," according to historian Kenneth R. Andrews.

> So far they had lost only a few ships; now many more were wrecked—probably as many as twenty on the Irish coast alone—and thousands of men died by drowning, starved to death or were captured ashore and slaughtered. In all some fifty vessels of the original fleet failed to return, and many of those which made Spanish ports were beyond repair.[16]

The English victory was spectacular, and it was celebrated as the triumph of Protestantism over England's enemy, Catholic Spain. Even though the 1588 battle inspired Spain to build up its naval strength and continue its assault on England, the 1580s were a decade of adventure, prosperity, and intense national pride, presided over by "a sovereign whose personality and showmanship managed to ignite the fire of boundless loyalty in most of her subjects,"[17] in the words of Lacey Baldwin Smith. The war with Spain was not officially concluded until Elizabeth's successor, James I (son of Mary, Queen of Scots), negotiated a peace treaty with Spain in 1604; nevertheless, the success of English privateers during the long sea war with Spain established England's reputation as an enterprising and formidable maritime power.

Exploration and Settlement

England's success at sea, and the willingness of entrepreneurial merchants to support and benefit from this success, aided the colonial ventures in the New World and in Ireland. It is not surprising that both colonization plans were related to English-Spanish foreign relations. Pope Alexander VI had issued a bull in 1493 that had divided the New World between Spain and Portugal, and both countries intended to keep their claim to the New World. Sir Walter Raleigh knew the risks involved in attempting to win the New World from Spain, but he sent an exploratory expedition to present-day North Carolina in 1584, claimed the land from Florida to Newfoundland for England, and convinced the queen that this newly claimed land should be named Virginia in her honor. Raleigh's friend, Richard Hakluyt, wrote a treatise to persuade Elizabeth that English colonization of the New World was in fact in England's national interests, and Elizabeth agreed to support Raleigh's colonizing plan. Not wishing to openly defy Spain's claim to the New World, Elizabeth assigned responsibility for the colony to Raleigh. Raleigh's cousin, Richard Grenville, led the 1585 Virginia voyage that established a colony of 107 men on Roanoke Island. Although the colony sustained itself for only a year—and the disenchanted settlers were rescued by Sir Francis Drake and taken back to England—Raleigh continued his efforts to establish an English colony in the New World. The second Virginia colony, established in 1587, had disappeared by 1590, and a permanent English colony at Jamestown would not be established until 1607, during James I's reign; nevertheless, Raleigh succeeded in connecting forever the name of Elizabeth the Virgin Queen to Virginia in the New World.

English settlement in Ireland was a response to a perceived threat. Turbulent, Catholic Ireland was considered a threat to national security not only because of the subversive manifestations of popery in Ireland itself but also because Catholic Spain might consider Catholic Ireland a convenient backdoor for invasion of England. Colonial settlement in Ireland was justified as a means to minimize the Catholic and Spanish threats while also providing a convenient place for resettling increasing numbers of poor from England. In addition, Ireland was perceived as a source of natural resources and an outlet for exports. During Elizabeth's reign the most extensive colonial project in Ireland was the Munster plantation. Between 1586 and 1598, fifteen thousand English were resettled in Munster, the southern province of Ireland. The plantation was not successful. In 1596 the Ulster (northern province of Ireland) lords and some of the Munster chiefs and Connaught (western province) chiefs rose up against England. The uprising was aided in 1601 by the Spanish, but the joint forces of the Irish and Spanish were defeated by the English just six days after the death of Elizabeth in 1603. This English success prepared the way for more extensive English plantation and conquest in Ireland during the seventeenth century.

The English Literary Renaissance

Like other European monarchs, Elizabeth welcomed to her court the intellectuals, artists, poets, and statesmen who would propagate the image she wished to project. Patronage was the social institution through which these courtiers were rewarded and by which they could in turn dispense favors to others. Professor Gary Waller explains that the patronage system was used by the queen and her court to promote writers who supported Elizabeth's stated social and political goals: "civil order, obedience, and a patriotism focused on the crown." As a result of the cultural control exercised by the court through the patronage system, the poetry written before 1580 is primarily, in Waller's words, "versified Protestant and civic propaganda—moral commonplaces, precepts, encomia, epitaphs, expostulations on patriotism, exposures of moral dangers."[18]

Sir Philip Sidney, one of Elizabeth's courtiers, supported the queen's goals and was, in addition, a gifted writer. He is often identified as the initiator of the literary renaissance. According to literary critic Kenneth Muir, Sidney believed that "the function of poetry was to teach delightfully," and his *Defense of Poesie* (written c. 1580; published 1595) eloquently argues that the poet is a more effective teacher than either the philosopher or the historian. Sidney's prose romance *Arcadia* (written c. 1580; published 1590) reveals, as Muir asserts, that the "poet's method is to teach indirectly by means of a story," and *Arcadia* "covers the whole range of private and public morality."[19] Muir explains:

> We see the operations of lust, pride, ambition, anger, and egotism no less than those of love, friendship, courtesy and valour. We see the evils of superstition, tyranny and anarchy, as well as the value of magnanimity, justice and good counsel. We see how rebellion is caused by bad government, how courtesy and injustice, love and egotism can be embodied in a single character.[20]

Sidney and his fellow poet Sir Edmund Spenser spent much time experimenting with different forms of meter in their own poetry; Sidney's sonnet sequence *Astrophel and Stella* (written 1580–1584; published 1591) is one of the seminal works of poetry in the sixteenth century. Not only did it inspire a host of sonneteers, among them William Shakespeare, but it also captured a variety of moods within a coherent dramatic structure in a way unrivalled by others who experimented with the sonnet genre.

Edmund Spenser's epic poem *The Faerie Queene* is perhaps

the most remarkable poem of the Elizabethan period. It clearly intends to celebrate and justify Elizabeth, her court, and her sociopolitical goals. Waller contends, however, that the structure of the poem and the content of its later books reveal an unsettling truth about how power was actually exercised in Elizabeth's court: In spite of the image she projected and the goals she supported, conflict was often resolved by brute force.

Elizabethan Drama

"The crowning glory of the Elizabethan Renaissance was drama,"[21] according to historians Youngs, Manning, Snyder, and Reitan. The flowering of Elizabethan drama in the 1580s is variously attributed to court patronage of professional acting companies, the building of the first public theaters, and the dramatic innovations of a group of young university-educated playwrights. No doubt the convergence of all three initiated the great age of Elizabethan drama. Encyclopedist Charles Boyce says that "Elizabeth herself was the most important patron of the Elizabethan theater; her influence was essential in protecting the theatrical profession from Puritan-inspired prohibition, and her court provided an important source of income and prestige for the leading London acting companies."[22] One longtime patron of theater, Robert Dudley, earl of Leicester, had supported a company of actors since 1559. In 1572, when actors were proclaimed vagrants unless supported by noblemen, Leicester formally defined the company as Leicester's Men. Two years later the queen proclaimed Leicester's Men to be "members of her household and thus exempt from London's laws against performing plays,"[23] according to Boyce. The first public theater, simply called the Theatre, was built by James Burbage in 1576 for Leicester's Men. The Curtain was built a year later, and several other public theaters, including the Rose, the Swan, the Globe, and the Fortune, were built during Elizabeth's reign.

Seven young men, whom modern scholars call "the University Wits," together transformed and refined comedy and tragedy in the 1580s. With their advanced educations, individual innovations and witty inventiveness, these men created plays that departed dramatically from earlier forms of English drama. Christopher Marlowe is commonly considered the greatest of this group, but the experiments of Thomas Kyd in tragedy and John Lyly in comedy are also important when considering the emergence of the new and popular Elizabethan drama. Marlowe used the form of verse that he developed to perfection, blank verse, to present his character, Doctor Faustus, the epitome of the Renaissance hero who aspires to infinite knowledge and power. Kyd's *The Spanish Tragedy* may be the first modern revenge tragedy, the first play that contains a play-within-a-play, and the first that uses a double-crossing Machiavellian villain. Kyd's adaptation of the structure and style of the classical Roman writer Seneca is apparent in this work, which also contributed to the anti-Spanish polemic of the 1580s. Lyly's crucial innovation in comedy was the euphuistic style, distinctive for introducing mythological and historical references, for using elaborate rhetorically balanced sentences, and for excessive alliteration. The affectations and absurdities of euphuism were mocked by Lyly's contemporaries, but his distinctive form of imaginative comedy marks him as an important early innovator.

Shakespeare in the 1590s

The variety, excellence, and sheer volume of poetry and plays produced in the 1590s may have been prompted by the exuberant spirit of the age, the growth of the printing industry, and the new national school of musical composition. One writer, however, William Shakespeare, acquired a reputation that few other writers can claim. In the 1590s he completed his sonnet cycle and two long narrative poems; he also wrote the history plays, comedies, and early tragedies that have been ranked among the masterpieces of English literature. Shakespeare's two tetralogies of history plays, which concentrated on the Wars of the Roses and the genesis of this thirty-year dynastic struggle for the English throne, were enormously popular. Such comedies as *The Taming of the Shrew*, *A Midsummer Night's Dream*, *The Merchant of Venice*, and *Much Ado About Nothing* display Shakespeare's genius in revealing the forms and fun of love, the complications produced by money and social class, and the significance of roles and role-playing. Shakespeare's early romantic tragedy *Romeo and Juliet* and his seminal study of the moody Dane *Hamlet* solidified his reputation as a master of tragedy as well. Shakespeare's uncanny knack for revealing the complexities of human character, his unique ability to embody the conflicting values and standards of his age in plays that were both entertaining and thought-provoking, and his creation of the poetry that continues to inspire admiration today, distinguish him as the literary genius of the Elizabethan age. The tragedies and romances Shakespeare wrote during the early years of James I's reign enhanced the reputation he had already established during Elizabeth's reign and merited him the words of praise from his friend and rival Ben Jonson, which are often quoted today: "He was not of an age, but for all time."[24]

An Image of Wealth During a Time of Hardship

The wealth of poetry, prose, and plays in the 1590s and the number of ballads celebrating the queen and the successes of her reign suggest England's continuing prosperity and the queen's continuing popularity. In the play *Old Fortunatus* by Thomas Dekker, performed in 1599, an old man is asked, "Are you then traveling to the temple of Eliza?" and the old man replies in terms that deify the queen and make England Paradise:

> Even to her temple are my feeble limbs traveling. Some call her Pandora, some Gloriana, some Cynthia, some Belphoebe, some Astraea, all by several names to express several loves. Yet all those names make but one celestial body, as all those loves meet to create but one soul. . . . Blessed name, happy country; your Eliza makes your land Elysium.[25]

Historian Christopher Haigh explains, however, that the image created in the play belies the actual conditions suffered by the country and the queen during the final decade of her reign. The plague, which was seldom entirely absent from London, reached epidemic severity in 1592–1593,

1599, and 1603. "Bad harvests, soaring food prices, peasant unrest, high taxes, and an unprofitable war [in Ireland] afflicted the kingdom,"[26] historian Lacey Baldwin Smith reports. Furthermore, the question of the aging queen's successor remained unresolved.

Outbreaks of Plague

The Black Death, a virulent outbreak of the bubonic plague, had devastated Europe in the fourteenth century, claiming nearly a third of the population between 1347 and 1351. Although the bubonic plague never again caused the same level of fatalities across entire countries, it continued to take its toll of lives in individual cities. "The first great plague of [Elizabeth's] reign struck London in June 1563 and raged until the early months of 1564, with deaths over the whole period totaling more than 20,000,"[27] according to theater historian Glynne Wickham. The disease assumed epidemic proportions again in 1592–1593, 1599, and 1603. Social historian Paul Slack suggests that "the death rate was probably less than 12 percent in the majority of the outbreaks in London,"[28] but that figure places fatalities at around 15,000 in 1593 and 21,000 in 1603.

Since the Elizabethans were unaware of the bacilli carried by fleas from infected rats in London, Jo McMurtry claims they "assumed that plague was caused by an unfavourable judgment from God and recommended as a remedy the repentance of sin." Because not all people in an infected area succumbed to the disease, the view of the plague as divine retribution on the sinful seemed reasonable; because not all who succumbed to the disease died, the possibility of repentance as a remedy seemed equally reasonable. Since the disease manifested itself as great swellings of the lymph glands, particularly in the groin and the armpits, "other remedies included eating onions roasted with molasses and pepper, carrying cakes of arsenic under one's armpits, and wearing charms and amulets of all sorts,"[29] McMurtry says.

There was surprisingly little blind panic during plague time, historian Slack explains, because the plague was considered by the general populace punishment for individual sin. However, London city officials treated the plague as a contagious disease that could be transmitted from person to person. They therefore quarantined the infected in their houses (with other family members) and painted a cross on the door of the house. Theaters and other places for public gathering were routinely closed during times of plague to prevent the spread of the contagion. Although only pneumonic plague (in which the bacterium infects the lungs) can be transmitted directly from person to person without the intermediary flea, these public measures were partially successful when they limited human contact with fleas in the infested areas of London. The affluent, who were able to leave London during times of plague and retreat to the country, escaped fleas from the infected rats and thus most successfully avoided the disease.

Since the outbreaks of plague in London during Elizabeth's reign seemed to be concentrated in slums and suburbs and seemed to be spread by beggars and vagrants, social prejudice became more overt. According to Slack, "the contempt of the respectable for the masses who presented a threat to their health" was articulated in regulations against the poor and other suburban "sinners," such as prostitutes and beggars: "Anyone wandering out of an infected house could be whipped as a vagrant; if he had a plague sore on him, he could be hanged as a felon."[30] Recurring visitations of the plague, Allardyce Nicoll says, "formed the somber background for the silks and taffetas, the processions and the plays."[31]

Harvest Failures and the Poor Law

In addition to the periodic ravages of plague, Slack claims that

> harvest failures in 1586, 1595, 1596 and 1597 brought malnutrition, disease and further surges in mortality to the poorer suburbs of town and to more isolated rural areas. . . . Food prices rose everywhere. . . . Widespread distress was accompanied by a peak in crimes against property, by a similar high point in illegitimacy rates, and by food and enclosure riots.[32]

Vagrancy rates increased as well. According to Slack, "Economic conditions were deteriorating in the longer term and producing a gradual increase in the number of poor."[33]

One of the most important pieces of pre–nineteenth century social legislation emerged as a result. The 1601 Poor Law established a tax to finance relief for the "deserving poor"; specified punishment for vagrants and beggars; and authorized work plans for the unemployed but able poor. The material results of the legislation were negligible because the provisions of the new law were not often enforced, and, Slack contends, "economic growth not public welfare . . . alleviated social problems in the seventeenth century."[34] Nevertheless, the impact of the Poor Law on Elizabethan attitudes was substantial. It persuaded the poor that the government shared their concerns, it reassured the middle ranks of society that deviant vagrants were being properly identified and punished, and it worked effectively to satisfy the socially concerned that the government accepted its responsibility to intervene in and direct public charity while still performing its traditional function: to maintain social discipline by punishing the disorderly.

The 1601 Poor Law, which, according to Slack, "persisted without fundamental alteration until 1834,"[35] both sustained the Tudor view of the class system and embraced humanitarian relief. In the words of Lacey Baldwin Smith, the Poor Law

> rested on the logic that if God ordained every man and woman to live without envy or malice in that station into which they had been born, then society could not risk revolution by allowing the victims of economic dislocation, human greed, and natural calamity to die miserably in their peasant hovels. Some help, if only reluctant and minimal, had to be offered.[36]

Even though this law enforced the class structure and supported the Tudor vision of paternalistic government, it also established the fundamental obligation of the government to see that some provision was made for those in distress. This obligation was sustained for over two hundred years.

During the last decade of her reign, Elizabeth was confronted with continuing conflict in Ireland. The Irish War, which began in 1596 with a revolt led by Hugh O'Neill, earl of Tyrone, forced the queen to sell Crown lands, valued at £120,000, to raise money to wage war. She also used £2 million from parliamentary funds and accrued a debt of £473 thousand pounds to further finance the war. In 1599 Robert Devereux, the earl of Essex and one of the queen's favorite courtiers, "demanded that Elizabeth allow him to lead an army into Ireland to redeem English honor and crush the Tyrone rebellion," according to Smith. "Instead of finding glory," Smith says, "Essex revealed his incompetence and latent treason."[37] He came to terms with Tyrone against Elizabeth's orders and was placed under house arrest. Angry and perhaps unstable, he staged an unsuccessful rebellion against the queen in 1601 and was beheaded for the attempt.

The Succession and Elizabeth's Death

The problem of the succession also haunted the final years of Elizabeth's reign. In 1601 the sixty-seven-year-old queen still refused to name a successor, so shortly after the execution of Essex, Elizabeth's principal secretary, Sir Robert Cecil, began private negotiations with James VI, king of Scotland. Cecil chose him because, as son of Mary, Queen of Scots, who was Elizabeth's cousin, James was in fact Elizabeth's nearest living relative. Cecil also wished to avoid a premature attempt by the Scottish king to claim the English throne, and he wished to negotiate a succession that would allow him to retain his position as chief minister. The secret negotiations proceeded smoothly during the next year and a half, and Cecil was able to garner the support of the nobility and the Privy Council early in 1603 during what turned out to be Elizabeth's final illness.

In February 1603 Elizabeth began to suffer from "insomnia, loss of appetite, and physical frailty," according to historian John Guy. "For twenty days she barely slept, refusing the attention of her physicians."[38] Biographer Alison Weir suggests that "the main trouble seemed to be slight swellings—probably ulcers—in the throat, accompanied by a cold."[39] Perhaps the queen developed bronchitis or pneumonia, and certainly her condition "had deteriorated alarmingly" by March 18. Elizabeth suffered a high fever on

March 20 and slipped into unconsciousness on March 23.
"She died," Guy says, "shortly before 3 A.M. on the 24th, attended by privy councilors and bishops."[40] She was sixty-nine
years old. Despite whether Elizabeth actually named James
her successor on her deathbed, Cecil had paved the way for
a peaceful succession. Three hours after Elizabeth's death,
the Privy Council formally approved the proclamation of
James's accession.

Elizabeth's Legacy

In spite of the difficulties of her last years and the eagerness
with which some citizens welcomed Elizabeth's successor,
James of Scotland, Elizabeth's reputation recovered shortly
after her death. It became clear that James could not solve
the problems that Elizabeth had bequeathed to him, and, according to historian Christopher Haigh, "history was rewrit-
ten for political purposes."[41] Compared to James, Elizabeth
seemed the symbol of peace and prosperity to her first biographer, William Camden. Although the image of Elizabeth I
has been embellished by some historians and diminished by
others in the nearly four centuries since her death, historian
Charles M. Gray declares her a net success:

> Perhaps she was not the political genius some of her admir-
> ers depict; her reign was not the Golden Age that it appeared
> to be in the troubled perspective of the seventeenth century
> or the romantic one of later times. But . . . she built up a
> great fund of credit in her subjects' affections. Even those
> she exasperated respected her; she played up to those whom
> patriotism, chivalry, and imagination disposed to idolize her;
> she was a woman of unmistakable intelligence and com-
> manding personal presence.[42]

Notes

1. Christopher Haigh, ed., *The Reign of Elizabeth I*. Athens: University of Georgia Press, 1985, p. 8.

2. Lacey Baldwin Smith, *This Realm of England, 1399 to 1688*, 7th ed. Lexington, MA: D.C. Heath, 1996, p. 175.

3. Smith, *This Realm of England, 1399 to 1688*, p. 191.

4. John Guy, *Tudor England*. Oxford, England: Oxford University Press, 1988, p. 41.

5. Guy, *Tudor England*, p. 62.

6. Frederic A. Youngs Jr., et al., *The English Heritage*, vol 1. Wheeling, IL: Harlan Davidson, 1999, pp. 118–19.

7. Youngs, et al., *The English Heritage*, p. 120.

8. Smith, *This Realm of England, 1399 to 1688*, p. 175.

9. Sara Mendelson and Patricia Crawford, *Women in Early Modern England, 1550–1720*. Oxford, England: Clarendon, 1998, p. 354.

10. Mendelson and Crawford, *Women in Early Modern England, 1550–1720*, p. 356.

11. Susan Doran, *Monarchy and Matrimony: The Courtships of Elizabeth I*. London: Routledge, 1996, p. 218.

12. Smith, *This Realm of England, 1399 to 1688*, p. 177.

13. Smith, *This Realm of England, 1399 to 1688*, p. 185.

14. Kenneth R. Andrews, *Trade, Plunder, and Settlement: Maritime Enterprise and the Genesis of the British Empire, 1480–1630*. Cambridge, England: Cambridge University Press, 1984, p. 229.

15. Quoted in Smith, *This Realm of England, 1399 to 1688*, p. 208.

16. Andrews, *Trade, Plunder, and Settlement*, p. 234.

17. Smith, *This Realm of England, 1399 to 1688*, p. 199.

18. Gary Waller, *English Poetry of the Sixteenth Century*. London: Longman Group Limited, 1986, p. 41.

19. Quoted in J.W. Robinson, ed., *British Writers and Their Work: No. 8*, Lincoln: University of Nebraska Press, 1965, pp. 102, 103, 105.

20. Quoted in Robinson, *British Writers and Their Work*, p. 105.

21. Youngs, et al., *The English Heritage*, p. 117.

22. Charles Boyce, *Shakespeare A to Z: The Essential Reference to His Plays, His Poems, His Life and Times, and More*. New York: Facts On File, 1990, pp. 171–72.

23. Boyce, *Shakespeare A to Z*, p. 174.

24. Ben Jonson, "To the Memory of My Beloved, the Author Mr. William Shakespeare," prefixed to the Shakespeare First Folio of 1623.

25. Quoted in Haigh, *The Reign of Elizabeth I*, pp. 5-6.

26. Smith, *This Realm of England, 1399 to 1688*, p. 224.

27. Glynne Wickham, Herbert Berry, and William Ingram, eds., *English Professional Theatre, 1530–1660*. Cambridge, England: Cambridge University Press, 2000, p. 54.

28. Quoted in Arien Mack, ed., *In Time of Plague*. New York: New York University Press, 1991, p. 113.

29. Jo McMurtry, *Understanding Shakespeare's England*. Hamden, CT: Archon Books, 1989, pp. 99–100.

30. Quoted in Mack, *In Time of Plague*, pp. 125–26.

31. Allardyce Nicoll, *The Elizabethans*. London: Cambridge University Press, 1957, p. 66.

32. Quoted in Haigh, *The Reign of Elizabeth I*, p. 226.

33. Quoted in Haigh, *The Reign of Elizabeth I*, p. 227.

34. Quoted in Haigh, *The Reign of Elizabeth I*, p. 240.

35. Quoted in Haigh, *The Reign of Elizabeth I*, p. 221.

36. Smith, *This Realm of England, 1399 to 1688*, p. 194.

37. Smith, *This Realm of England, 1399 to 1688*, p. 225.

38. Guy, *Tudor England*, pp. 542–43.

39. Alison Weir, *The Life of Elizabeth I*, New York: Ballantine Books, 1998, p. 481.

40. Guy, *Tudor England*, p. 453.

41. Haigh, *The Reign of Elizabeth I*, p. 8.

42. Charles M. Gray, *Renaissance and Reformation England, 1509–1714*. New York: Harcourt, Brace, Jovanovich, 1973, p. 74.

Chapter 1

Political and Social Turning Points

Turning|Points
IN WORLD HISTORY

A *Woman* on the English Throne

Sara Mendelson and Patricia Crawford

In sixteenth century England, when women were considered naturally inferior to men, the prospect of being ruled by a woman created considerable anxiety. Mary (daughter of Henry VIII and Catharine of Aragon) was actually the first woman in English history who was acknowledged as the reigning monarch, the "Queen regnant," and her short reign (1553–1558) increased popular anxiety. When Mary died in 1558, her half-sister Elizabeth became the second "Queen regnant." Elizabeth I (daughter of Henry VIII and Anne Boleyn) reigned for nearly half a century (1558–1603). During her long reign, Elizabeth, who never married, confronted the prevailing belief at the time that females were naturally inferior to males by creating an image of herself as both "male" and "female."

In this selection from their book *Women in Early Modern England*, Sara Mendelson and Patricia Crawford explain how Elizabeth I countered her subjects' anxiety at the prospect of female rule by "manipulating contemporary images of monarchy and gender": she dramatized the "male" attributes she shared with her father—bravery and intellectual skill—and she also encouraged a sacred and magical "female" aura by allowing comparisons of herself with the Virgin Mary and Diana, goddess of chastity. Ironically, Elizabeth's success as a monarch did not change the generally accepted view that females were inferior to males.

Both Sara Mendelson and Patricia Crawford have published works independently on women in Renaissance England. Mendelson's work includes a book-length study, *The Mental World of Stuart Women*, and Crawford's previous book is *Women and Religion in England*.

In early modern Europe, issues of gender were everywhere regarded as vital to the workings of monarchy. In a society which assumed that females were naturally inferior to males and were subject to them by divine law, the prospect of female rule aroused men's deepest anxieties. Europe's intellectual elite had inherited a belief in women's incompetence for state affairs from classical writers such as Aristotle, who declared that women's involvement in politics was unnatural. Contemporary statesmen echoed Aristotle's opinion: Sir Thomas Elyot noted the common belief that 'in the partes of wisedome and civile policy, [women] be founden unapt, and to have litell capacitie'.

The problems entailed by female rule were legal and practical as well as psychological and symbolic. Female heirs to the throne were aware that men foresaw intractable difficulties for a queen regnant in both political and religious spheres. How could a woman lead troops in battle, manage Parliament, or negotiate with foreign kings? If women must not speak in church, as Paul had instructed the Corinthians, how could the queen command her bishops as head of the Anglican establishment?. . .

Women's ambiguous status and unsuccessful history as royal heirs helps explain Henry VIII's desperate concern to beget a male heir. Indeed, the English Reformation can be understood in part as the consequence of Henry's efforts to avoid a female heir. Henry did not doubt women's practical ability to govern: he depended on his wife Catherine's advice, and left home rule to her management when he was at war abroad. But no counter-example could refute the perceived disadvantages of a queen regnant.

The Monarch's "Two Bodies"

In sixteenth-century debates about queenship, the paradoxical status of female monarchs was rationalized in theoretical terms as an instance of the medieval principle of the monarch's 'two bodies'. According to this doctrine, even if the king's personal body was defective, as in the case of an under-aged or senile male heir to the throne, the monarch's 'body of state' was secured against human weakness through

God's grace, with the aid of privy counsellors and the rest of the political nation. In the case of females, the notion of the queen's 'two bodies' was extended to reconcile the incongruity between women's subordinate role and the requirements of sovereignty. As Sir Thomas Smith remarked, such considerations explained why a queen by 'blood and progenie' had the same authority as a male monarch.

> For the right and honour of the blood, and the quietnes and suertie of the realme, is more to be considered, than either the base age as yet impotent to rule, or the sexe not accustomed (otherwise) to intermeddle with publicke affaires, being by common intendment understood, that such personages never do lacke the counsell of such grave and discreete men as be able to supplie all other defaultes.

England's initial resolution of the gender issue was embodied in two documents of Henry VIII's reign, the third Parliamentary succession statute and Henry's own will. Both documents specified that any male heir was to be given precedence; if none existed, first Mary and then Elizabeth was to succeed to the throne. When Edward died, constitutional uncertainty lay not in who was his rightful successor, but on what terms and with what powers a female monarch would rule.

In 1553 Mary I succeeded to the English crown as its first acknowledged queen. By the time Elizabeth I died in 1603, England had experienced half a century of female rule. . . .

Elizabeth's Strategy

Because she was a Protestant, and chose not to take a husband to share her rule, Elizabeth was the first English queen to confront head-on all the paradoxes created for the English Church and State by an independent female monarch. Although her pioneer role provoked tension with male counsellors, who continually urged her to marry and bear an heir, the novelty of her situation gave Elizabeth the opportunity to experiment, to forge an individual solution to the problems of female power.

Elizabeth founded her personal supremacy over Church

and State on traditional, non-gendered grounds: her God-given right by inheritance, a pre-rogative to which all her subjects must swear allegiance. Going beyond the notion of divinely ordained rule, however, Eliza-beth strengthened her authority and promoted popularity among her subjects by manipulating contemporary images of monar-chy and gender. Elizabeth dealt with her subjects' anxieties, and with the weaknesses and ambi-guities of her position, by push-ing the notion of the monarch's

Queen Elizabeth

'two bodies' to its symbolic and psychological limits, repre-senting herself as both queen and king. To express her unique status, the queen employed rhetoric and imagery appropriate to both sexes, describing herself alternately in feminine and masculine terms.

In masculine milieux like the battlefield, Elizabeth por-trayed herself as repressing her female aspect to allow 'male' qualities to emerge. The queen's famous remarks allegedly addressed to the troops at Tilbury in 1588, just prior to the Armada crisis, highlighted her manly attributes: 'I may have the body of a weak and feeble woman, but I have the heart and stomach of a king.' On this occasion she further drama-tized her male persona through visual imagery, appearing in breastplate and helmet, mounted on a charger. In general, without surrendering her femininity, she stressed those mental and physical traits she shared with her father Henry VIII, such as her bravery and her linguistic proficiency. In the religious realm, like the other three Tudor-Stuart queens [Mary Tudor, Mary Stuart, and Anne Stuart], Elizabeth con-tinued the kingly tradition of 'sacred monarch', whose heal-ing powers confirmed her divine and majestic status.

As 'sacred monarch' and virgin queen, Elizabeth also cre-atively elaborated upon a repertoire of female images. Her virginity served as a potent symbol of female power, enhancing the magical and religious aura that surrounded her. Such imagery was initiated with her accession portrait, in which Elizabeth was shown with her hair down, attired as a virginal maiden. At times depicting herself in the guise of the Virgin Mary, the queen appropriated those divine attributes that could be embodied in a woman. Similarly, in her persona as Diana the chaste goddess and as the Fairy Queen, Elizabeth created a stage setting in which her subjects' obedience was translated into the romantic language of chivalry. 'Courtly love' rendered male subservience to a woman acceptable to noble courtiers; in any other context, subjection would have been experienced as demeaning or even unmanning.

Elizabeth also capitalized on her 'feminine' characteristics to achieve well-defined goals of statecraft. For a sixteenth-century regime, her reign saw very few executions, and the queen agonized over those to which she was obliged to consent. Elizabeth's preference for 'mild and merciful rule' towards her political rivals, in contrast to the ruthless policies of her father and sister, was seen as an expression of her feminine compassion. The queen's legendary meanness was represented as the frugality of the conventional housewife applied on a national scale. Elizabeth carefully deployed her alleged vanity, sexual jealousy, and passionate temper to manage her councillors and suitors. Cultivating the myth that she could 'never keep a secret', she played her councillors against each other in a strategy of 'divide and conquer'.

Elizabeth's manipulation of contemporary assumptions about gender attributes is shown clearly in her management of her official courtships. Courtship had complex significance for the queen as a game, a strategic political tactic, and an entire social and cultural milieu. As a strategy, courtship became the queen's method for sidestepping the choice between two equally problematic alternatives, wedded subservience and barren virginity. Elizabeth appealed to the feminine quality of 'shamefastness' to delay and ultimately to avoid matrimony. At the same time, her advisers' construction of female sexuality, encouraged by Elizabeth's ambiguous behaviour towards unofficial suitors like the earl of

Leicester, seemed to confirm the queen's right to choose or reject each potential suitor.

General Vision of Women Unchanged

Elizabeth's outstanding political skills were employed not only to run the kingdom, but also to demonstrate that she was an exception who was superior to the usual disabilities that afflicted ordinary women. Paradoxically, her success as a female ruler depended on putting a distance between herself and all other women, because of the central problem of female authority. Although some historians have labelled Elizabeth patriarchal or even misogynistic, it is anachronistic to attribute her behaviour to an anti-female bias. The queen could not afford to be receptive to other women's claims for power, for fear of undermining her own position. Moreover, Elizabeth's apparent 'hostility' to other women's political pretensions was not necessarily inconsistent with female friendship on a personal level, or royal favour and bounty in the form of patronage.

Although relatively less popular in the final years of her reign, Elizabeth evoked a good deal of sentimental regret during the first half of the seventeenth century, especially when her prudence and parsimony were contrasted with Stuart excess and misjudgement.

> The honor, wealth, and glory of the nation, wherein Queene Elizabeth left it, were soone prodigally wasted by this thriftlesse heire, the nobillity of the land utterly debas'd by setting honors to publick sale . . . Then began Murther, Incest, Adultery, drunkennesse, swearing, fornication, and all sort of ribaldry to be no conceal'd but countenanc'd vices . . . because they held such conformity with the Court example.
> [L. Hutchinson]

The enduring popularity of Elizabeth's image as monarch can be traced in the seventeenth-century nostalgia for a mythical 'Merrie England' in which England's honour and prosperity as a nation had reached their greatest heights.

Yet even with Elizabeth as a successful exemplar of female monarchy, the belief persisted that women as a sex were naturally unfit for political rule. While we might have expected Elizabeth's achievements to have transformed the axioms of misogyny into more positive notions about the potentialities of queenship, it is clear from contemporary commentaries on her reign that notions about female political rule were not tied to the empirical performance of any particular queen. On the contrary, even her warmest female admirers discounted evidence of Elizabeth's independent abilities. In denouncing Henrietta Maria for her 'fatal' influence on her husband Charles I, Lucy Hutchinson interjected a general condemnation of female political power. [Henrietta Maria encouraged her husband to oppose Parliament, resulting in civil war and the beheading of Charles I in 1649.] No place is ever happy, she remarked, 'where the hands that are made only for distaffes affect the management of Sceptres'. And if anyone objected the recent counter-example of Queen Elizabeth, 'let them remember that the felicity of her reigne was the effect of her submission to her masculine and wise Councellors'.

Elizabeth Unifies England by Establishing a National Church

Roger B. Manning

Although Elizabeth's father, Henry VIII, created an independent English Church under royal authority rather than papal authority, the English Church during Henry VIII's reign retained the doctrine and liturgy of the Roman Catholic Church. During the short reigns of Elizabeth's half-brother, Edward, and half-sister, Mary, the English Church underwent dramatic changes and reversals. In Edward's short reign (1547–1553), monumental changes in doctrine and liturgy were imposed, and the English Church became Protestant; Mary returned England to Catholicism, and during her short reign (1553–1558) many Protestant leaders left England and nearly 300 Protestants who stayed were burned at the stake as heretics. Elizabeth inherited a legacy of confusion, suspicion, and bitterness when she ascended the throne in 1558. A remarkably intelligent, popular, and secular-minded woman, Elizabeth I was able to unify the country by promoting nationalism over religious factionalism. Using her personal popularity and her political savvy she was able to contain both fear of Catholics and threat from radical Puritans. Her efforts allowed the Church of England time to develop the unique doctrine and liturgy known as Anglicanism, "the middle way" between unreformed Catholicism and radical Protestantism.

In this selection from *The English Heritage*, Professor Roger B. Manning of Cleveland State University explains the basis of what has become known as the "Elizabethan Settlement," and he outlines the manner in which Elizabeth contained threats from both Catholics and Puritans.

Excerpted from *The English Heritage*, 3rd ed., vol. 1, pp. 103–124, edited by Frederick A. Young Jr., Roger B. Manning, Henry L. Snyder, E.A. Reitan. Copyright © 1999 by Harlan Davidson, Inc. Reprinted by permission of Harlan Davidson, Inc. All rights reserved.

The English defeat of the Spanish Armada in 1588 was therefore interpreted at the time as not only a political victory but also a resounding triumph for English Protestantism over Spanish Catholicism.

Elizabeth was remarkably secular-minded in a century of religious passion. France was torn by religious civil wars, and the advancement of Catholicism was a principal motive of Spain's foreign policy; in contrast, Elizabeth made her church serve England first, then Protestantism.

When Elizabeth came to the throne of England conditions did not favor a female monarch. Neither Edward VI [who was Protestant] nor Mary [who was Catholic] had ruled long enough to unite the realm under one religion or the other, and England remained prone to factionalism and disorder. Her task was to unify the country and avoid the more extreme religious settlements of the previous two reigns. That she was able to do so and avoid civil war in an age of almost universal religious war is a tribute to her political skills, wisdom and judgment. She demonstrated an extraordinary ability to choose first-rate royal councillors who possessed administrative and fiscal talents and knew how to manage parliaments so as to minimize opposition. In an age when John Knox and other Protestant reformers thought that female government was "monstrous," Elizabeth knew how to intimidate male courtiers and master the factionalism which was always to be found in her Privy Council. . . .

The Elizabethan Settlement

Elizabeth sought a religious settlement which would bind the English people together in a national church and avoid the mistakes of the mid-Tudor period [1547–1558, when Protestant Edward VI, then Catholic Mary I reigned]. She was mainly interested in reasserting royal control of the Church of England, and the Act of Supremacy of 1559 named her supreme governor of the English Church. . . .

The Elizabethan Religious Settlement, as enacted by Parliament in 1559, was intended to promote unity by compelling every person in the realm to attend Anglican services performed according to the *Book of Common Prayer* in every parish church. It was axiomatic to statesmen of this period that the ruler's sovereign authority could be maintained only by the establishment of a single, national church. The advocacy of toleration was equated with blasphemy and political disaffection, but during this period, growing religious discord and the revival of religious wars abroad made it increasingly difficult to include all English people within the Church of England.

Outwardly, the Church of England, legally established by Act of Parliament, resembled the medieval Catholic Church insofar as it retained episcopal government, or rule by bishops, who presided over territorial dioceses, which were further divided into parishes—the basic unit of both ecclesiastical and civil government. In the time of Henry VIII, royal authority had been substituted for papal authority, but the royal supremacy in ecclesiastical affairs was now shared with Parliament to a considerable extent. Elizabeth took the title "supreme governor" in deference to those members of Parliament, who objected to a woman being "supreme head" of the church as Henry VIII had been styled. She governed the church indirectly through the hierarchy of archbishops and bishops with occasional interference from Parliament.

The doctrine of the Elizabethan Church of England was Protestant but not yet distinctly Anglican. The liturgy of the church, prescribed by the *Book of Common Prayer* of 1559, looked Protestant to Catholics, but retained far too many medieval Catholic rituals and ecclesiastical vestments for Puritan tastes. The medieval Catholic Church's lands and revenues had been plundered by the Tudor monarchs and their courtiers, and numerous lands formerly belonging to monasteries, chantries and bishoprics had been expropriated by the crown and many sold into lay hands. Elizabeth continued to profit at the expense of the church, sometimes delaying the appointment of new bishops to dioceses where the previous bishop had died so that the crown could enjoy the revenues of that diocese in the interim, and sometimes forced church officials to exchange more profitable church lands for less remunerative royal lands.

The Elizabethan religious settlement placed Catholics in a difficult position. Some, known as "church-papists," compromised and continued to attend Anglican services in their parish churches. In some cases they were actually advised to do so by aging Catholic priests, who survived from the reign of Mary. But younger Catholic clergy, who had caught the spirit of the Catholic Reformation from abroad, dissuaded Catholics from attending Anglican Churches. From their refusal to conform to the established church such Catholics became known as "recusants" [from the Latin *recusare*, meaning "to refuse"]. . . .

Elizabeth: Symbol of National Unity

In this excerpt from The Norton Anthology of English Literature, *Hallett Smith and Barbara K. Lewalski identify the personal qualities that made Queen Elizabeth not only a successful leader but also a symbol of English national unity during the age that bears her name.*

Queen Elizabeth I, who ascended the throne in 1558 and ruled until 1603, was one of the most remarkable political geniuses England has ever produced. Vain, difficult, and headstrong, she nevertheless had a very shrewd instinct about her country's strengths and weaknesses, and she identified herself with England as no previous ruler had done. . . .

England's strength lay in its power to sway the balance of power in Europe: it could throw its weight either way in the ongoing power struggle between Spain and France; and it could support or fail to support the Protestant uprisings against Spain in the Low Countries. Moreover, Elizabeth made adroit use of her situation as an unmarried monarch generally expected to marry so as to provide a legitimate heir to the throne. She kept all Europe guessing as to her intentions, skillfully playing her several suitors off against one another—and at length insisted that England alone was her spouse. By the time it was too late for her to marry and bear children, England was strong and united.

Ironically, the papal bull (decree) of 1570, excommunicating

While Catholic recusants wished to withdraw from the established church, Puritans emphatically wished to remain within the Anglican Church, but, at the same time, to reform it according to the pattern of the Calvinist Church of Geneva. The term "Puritan" was pejorative and was used by Catholics or more moderate Protestants to describe a wide variety of opinions, including proponents of moderate reform. While some Puritans were willing to accept government by bishops, most belonged to the presbyterian party and wished to replace episcopal government with rule by "classes," or councils composed of ministers and lay elders. Thus, presbyterian church government sought to reduce

Elizabeth and relieving her subjects of their loyalty to her, contributed greatly to that unity. This bull was intended to bring to the throne Mary Stuart, Queen of Scots, who was Catholic by faith and French by culture—an insupportable thought. The English rallied to their queen, and she became a symbol of Englishness and nationalism. The adulation of her, in the face of trouble on the Scottish border, near-chaos in Ireland, and continued threats from the Continent, took on religious intensity. Her reputation for beauty (which was exaggerated) and for wisdom (which was not) became articles of faith. In 1588 God himself seemed to testify to her divine mission to guide England: Philip II of Spain sent out the mightiest invasion fleet ever mounted against England, but that Spanish Armada was almost wholly destroyed by a violent storm, which seemed an act of God. . . .

The mere survival of Elizabeth for so long provided the opportunity for nationalistic consciousness to become firmly established. When she came to the throne in 1558 she was only twenty-five years old, and she remained queen for almost forty-five years. It is wholly appropriate therefore that the second half of the sixteenth century bear her name, the Elizabethan Age.

Hallett Smith and Barbara K. Lewalski, "The Sixteenth Century," in *The Norton Anthology of English Literature*, Fifth Edition, vol. 1. General Editor, M.H. Abrams. New York: W.W. Norton & Company, 1986.

clerical influence in the church and to increase the influence of laymen drawn from the landed gentry and merchant oligarchies in the towns. Puritans disliked the Anglican *Book of Common Prayer* because it retained Catholic liturgical practices such as using the sign of the cross as well as requiring clergymen to wear the surplice when ministering the sacraments. Indeed, Puritans wished to abolish all practices, such as the observance of Christmas, for which no warrant existed in Sacred Scripture. Their beliefs were drawn exclusively from the Bible, and they wished to make sermons based on a biblical text the focal point of Anglican worship.

In the reign of Elizabeth there were no doctrinal differences between Anglican and Puritan; both shared the same Calvinist theology, and their differences grew out of matters such as church government, liturgy, and clerical dress. Thus, Puritanism should not be regarded as a deviant form of Protestantism; it remained well within the mainstream of English and European Protestantism. As such, Puritans are to be distinguished from separatists, those sects such as the Brownists and members of the Family of Love who did not adhere to the Church of England. What made the Puritans dangerous in the eyes of Elizabeth and the Anglican bishops was that they ultimately posed a threat to royal control of the Anglican Church and the monarchy itself through their attacks on church government by bishops. Many critics of Puritanism came to believe that if you scratched a Presbyterian, you would find a Republican underneath.

The Fear of Catholicism in the 1570s and 1580s

The popular fear of Catholicism became a permanent feature of English politics in the middle years of Elizabeth's reign and thereafter. It derived from two perceived threats. The first was the arrival of the first seminary priests in 1574 from the English Colleges on the Continent. These missionaries intended not only to minister to the spiritual needs of the English Catholic community, but also to reconcile lapsed Catholics and convert Protestants. Since the very act of being a priest, ordained abroad since September 1559, was defined by a parliamentary statute of 1585 as high treason, as was also the act of reconciling a lapsed Catholic, these seminary priests were obliged to enter the country secretly and in disguise. A traitor's death was almost certain if they were caught, so the missionary priests came psychologically prepared for martyrdom. Because the English Colleges were also located in Spanish or Papal territories, the seminary priests were perceived as being agents of hostile foreign powers which were actively planning an invasion of England during this period and were at war with England after 1585.

The most feared of all the English seminary priests were the Jesuits, the largest and most effective of the new religious orders founded during the Catholic Counter-Reformation. Like their rivals, the Puritans, the training of Jesuit priests emphasized learning and preaching, and they had already established a formidable reputation by their successes in re-catholicizing parts of continental Europe, which had earlier become Protestant. Although their numbers were never sufficient to pose such a threat in England, the seminary priests and Jesuits did stiffen the resistance of the English Catholic laity. Since the latter included a disproportionate number of peers and country gentry, their missionary efforts were always viewed as posing a political threat to England. This was especially true during the war years at the end of the reign, when the Spanish made several attempts to invade England and Ireland.

While Catholic seminary priests were branded as traitors, parliamentary legislation against Catholic laymen sought their financial ruin rather than physical punishment. The Recusancy Laws, especially that of 1585, intended to cripple the Catholic gentry by striking at their patrimony and eroding their social status. Heads of Catholic gentry households were subjected to crippling fines of £20 per lunar month (there were thirteen lunar months in a year) for failure to attend Anglican worship. Particularly stubborn individuals might be imprisoned and compelled to attend Anglican sermons; two-thirds of their estates might also be confiscated. Persecution, propaganda, and financial pressure did cause many Catholics to conform, at least occasionally, but the supply of missionary priests never ceased and, eventually, an irreducible hard core of the Catholic population emerged who could not be swayed by any amount of pressure. However, when the Spanish Armada of 1588 attempted an invasion of England, the English Catholics remained loyal to the queen.

The Threat from Puritanism in the 1570s and 1580s

Puritanism involved less of a confrontation but more of a sustained threat. Because the Marian Catholic bishops had fled on Elizabeth's accession in 1558, the new queen had had to rely greatly on those returning self-exiles who had spent Mary's reign abroad, the greater part in Geneva where they had become strongly Calvinistic. Equally as great a reason for Puritanism's success was that laymen as well as churchmen shared its leadership, so that its pressures for reform were made not only in the church but also in Parliament, where a disproportionate number of reformers were elected, and even in the royal court, where sympathizers such as Sir William Cecil and Robert Dudley were very influential.

The early efforts at reform in the 1560s had been piecemeal, seeking the removal of pre-Reformation religious practices. The reformers believed that the queen favored further reform, and they sought to hasten matters by making proposals in the church's convocation and in Parliament. They were surprised when she refused to let the proposals be discussed in the House of Commons, arguing that, as head of the church, its reform was her exclusive right. Some in the Commons recalled contrary precedents for parliamentary initiatives in the two earlier reigns, but Elizabeth refused to let a religious matter become a constitutional issue and promised to make reforms herself.

In the early 1570s Thomas Cartwright, a professor of divinity at Cambridge who came to Presbyterianism by an academic route, and other Presbyterian leaders who had learned at the feet of Calvin himself at Geneva, began to write and surreptitiously print books urging change. Not only Cartwright but even Archbishop Edmund Grindal lectured the queen on her religious duty to delay a "complete" and thoroughgoing reformation no longer. Elizabeth struck back by ordering the enforcement of religious uniformity against Puritanism.

Not unnaturally the movement went underground but resurfaced in the 1580s in more threatening guises. A clandestine Presbyterian organization was established in some parts of England, particularly in eastern England where Puritanism was strongest, alongside of and completely ignoring the bishops' authority. The pressure within Parliament to replace Anglicanism with Presbyterianism or at least a milder form of Puritanism was as unrelenting as it was unsuccessful. Elizabeth's counterattack triumphed when her anti-Puritan new archbishop of Canterbury, John Whitgift, made his own diocesan tribunal into a nationwide Court of High Commission in which Puritan churchmen were charged, tried, and removed from office and influence. Laymen who wrote books urging reform were branded "seditious," and thus, for example, John Stubbs, a Puritan author who wrote against the queen's consideration of marriage to a French Catholic prince, had his right hand cut off. More important, government agents sought out and suppressed the growing Presbyterian underground counter-church, so that by the late 1580s Puritanism was rendered less effective.

Meanwhile, three decades of internal growth had enabled Anglicanism to develop and enunciate its principles. The most mature expression was in Richard Hooker's *The Laws of Ecclesiastical Polity*, an argument that Anglicanism was a *via media*, a "middle way" between unreformed Catholicism and radical Protestantism. Anglicanism accepted as a valid norm for the church not only the Bible but also the tradition of the first five centuries of the church before the great growth of papal influence—thus it accepted the episcopal form of government, creeds, and practices, which had flourished in the early Christian church during and after the Biblical first century, and rejected the belief of Puritans and others that man's will was not free. . . .

The Defeat of the Spanish Armada

A state of war between England and Spain existed from 1585 to 1603. Its causes were long-standing: Elizabeth sent money and troops to help the Protestant Dutch who were fighting for their independence from the Spanish Netherlands; English seamen tried (unsuccessfully) to intercept the annual treasure fleets returning from the New World; English merchants attempted to break the Spanish monopoly on trade with America; and, most importantly, King Philip II sought the triumph of his cause over the Protestant queen.

The major campaign of the war was the attempted invasion of England in 1588, when the Spanish Armada, a fleet of about 130 ships, sailed to rendezvous with soldiers under Spanish command in the Netherlands and then to ferry them across for the invasion. The plan was beyond the capabilities of the time: communications were inadequate, there was no deep water in which the Spanish ships could anchor to pick up the soldiers, and the prevailing winds from west to east were likely to prevent the westward attack even if the troops reached the ships. The English seized the initiative by moving upwind, and with the wind at their backs they could harry the Spanish fleet, let the English heavy guns wreak havoc, and then even send unmanned fire ships into the moored Spanish fleet. Unable to retreat westward, the Spanish had to turn northward and circle Scotland, returning past Ireland. Philip had trusted God to overcome the obstacles his commanders had pointed out; the English felt the "Protestant wind" was their best ally. . . .

England had stood off the mightiest nation in the world, the political champion of the Catholic Counter-Reformation. There could have been no greater boost to English self-esteem. The trials of battle had proved that early-modern England was of age—flourishing, proud, successful. It was a remarkable heritage to pass on.

The Power of Parliament in Elizabethan England

Charles M. Gray

When Elizabeth became queen, she inherited a distinctive political tradition. England was a monarchy, but the power of the monarch was limited by the English constitution. Although the monarch had the power to convene and dissolve Parliament, laws could not be changed without the Parliament's consent. Despite this limitation, the monarch retained considerable power because he possessed an absolute veto. He could also confer titles on whomever he pleased, thus conveying the right to sit in the House of Lords, and he could invite new boroughs to send members to the House of Commons.

In this selection from his book, *Renaissance and Reformation England*, University of Chicago professor Charles M. Gray explains the decisive changes in the relationship between monarch and Parliament during Elizabeth's reign. Elizabeth created few new noblemen, but the House of Commons grew both in numbers and in power during her reign. From the conflict between the queen and the House of Commons there emerged both a stronger Parliament and a more carefully delineated vision of the power of the monarch. Parliament gained "corporate strength," and Elizabeth's restructuring of her Privy Council enhanced the powers of the monarch as a political administrator.

Gray's other books include *The Costs of Crime* and *Hugh Latimer and the Sixteenth Century*.

The sixteenth century was a decisive period in the history of Parliament. The Tudors did not alter the basic rules: Parlia-

Excerpted from *The Harbrace History of England*, Part 2: *Renaissance and Reformation England, 1509–1714*, by Charles M. Gray. Copyright © 1997 by Harcourt, Inc. Reprinted by permission of the publisher.

ment's right to consent to taxation and legislation, its dependence on the king. They did permit it to become a different kind of institution with an altered sense of itself. They helped Parliament become a stronger embodiment of the *politicum* [populace], a more active counterforce to the *regale* [reigning monarch]. . . .

The Elizabethan phase of Parliament's development was nourished by conflict. The queen held a conservative view of Parliament's role in the face of an emergent counteropinion, which divisive religious issues stimulated. Although Elizabeth tried to avoid too many Parliaments, she fully recognized the wisdom of taking counsel with her subjects and of allowing members of Parliament to have their place in the sun. But when Elizabeth faced Parliaments, she faced troublemakers, which is close to saying that she faced Puritans. Those who wanted further reformation in the Church were represented in Parliament. Hard-line Puritans were a small minority, but their zeal made them persistent; their determined interest in their program made them act in a more partylike way than was quite respectable in sixteenth-century politics. The queen refused to consider the Puritan demands in substance, and, in addition, she took the position that religious affairs, being subject to the monarch as sole Supreme Head, should not be discussed in Parliament without invitation. In short, the queen made an issue. Perhaps it would have been wiser not to have done so, for where there was a constitutional issue, opposition to the monarch's point of view would spread beyond those intent on revising the Church settlement.[1]

Separation of Powers Provokes Conflict

Elizabeth's general theory was that Parliament should not discuss matters within the areas left to the royal prerogative. Unless invited to do so, they should not discuss those matters with a view toward legislating; much less should they

1. a 1559 act of Parliament intended to settle the dispute between Catholics and radical Puritan Protestants by establishing a national church with a unique doctrine and liturgy known as Anglicanism, the "middle way" between unreformed Catholicism and radical Protestantism

discuss them merely to register dissent or to prod the monarch with unwanted advice. The queen's theory provoked an answer: Parliament's traditional freedom of speech means that members have a right to introduce legislation on any topic and to say what they think in connection with any proposed legislation. For that matter, freedom of speech includes the right to resolve, to address the monarch with expressions of solicitude for the nation, and simply to discuss. Surely the representatives of the country meet to let it be known what the country is worried about, to make the unity of monarch and people a reality based on communication.

Parliament men who were not Puritans were attracted to the theory that expressed the greater trust in Parliament's capacity for participation. Issues beyond the Church extended the conflict between the royal position and Parliament's corporate pride. Parliament men shared with other subjects the hope that the queen would marry, or at least that she would settle the succession. That hope was most intense among the staunchest Protestants, for whom the danger of a Catholic claimant was most terrifying, but one did not have to be a Puritan to dread the Pope and civil trouble. While Parliament publicly urged the queen to marry and to do something about the succession, Elizabeth maintained that those matters were outside its jurisdiction. She naturally felt her marriage to be a personal concern, and she may have had qualms about usurping the place of God in choosing her successor. The real strength of her position, however, was that negotiations for a royal marriage belonged to foreign policy. The question of succession also had diplomatic implications. Such matters had to be governed by considerations of "policy"—in Elizabethan usage, a word close to "strategy," requiring secrecy. The queen had excellent reasons for her attitude, but her theory of Parliament's role was hard for its members to accept.

Conflict carried the maturation of Parliament forward in Elizabeth's reign as the absence of conflict had fostered its growth before. Parliamentarians thought and cared more about their privileges as they were challenged. Parliament's earlier participation in religious affairs (and also its recognition of royal marriages and its settlement of the succession) put the queen in a reactionary light. The enhanced sense of national unity in a common Protestant faith made the queen's insistence on separating the spheres of monarch and people seem gratuitous. Meanwhile, other changes reinforced Parliament's accumulating self-confidence.

The House of Lords

The royal power to create noblemen, and so add to the House of Lords, was used sparingly by the Tudors. At the beginning of the Tudor period [1485–1509], bishops and abbots, essentially royal appointees, were a majority of the House of Lords; the number of lay peers was low. The Reformation changed the picture by sweeping the abbots away. New growth by the ennoblement of laymen was slow. Elizabeth was reluctant to create noblemen with status beyond their resources, and she did not want to spend her own resources to endow new nobility. There were great advantages in having no more titled noblemen than one could take care of. A moderate number of peers could be provided with public employment and dignities; each could have his share of privilege, graft, and patronage without impoverishing the Crown or making slighted grandees restive. The Elizabethan nobility was small enough for most noblemen to have a role in the government and hope of serving their self-interest by court politics. Most new creations earned their titles and riches in the queen's service, and most noblemen identified with the government's policies and with its executive distaste for parliamentary meddling.

Conflict with the House of Commons

The story of the House of Commons is different. Conflict with Queen Elizabeth was concentrated there, for the lower house was emerging into unprecedented independence and standing. Elizabeth's reign was the chief period of the house's quantitative expansion, and qualitative changes accompanied it. Basically, the supply of borough seats was increased to meet demand. The demand did not come from people who lived by their trades in the towns, which were nominally represented, but rather from gentlemen who wanted seats for themselves and from noblemen who wanted seats for their clients, relatives, and factional confederates. Gentlemen were better educated and more aspiring to a public role. London and the court grew more sophisticated and exciting as gentlemen grew less content with country life from birth to death. The regular royal service could not accommodate all the well-born people who hankered for a wider stage than their manors and local societies furnished, nor all those whom noblemen and courtiers might wish to favor. Many of these born into the fast-breeding gentry managed to stay gentle, while others less well-born bought their way into land and gentility. There were large "county societies" of socially prestigious and wealthy people—"nests of gentlefolk"—competing with each other and forming factions. New ways to compete and new ways to score in the scramble for status, whether for oneself or for a noble patron, were needed. More seats in the Commons were a good way to satisfy these needs. They cost the Crown nothing in money.

A larger House of Commons, with more men of notable ability and men who enjoyed the confidence of class and local success, naturally took a more generous view of the house's privileges than the queen did. Even so, conflict stayed within bounds during Elizabeth's reign. Aggressive dissenters remained a minority. Many aristocratic M.P.s [members of parliament] were uninterested in politics, uncertain of their opinions, and unwilling to offend the queen. They could often be swayed by oratory, but in the end they could usually be brought around by governmental pressure, including the queen's special blend of sweet talk and tantrum, and by the managerial arts of Parliament's most professional members, the queen's privy councillors. Basically, the government had a reliable majority without resort to the hard-nosed game of electioneering and party building by patronage that politicians of a later day would master. Queen Elizabeth would not have approved of that game, for her theory of Parliament came to a "separation of powers" position: Parliament and the monarchy should stay in their respective territories; each should be free in its sphere. The mutual trust required to make such a system work was basically present in Elizabeth's reign, although by insisting on her theory the queen helped Parliament develop counterattitudes that later subverted it. . . .

The Privy Council

The most striking governmental change—a basic reorganization of the king's council—was pioneered under Henry VIII and confirmed under Elizabeth. The council was greatly reduced in size and compartmentalized to perform two functions separately. It is conventional to speak of the shrunken body as the privy council. In its Elizabethan heyday, the privy council was small enough (a dozen plus) to function continuously as a unit. Its members—some leading officeholders, some professional royal servants whose main job was to serve on the council, some noblemen—were expected to work regularly at the two aspects of their assignment. The privy council met frequently, almost daily much of the time, to perform the first of its functions, political and administrative duties. The same men also met at regular times (certain days of the week during the periods of the year when the ordinary law courts were in session) to perform the council's second function, the judicial. When serving as a court, it came to be called (after its meeting-place) the Court of Star Chamber.

As an organ of administration, the Elizabethan privy council was a distinctive institution. The monarch did not attend the council's regular meetings. It was not a standing committee to give the queen direct advice on the matters she had to decide. The tradition of informality still prevailed at the top. (One official, the secretary, grew in importance as the monarch's direct assistant.) Although the privy council discussed high affairs of state and many lower-level matters that reached it by one route or another, its formal role was chiefly to handle the stream of complaints that flowed to the Crown and to serve as an "internal security" board. Complaints that required judicial disposition were redirected to the regular courts (including the Star Chamber, for some misdemeanors and trespasses), but many private quarrels, official malfeasances, disputes over economic privileges, and the like that were brought before the council could be dealt with in a sub-judicial (although often nearly mandatory) way. In addition, much of the council's energy went into searching out and investigating reports of spies and conspirators—in other words, performing a police function in a police-less society, including the exaction of confessions by torture. Apart from its specific work, the reorganized privy council was an advantage for royal government, for it assumed some of the queen's burdens without threatening her control. By functioning regularly and collectively, it gave the government a sense of oneness and enlarged the aura of the state. A board of dignitaries with power presented a solemn symbol to those who came into its presence, whether a trembling subject or an honored ambassador.

The Gains of Parliament and Queen

To summarize, Parliament gained corporate strength in the sixteenth century, but its subordination to the Crown was never more insisted on than under Queen Elizabeth. The administration became more institutionalized, but thereby it enabled the monarch to govern an increasingly complicated society more effectively. Royal government rose to the challenge of a larger population than the kings of the past had had to keep in order. Internal peace and law-abidingness probably surpassed the medieval norm. Although conflict was more widespread than ever—there were more people jostling each other, in their native quarrelsome spirit, within a richer web of economic interests and social ambition—that conflict was increasingly channeled into litigation and political rivalry. The government was able to expand the facilities for peaceful contention and to crack down on lawless violence. The royal side of government—executive and legal—needed to be asserted; it was asserted in new ways without becoming less royal.

The Political Significance of the Queen's Courtships

Susan Doran

Elizabeth was urged to marry by her Privy Council, Parliament, several bishops, foreign diplomats, and countless writers—and she was urged to marry for various reasons: to resolve the problem of succession, to form a beneficial political alliance, to protect England from its enemies, and to please her subjects. Why then did Elizabeth not marry? Various theories have been suggested, ranging from the biological (some physical impediment to intercourse or some mysterious disease) and psychological (a pathological aversion to marriage) to the feminist (a conscious choice of career over marriage and motherhood) and egotistical (a reluctance to share power with a husband and a desire to appear personally exceptional). Historian Susan Doran contends, however, that Elizabeth *did* wish to marry, twice, and that she was at least willing to enter marriage negotiations in two additional instances.

In her book-length study of the courtships of Elizabeth I, *Monarchy and Matrimony*, Doran traces the complex debates surrounding the courtships and the political tactics employed by the opponents of the various matches to reveal why Elizabeth remained single. In this selection from the conclusion of the book, Doran retraces her central argument and clarifies two central points: Elizabeth was too cautious and politically adept to insist on her personal preferences when her leading councillors opposed the match, and she was willing to marry only if her council reached consensus concerning a suitor. The story of the queen's courtships is finally less a narrative of her "matrimonial diplomacy" in foreign affairs and more a revelation of her desire to mediate political rivalries and retain her power at home; this latter desire led her to reject all controversial suitors and therefore to remain single.

Until 1581 Elizabeth's marriage was a dominant and often divisive political issue in England, and was treated with such importance by contemporaries that it provoked both polemical debate and political unrest. Elizabethan observers realised, even if later commentators have since forgotten, that the final outcome of the courtships was uncertain and could affect the political stability of the realm, determine its religious future, and influence the direction of England's relations with her neighbours abroad. By focusing on the matrimonial issue, therefore, a new window is opened onto the outlook and concerns of early Elizabethan England. Furthermore, only a detailed examination of the individual courtships can provide a full explanation of why Elizabeth did not marry. Certainly there is very little evidence to support the view, which appears in so many biographies, that from the very beginning of her reign the queen had made a conscious decision to remain unwed either because of her implacable hostility to matrimony or her determination to rule alone. . . .

Indeed, I question whether Elizabeth *chose* at all to remain single. It is clear to me that she did want to marry on two occasions: once on the death of Lord Robert Dudley's wife in September 1560 when most contemporary observers believed that she was seriously contemplating marriage to her favourite, and again in 1579 when she demonstrated a strong desire to wed Francis duke of Anjou. Furthermore, in response to intense pressure from her councillors and parliaments, she showed a readiness to marry two other suitors, though admittedly without the enthusiasm displayed during the Dudley and Anjou courtships. In the mid-1560s she agreed to open negotiations with the archduke Charles of Austria and from late 1570 through to the autumn of 1571 she encouraged matrimonial negotiations with Henry duke of Anjou. On both these occasions there was no dallying with her suitors for political advantage; on the contrary Elizabeth exhibited a serious intent to get down to the business of drawing up an acceptable matrimonial contract and at times was ready to offer concessions on areas of disagreement. . . .

The Council's Central Role

Why then did Elizabeth I not marry? Elizabeth's personal preferences provide no answer here, for there was little room for them to operate in this crucial area of policy. Had her Council ever united behind any one of her suitors, she would have found great difficulty in rejecting his proposal; likewise, without strong conciliar backing Elizabeth would not or could not marry a particular candidate. In the case of those men whom she had no particular wish to wed, opposition from within the Council allowed her to elude their suits. Thus, it had required concerted conciliar pressure to force her into negotiations for a marriage with the Archduke Charles, and it was only when a significant number of councillors spoke out against accepting Habsburg demands for a private Mass in November 1567 that she felt able to bring the courtship to an end. Similarly, in 1572 she was able to slip out of the negotiations with the duke of Montmorency for a marriage alliance with Francis duke of Alençon on the grounds that her Council was divided over whether or not to accept the French terms on religion. As she herself said on several occasions, she was only thinking of marriage to satisfy her subjects, so there was no point at all in taking a husband who would displease a significant number of them. In part such statements provided a convenient excuse to avoid the responsibility for the failure of particular sets of negotiations, but they also contained more than a grain of truth. Furthermore, on the practical side, she needed full conciliar support for a match so that the matrimonial treaty would not run into difficulties when presented to parliament for ratification.

At other times, however, when Elizabeth appeared to be close to accepting the hand of her favoured suitors, first Robert Dudley and then Francis of Anjou in 1579, the active opposition of some leading councillors convinced her that it would be definitely unwise and perhaps disastrous to proceed with the match. She was all too aware that both Wyatt's

Rebellion in Mary I's reign and Mary Stuart's deposition in 1567 had occurred when a queen regnant insisted upon taking a husband against the wishes of her important subjects. Elizabeth was far too cautious and politically adept to make the same mistake. There is every reason to suppose that had her councillors overwhelmingly supported either Dudley in late 1560 or Anjou in 1579, she would have gone ahead with the wedding.

Little to Recommend Early Suitors

But why could no suitor ever command the overwhelming support of her councillors? As far as most of the early matrimonial candidates were concerned, the answer is that there was little to recommend any of them: Philip II was unacceptable in England as the man held responsible (admittedly most unfairly) for the disastrous French War and the persecution of Protestants during the previous reign; marriage to him, moreover, was clearly incompatible with the radical changes in religion favoured by the queen and her new Council. Charles IX was out of the question because of his age; in 1564 when his suit was first raised he was only fourteen to the queen's thirty-one years. While Elizabeth herself was worried that she would look ridiculous at the wedding, like a mother taking her child to the altar, her councillors were more concerned that the young king would be unable to consummate the marriage for several years and that the match would thus fail to resolve immediately the succession problem.

Almost all the remaining early candidates were simply not thought good enough for a reigning monarch. As the Spanish ambassador in France said of the earl of Arran in 1560, these suitors brought nothing with them but their own person. Although the dukes of Saxony, Holstein, Ferrara and the rest might meet the requirement of siring an heir, the queen would gain no prestige, riches or valuable foreign alliance by wedding them. On the contrary, there was the strong likelihood that as consorts they would prove a drain on the queen's resources and bring her enemies rather than powerful friends. In addition, the disparagement involved in marrying a mercenary, such as Holstein, or even an elected king, such as Eric XIV [of Sweden], was not insignificant for a queen who had been pronounced a bastard and whose title to the throne was challenged by Mary Stuart and her allies. Elizabeth's preference for a husband of royal blood, therefore, was not just snobbery, as is frequently claimed, but a considered means of enhancing her own status and authority.

Opposition to Robert Dudley

Robert Dudley, of course, should have been viewed as a candidate in this category, for as Cecil rightly noted: 'Nothing is increased by Marriadg of hym either in Riches, Estimation, Power.' It was frequently said that the nobility despised him as a 'new man', whose father and grandfather had been attainted for treason, and that they considered the queen's marriage to a commoner as disparagement. Again, such thoughts went beyond the social elitism that was undoubtedly present; Elizabeth's child might well have to compete for the throne against Mary Stuart or any son she might have, and would be at a disadvantage with only one grandparent of royal blood, especially as some Catholics persisted in questioning whether Henry VIII had indeed fathered Elizabeth. The queen's deep affection for Dudley, however, outweighed these obstacles, while his own abilities as a self-publicist and politician helped him gradually to win over many initial opponents of his suit. As a result, he was considered a serious candidate by contemporaries until the mid-1560s and beyond.

Dudley's main handicap in courting the queen was the mysterious death of his wife. Although the coroner's court judged Amy Robsart's fall down the staircase at Cumnor Place to be 'death by misadventure', many clearly believed otherwise. Consequently, Elizabeth had good reason to fear that her marriage to Dudley would confirm the rumours that he had conspired to bring about his first wife's death, that she too was implicated in the murder, and that she and Dudley had long been lovers. Councillors like Cecil and royal servants like Throckmorton who opposed the marriage played on this anxiety by bringing to her attention the scurrilous comments circulating both at home and abroad about her relationship with her favourite.

The single most important reason for their hostility to Dudley's suit, however, was political self-interest. Most of Elizabeth's councillors and nobles distrusted Dudley as a potential faction-leader who would promote his own men and take revenge on the enemies of his father, the late duke of Northumberland. 'He shall study nothing but to enhanss his owne particular Frends to Welthe, to Offices, to Lands, and to offend others', wrote Cecil when listing his reasons against a Dudley marriage. Cecil was also no doubt well aware that his own political power would be most at risk if Dudley became royal consort. Like the favourite and unlike his aristocratic colleagues, Cecil had little power-base of his own in the early 1560s and his position depended entirely on the queen. Thus, in contrast to Dudley's earliest enemies, Arundel, Norfolk and Pembroke, Cecil was never won round to the match or seduced by the belief that it would be preferable for the queen to marry her Master of the Horse than to remain single. He, therefore, worked quietly but consistently behind the scenes to subvert Dudley's Spanish strategy in the springs of 1561 and 1562.

Dudley's Opposition to Other Suitors

The opposition within the Council to the other strong candidates for Elizabeth's hand was also based to a large extent on political self-interest. Dudley's hostility to the suits of Eric XIV, Archduke Charles and Francis of Anjou owed much to his anxieties that his own political position would be adversely affected by a royal marriage, for his intimacy with Elizabeth, the main source of his political influence and material rewards, could hardly continue once she had a husband. Furthermore, his political rivals, who were promoting these matches, would be likely to benefit if the queen married their favoured candidate. Sussex made this point in late 1567 when he told the Spanish ambassador at the Imperial court that 'if he concluded the marriage it would help him greatly against his political enemies'. For these reasons, Dudley took the lead in opposing these three matrimonial projects. In 1560 and 1561 he encouraged propaganda against a foreign consort in order to foil his Swedish rival. In the mid-

1560s he helped the French to present Charles IX as an alternative candidate to the Archduke Charles in an attempt to cloud the issue and divide the Council; when that failed, he opposed the match in the Council on religious grounds, and he may well have been behind the anti-Catholic scare whipped up in late 1567 and early 1568 to warn Elizabeth of the dangers in conceding a measure of religious toleration to the archduke. Between 1578 and 1579, his hand can again be detected behind many of the strategies designed to warn Elizabeth off a marriage to Francis duke of Anjou.

On each occasion Dudley was ultimately able to count on the active support of other councillors because of the nationality and religion of the suitors. For the queen and the supporters of the Habsburg and Anjou matches, marriage to a foreign prince was desirable as a means of placing a protective mantle around the realm. A match with the Archduke Charles was expected to bring with it an informal alliance with both the emperor and king of Spain; while the marriages to Henry of Anjou in 1571 and Francis of Anjou in 1579 were intended to bind England and France in a defensive league against Spain. Yet many at court disliked the prospect of the queen marrying a foreigner. Besides xenophobic prejudices, they shared a genuine apprehension about the practical political problems that seemed likely to arise from any union between Elizabeth and a foreign prince. Her consort, it was feared, might draw the queen into wars of his own making and expect her subjects to pay their cost; he might take his wife abroad to live in his own territories, leaving England to be governed by a viceroy; worse still, the birth of a male child would put at risk England's national independence. Furthermore, if Elizabeth were to die in childbirth, her husband would act as regent with the authority to rule until the child reached maturity. Even though a number of these concerns could be dealt with in a carefully worded marriage-contract, as indeed they had been in Mary I's matrimonial treaty, these alarming prospects influenced many to speak out against Elizabeth's foreign candidates. Anxieties were expressed both in Council meetings and political tracts, such as the discourse of Thomas Smith directed against the

Swedish and Habsburg candidates and the pamphlet of John Stubbs attacking the Anjou project.

The Anti-Catholic Scare

The greatest objection of all to the Austrian and French candidates, however, was their Catholicism. In each case, the promoters of the marriage believed that in time Elizabeth's consort would change his religion. Thus, when Cecil opened negotiations with the Archduke Charles of Austria in 1563, he was under the mistaken impression that the prince was sufficiently flexible to convert to Protestantism soon after the marriage. Similarly, it was hoped that Henry of Anjou would be educated into accepting the Protestant faith once he was removed from the influence of the Guises, and marriage negotiations with Francis of Alençon were initiated only in 1572 because he was held to be 'more moderate' and 'not so obstinate' in religion. Although some extreme Protestants opposed marriage to a Papist on ideological grounds, the majority view in the Council appears to have been that it would be acceptable provided that there were sound expectations of a conversion to Protestantism.

In the meantime, however, difficulties existed over the terms on which a Catholic consort could live in Protestant England. There were three main issues to be resolved. Was the wedding ceremony to follow the Catholic service or the English Prayer Book, and was it to be presided over by a priest or minister? Did Elizabeth's husband have to attend English Protestant services? Would he and his household be allowed to hear the Mass? Attempts to reach agreement on these issues bedevilled all the matrimonial negotiations. Henry of Anjou's refusal to make any concessions at all and his insistence both on non-attendance at Protestant services and freedom to hear public Mass ended his suit. Both the Archduke Charles and Francis of Anjou, however, were more accommodating and after tough negotiations Elizabeth was able to reach a compromise with them on the first two points which was satisfactory to the majority of her councillors. It was on the question of the Mass that the Council divided. On this issue, both suitors were again more flexible than Henry, in that they agreed to forgo public celebrations of the Mass provided that they and their fellow countrymen could hear it privately. But while this demand seemed reasonable to some councillors, it was totally unacceptable to others.

The division in the Council on the issue of the Mass was in part ideological. The councillors who recommended a limited toleration were on the whole conservative in religion: Sussex, Norfolk, Howard of Effingham, Croft and Hunsdon. On the other hand, Protestant zealots and Puritan patrons like Walsingham, Mildmay and Knowles viewed the Mass as extreme idolatry: 'The highest treason that can be against the lord's own person.' For them and many other Protestants outside the Council, it was Elizabeth's religious duty to take up the sword against this 'pagan rite', and not to allow it to be set up 'on the highest hill of the land, in London, which is our Jerusalem'. None the less the Council did not split cleanly along religious lines. Dr Thomas Wilson, a Marian exile and supporter of an interventionist Protestant foreign policy, gave his support to the Anjou match in 1579; whereas Sir Christopher Hatton, Archbishop Whitgift's patron and a noted conservative, came out as a leading opponent. Wilson's fear of an international Catholic league led him to accept the Anjou match as a necessary evil; Hatton, on the other hand, had more faith in England's power to withstand the international threat but feared the internal consequences of allowing Anjou liberty of worship. Cecil, whose deeply ingrained anti-Catholicism reflected an apocalyptic world view, nevertheless consistently promoted Catholic marriages for the queen on terms which would allow her consort a private Mass. His promotion of the Archduke match was mainly motivated by his worries about the succession, while in 1571 and 1579 he advocated a French match as a way to protect England against an international Catholic league. Nor were more self-interested political considerations ever entirely absent from his thinking.

Opposition to Francis of Anjou

In late 1567 Elizabeth did not need much convincing against the Archduke match, for she had her own doubts about agreeing to the Austrian's terms on both legal and political grounds. Conciliar opposition, however, bolstered her resolve and enabled her to reject the Archduke's request for a private Mass, thereby bringing the negotiations to a close. At the time of the Francis of Anjou matrimonial negotiations, however, Elizabeth strongly favoured the duke and was even ready to pass over the issue of the Mass in order to marry him. The overwhelming advantages of the Anglo-French matrimonial alliance seemed to outweigh the dangers of allowing Anjou the restricted exercise of his religion; it is also probable that she believed that, once married and under her influence, he would soon cease to hear Mass. On this occasion, therefore, the conciliar opposition to the match had to move into higher gear to persuade the queen against the marriage on these terms; led by Leicester and Walsingham, councillors against the match helped to mobilise a widespread propaganda campaign which Elizabeth could not ignore. . . .

Between 1558 and 1581 personal antagonisms, political rivalries and policy differences were at least as much a feature of the court scene as co-operation and consensus. Disagreements over the question of the queen's marriage and foreign policy exacerbated personal conflicts amongst courtiers and councillors, which could easily get out of hand and disrupt political stability. In late 1560 the threat of armed conflict between Dudley and the earls of Arundel and Pembroke shook the court. In 1562 a meeting of the Knights of the Garter around the time of St George's Day was disrupted when Arundel and Northampton stormed out in protest after a petition in favour of Dudley marrying the queen was approved. In 1566 rival followers of the Howards and Leicester wore distinctive colours to show their group loyalty and the danger of armed violence between Sussex and Leicester was so great that the queen was forced to intercede between them. In 1579 the divisions generated by the Anjou matrimonial project nearly resulted in a 'palace revolution' when Leicester and Walsingham were banished from court and the queen considered bringing some Catholics onto the Council. Nor were these disputes always confined to the court. Both the 1563 and 1566 parliaments were affected by divisions within the Council on the marriage and succession, while in 1579 preachers and polemicists brought a wider public into the debate on the Anjou marriage.

Elizabeth Prefers Consensus Politics

There is little evidence that Elizabeth encouraged these disputes and divisions by pursuing [what biographer Wallace MacCaffrey calls] 'a divide and rule' policy which gave her 'freedom of action' and turned her into 'an umpire to whose judgment the contenders would always have to bow'. Too much weight has been placed on the report of the Jacobean Sir Robert Naunton that Elizabeth made and unmade factions 'as her own great judgment advised'. On the contrary she usually encouraged rival politicians to work together to formulate and execute policy, and attempted to calm down passions which arose from their disputes. Thus Cecil was brought into the negotiations with de Quadra and Dudley in 1562 concerning England's representation at the Council of Trent, a move which in the event allowed her Secretary to outmanoeuvre both queen and favourite. In 1571 she left the day-to-day negotiations with the French to be handled by Leicester and Burghley in tandem. In October 1579 she tried to obtain the consent of the whole Council to the Anjou match; only later did she seek out councillors' individual written views as a way of breaking down the opposition to her plans. On the whole, then, Elizabeth preferred 'consensus' politics to 'divide and rule'; and the divisions at her court were a mark of political failure not a means for securing freedom of action. Indeed, it is questionable whether Elizabeth experienced very much 'freedom of action' in the area of matrimonial policy.

The queen who emerges from the pages of this [analysis] has less control over politics and policy-making than the Elizabeth of earlier studies. Even when we look at the creation of her public image, we can see that the iconography of chastity was imposed on her by writers, painters and their patrons during the Anjou matrimonial negotiations. Furthermore, in her dealings with foreign powers she appears far less adept at matrimonial diplomacy than her admirers have often asserted: there is little sign of the elusiveness and prevarication with which she is said to have dazzled and bewildered her suitors and their representatives for months, even years, on end. On the contrary, in practically all of her many courtships Elizabeth was straightforward and direct with those who wooed her, so much so that on several notable occasions Cecil intervened to advise a more cautious and evasive approach. In none of her negotiations, moreover, was Elizabeth herself successful in extracting major concessions from foreign courts.

On the other hand, the matrimonial negotiations also reveal Elizabeth's great strength as a ruler. Like all successful heads of state she had a highly developed instinct for survival: a sensitivity to public opinion and an awareness of what was politically possible. She listened and acted upon calls to marry; but turned down suits which proved unpopular or divisive. Only briefly during 1579 did her political intuition falter but even then she soon recovered and stepped back from the brink of the disaster which would surely have accompanied the Anjou marriage. She was not the Queenie of the television series *Blackadder* who could chop off heads at will or get her own way by throwing a tantrum. She was not the Glenda Jackson of *Elizabeth R* whose snarl could tame a cast of courtiers. She was not a tyrannical ruler who would ride roughshod over the views of the political nation. Aware of her own limitations, therefore, she listened to counsel, rejected controversial matches and in the event remained single.

The Emergence of an Ambitious Class of Tradesmen

Louis B. Wright

Although we tend to focus on the monarch and her court when we envision Elizabethan England, scholar Louis B. Wright contends that the Elizabethan tradesman was actually "the backbone of progressive enterprise" in Elizabethan England. A prolific scholar, Wright has published books on Shakespeare, Renaissance explorers, English colonization of North America, and several studies of life in colonial and frontier America. His wide-ranging interests inform and influence his study of enterprising tradesmen, *Middle-Class Culture in Elizabethan England*, first published in 1935. In this selection from the 1980 reprint of his book, Wright emphasizes the economic and social ambitions of the Elizabethan tradesman.

The development of industry and commerce during Elizabeth's reign "absorbed the activities of an ever increasing proportion of the population," Wright explains, and the financial success of individual members of this commercial class stimulated the economic ambitions of others in similar lines of work. This enterprising class of merchants, tradesmen, and craftsmen acquired a new spirit of independence and a sense of pride in the results of hard work.

With the increasing concentration of industry and trade in urban centers, especially London, large numbers of tradesmen were drawn to the cities during Elizabeth's reign. Unskilled urban laborers experienced grinding poverty, but business flourished, and many urban tradesmen became wealthy. Wright contends that the active life of ambitious tradesmen in London stimulated their desire not only for finer material possessions but also for education. Since the social ambitions of enterprising tradesmen included educating their sons, it is not surprising that several of the most celebrated Elizabethan writers were in fact sons of tradesmen.

We have created a conception of Elizabethan England as a land of dashing courtiers like [Sir Walter] Raleigh strewing coats in the mud for a queen to walk upon, of court intrigues, of maids of honor listening to sugared sonnets, of statesmen reading [Edmund] Spenser's *Faerie Queene* as a political document, of life spent in palaces or in high adventure on the Spanish Main. Of what the draper, the baker, the butcher, and their apprentices were reading and thinking we hear little.

But why consider the man in the street, dead these three hundred years? Perhaps he never read much, and thought less. If he did, what influence did it have? Why resurrect dead dullness? Is the taste of the average citizen of the present time not deplorable enough without unearthing the crudities of his ancestors?

We must remember, however, that the Elizabethan tradesman, the average citizen, was the backbone of progressive enterprise in England and the direct ancestor of a civilization soon to predominate on both sides of the Atlantic. His vigor and strength enabled England to take its place in the front rank of nations. As he pushed ahead, he developed new ideas of his own importance and bred an ambition for better things, material, spiritual, and intellectual. In the furtherance of his social ambitions, the Elizabethan business man evolved a philosophy of success, which emphasized thrift, honesty, industry, and godliness. Education, he found, was the key to advancement, and in the cultivation of his wits he foresaw the attainment of his ambitions. Substantial commoners, gathering strength in the sixteenth century, grew in intelligence and mental stature to become the power that was to conquer a new continent and make England great. The impetus gathered by the commercial classes swept England toward the Puritan Revolution of the mid-seventeenth century and the Whig supremacy of the eighteenth. Naïve, awkward, and crude as were the Elizabethan citizen's first attempts to take his place among the learned or the gentle, he possessed a strength of mind and character which gave vitality to his thinking and enabled him to propagate his ideas so luxuriantly that they have survived in all their vigor to become the clichés of modern civilization. The cultural interests, then, of so virile a group as the Elizabethan middle class deserve attention, for in these interests we may find much that explains our own culture.

Classes in Elizabethan Society

Elizabethan society may be roughly separated into three major divisions. The highest class consisted of the titled nobility, the landed gentry, and the more important members of the learned professions. The lowest class was composed of unskilled laborers, an illiterate peasantry, and those small artisans whose trades required little training and whose rewards were meager. Between these extremes was a great class of merchants, tradesfolk, and skilled craftsmen, a social group whose thoughts and interests centered in business profits. They made up the middle class, the bourgeoisie, the average men.

But the lines of distinction, even in the stratified society of the sixteenth and seventeenth centuries, were not distinct and mutually exclusive. The highest caste was eternally being recruited from the ranks of the rich merchants, and the lowest was always being swelled by economic derelicts. From both extremes the middle class absorbed new recruits. If the younger sons of the gentry regarded business as a refuge from the tyranny of primogeniture, poor youths, fresh from country toil, looked upon an apprenticeship in trade as the certain pathway to prosperity. If a rich merchant could aspire to a peerage or to lands and a coat of arms, many a daughter of a gentle house did not disdain a match with a tradesman who could offer her luxuries and the gaiety of the city. Professional men—preachers, lawyers, and physicians—frequently shared the ideals of the commercial group with which they were associated and from which, in many instances, they had come, and some of the yeomanry had much in common with the lower middle class. Nevertheless, despite the constant flux within the social order, the classes remained sufficiently independent of each other to be roughly distinguished, and preachers and lay writers constantly emphasized the necessity of the system of social degree.

The Middle Class

The middle class developed a way of life, a code of ethics, and a set of ideals which gave distinctness to its qualities. While the improvident poor degenerated into wretched misery, and the extravagant nobility ruined themselves with lavish entertainment, the middle class cultivated the virtues of thrift. "Put money in thy purse" echoed in the ears of every tradesman. Courtiers might fawn upon favorites for patents and monopolies, but enterprising business men, by dint of their own exertions, acquired not only wealth but a spirit of sturdy independence. Though not averse to profiting by political expediency, merchants and tradesmen learned that honesty and industry were the most certain ways to success. Having realized that wealth could be won by their own endeavors and that money would exalt their positions, tradesmen grew ambitious for further improvement. The ideal of progress—if not the word—was cultivated by the middle class in their desire for the improvement of their lot here below. If poets wished to pine over the lost golden age, it was merely proof of the impractical nature of poets. The tradesman set about gilding the age to his own taste. The middle class found that trade was not a tarnishing, shameful thing, but something to be proud of. Like his American descendant, the self-made man of Elizabethan England did not hide his light under a bushel. [Writers Thomas] Deloney and [Thomas] Dekker were fond of honest craftsmen who stood before kings and boasted of their labors. Thus many concepts of modern business life are traceable to the molding influence of Elizabethan bourgeois ideals. Utilitarianism was born of them and humanitarianism was a natural sequence. The materialistic dye which so deeply colors modern life was brewed in the cauldron of

Elizabethan business by tradesmen who believed that money and possessions were the proof of success. Even Calvin's grim theology did not discourage man from gathering material possessions. Instead, it was twisted to the profit of acquisitive society, for bourgeois religion, despite all its smoke and hell-fire, did not put away the world, and business expediency influenced the ethics evolved by the middle class. . . .

Economic Changes Increase Numbers of Middlemen

Economic changes of the sixteenth and early seventeenth centuries favored the development of industry and commerce, which absorbed the activities of an ever increasing proportion of the population. As the feudal agricultural system gave way to inclosures, farms and old corporate towns were depopulated, and a floating group struggled to adjust themselves to new conditions. The result was the swelling of the population of London and a few other industrial and trade centers, the development of new industrial villages and towns, and the spread of a system of cottage industries. The Statute of Apprentices of 1563 provided that all persons except gentlemen, scholars, and possessors of property must choose a trade from the crafts, the sea, or agriculture. Though it sought to prevent workers' wandering from one locality to another, it failed to stop their migration to industrial districts. The wool and cloth trade, which for centuries had been the core of English commerce, increased as England gradually wrung more trade from foreign markets and improved its means of distribution abroad through the trading companies that were so important in the expansion of Elizabethan business. As the demand for English cloth grew heavier, its production was stimulated by the increase in weaving in cottage and village. Since small manufacturers could not keep on hand a large supply of wool, there arose a class of middlemen who lived in the smaller towns and dealt in wool and cloth. For the benefit of such local tradesmen, legislation was repeatedly demanded to prevent London merchants and foreign buyers from purchasing directly from the small manufacturers; but so strong was the insistence upon the village weaver's right to sell where he wished, that restrictions on his trade were finally abolished. Not merely did the cloth trade expand and produce a host of related businesses, but such industries as iron founding, steel manufacture, the mining of coal, tin, lead, and gold, and a score of other industrial activities received new life in the later sixteenth and early seventeenth centuries. Thomas Sutton, founder of Charterhouse School, made a fortune in coal mining, and Bevis Bulmer succeeded so well with lead, tin, and gold that he won a knighthood and enlisted King James in a project for searching out gold in Scotland. Projectors, ancestors of the modern high-pressure salesman, swarmed in London with innumerable schemes for new businesses and industries, and inventors boasted of new processes for smelting iron with pit coal, making nails with a slitting machine, or even turning lead into gold. The romance or the tragedy of industrial development had begun, but such was the peculiar quality of Elizabethan industry that instead of centering business in the hands of a few great manufacturers with an army of slaves, as in the later Industrial Revolution, it multiplied the middle class.

Structure of Industry Inspires Ambition

The industrial development of the sixteenth and seventeenth centuries had this quality which distinguishes it from modern industry: the individual craftsman was closer to the completion and distribution of the product of his labor, and the apprentice or journeyman might look forward to becoming a master craftsman, who could, if he wished, combine the functions of manufacturer and retail or wholesale distributor of his finished products. The division of labor had not yet become so complex that the skilled laborer felt that he was merely a cog in an industrial machine. On the contrary, the system encouraged the development of a strong bourgeois spirit, for even a cottage weaver might employ one or two apprentices and journeymen weavers, who in turn might look forward to setting up as independent workmen. Though many journeymen continued to work for wages, the progression from apprentice to independent manufacturer was steadily going on to increase the number of small masters. Since the apprentice of today was the master of tomorrow, he was exhorted to cultivate the qualities that would make him a substantial and successful business man when he won his freedom and set up for himself. Although something like the factory system was foreshadowed in a few industries, such as cloth manufacturing, throughout the period the skilled craftsman could expect, provided he was industrious and thrifty, to become a manufacturer employing assistants to increase his output, and marketing directly his own handiwork. From the cottager with one apprentice to the employer of many journeymen, the economic points of view were similar. So overlapping were trades and business occupations that they combined to produce a middle class relatively far more extensive than modern industrial society permits. . . .

A New Urban Class

Although the widespread diffusion of industrial and commercial interests in Elizabethan England created a middle class who were not exclusively urban, yet as industry and trade tended more and more to concentrate in thickly populated areas, London and a few other towns became centers where large groups of citizens had an opportunity to develop an urban way of life and to taste the luxuries that further stimulated the pursuit of wealth and the acquisition of a set of social ideas prompted thereby. Port towns like Bristol, Plymouth, and Southampton grew into thriving marts. An industrial development prophetic of the future began in Birmingham, Sheffield, Halifax, Leeds, Wakefield, Manchester, and many other towns and villages, in which iron and cloth were the backbone of business. Even if foreign artisans—many of whom were brought in by the government—created intense animosity among native workers, they nevertheless taught Englishmen new trades and developed new industries which swelled the urban population. The manufacture of glass, paper, cutlery, and certain types of fabrics was improved by foreign immigrants, who settled in Canterbury, Sandwich, Norwich, Dover, and numerous other towns. Abundant as were the complaints in the sixteenth century about the decay of the old corporate towns, many new municipalities were laying the foundations for a commercial development that was soon to bring them size and prosperity.

Of all the urban developments of the sixteenth and seventeenth centuries, the growth of London was the most phenomenal and did the most to color the whole of Elizabethan civilization. In Chaucer's [poet Geoffrey, 1343–1400] prime, London had a population of probably fewer than 50,000 inhabitants. The population in 1563 has been estimated at 93,276; in 1580, 123,034; in 1593-95, 152,478; in 1605, 224,275; in 1622, 272,207; in 1634, 339,824. Since the population of the whole of England in 1600 was only about 4,460,000, the importance of London in relation to the rest of the country is at once apparent, for the capital was many times the size of any other city in the realm. In less than three-quarters of a century London more than trebled in size, expanding from a provincial walled town into a cosmopolitan city stirring with business, surrounded by busy suburbs. With the gradual decline of Venice and Genoa and the fall of Antwerp in 1585, London became the economic capital of Europe, a banking center, the seat of merchant princes, a distributing point for foreign and domestic goods. Its harbor teemed with ships whose tall masts astonished visitors. Its Royal Exchange, built by Sir Thomas Gresham in imitation of the Bourse at Antwerp, was the meeting place of traders from the ends of the earth. The gentry of England, who crowded to London to shine in the glory of the court, were followed by an army of tradesmen, great and small, who lived on the needs of the mighty. Cheapside, resplendent with shops, was a sight which travelers noted in their diaries. Rich silks from China, rare spices from the Indies, plate of hammered silver and gold, glassware from Venice, besides the endless array of articles of commoner use, filled the shops. The craftsmen, native and foreign, who plied their trades in and about the city were almost as varied in their occupations as the contents of the shops. Infinitely busy, London was forging ahead as the leading city of the world in commerce and industry.

Urban Aspirations

From country cottages, from small villages, from other industrial and commercial towns, tradesmen and craftsmen poured into London. The ambition of every provincial apprentice was to go like Dick Whittington to London, where he might grow rich and become an alderman or even lord mayor. Nor were the provincial gentry averse to apprenticing one or more of their younger sons to London tradesmen. With the world of commerce open before them and with a keen ambition driving them to success, these new citizens of London acted like a leaven to keep the fermentation of progress eternally at work. The result of their effort was evident in the prosperity of the city and in their personal achievements. Many did rise to positions of honor and authority, and a survey of the aldermen, sheriffs, and the lord mayors of the late sixteenth and early seventeenth centuries shows that a majority of them were of provincial birth, often of humble parentage. From all the counties of England came immigrants to settle in London and establish substantial families of industrious citizens. Though the plague might come like a holocaust to destroy the people, and though King James might pronounce a royal decree against crowding to the capital, the metropolis swelled until it burst its walls and overflowed into the suburbs, and approached the neighboring boroughs.

With the spread of commercial undertakings, the London citizenry, long famous for their sturdy independence, acquired new enterprise and daring. By the end of the sixteenth century trading companies were multiplying, and there were few citizens of even moderate means who did not have an interest in some of the ventures to the Indies, Russia, the Levant, or the New World. English ships pushed into strange ports and brought back stranger produce—sometimes to the disgust of the conservatives of the older generation, who looked askance at the traffic in luxuries that their fathers had got on without. As rumors of the profits from some of the trading ventures were bruited about and the appetites of investors were whetted, a rage of speculation swept England, until no scheme was too fantastic to find subscribers. . . .

Interest in Music and Art

The love of luxuries, which the traffic of business placed in reach even of small tradesmen, had tremendous esthetic effects. As citizens of London and other towns could afford it, they tore down their old houses and built new and finer homes with chimneys and glass windows and carved stairways. No longer, as in the days of their fathers, were tradesmen content with rude furnishings and bare necessities. Now they hung their walls with painted cloths and tapestries and had their portraits painted. As they grew richer, they laid out gardens and dreamed of country estates. Although diligence and industry were cardinal points in the tradesman's creed, he took time for honest pleasures, of which music was a favorite. Unlike his modern descendant, who turns a mechanical gadget and listens to a broadcasting crooner, the Elizabethan tradesman sang himself, either at his work or in the evening with his household. Folk songs were mingled with newer forms like the popular madrigal, introduced from Italy. For the singing of madrigals, Nicholas Yonge, a lay clerk of St. Paul's, was accustomed to bring together at his house "a great number of gentlemen and merchants . . . for the exercise of music daily." If so minded, the tradesman might play the lute, for even in barber shops he would find one provided for his convenience. With some misgivings, because the reforming preacher often railed at such frivolities, he might join in a dance with his friends and neighbors. The urban tradesman of the sixteenth and early seventeenth centuries was learning to cultivate the amenities of life, to enjoy the world about him, and to make it pleasanter for himself. . . .

Naïve though the artistic sense of Elizabethan commoners may have been, the esthetic consciousness of plain men and women was growing with a vigor stimulated by increasing wealth, which placed within reach of the multitude painted pictures, tapestries, and other handiwork of sundry native and foreign craftsmen skilled in the decorative arts. No longer content with smoky hovels and crude furnishings, citizens seeking the ornamental developed a taste for color and gorgeousness, which is reflected in all Elizabethan art, including literature.

Intellectual Awakening

The immense activity of the business life of London stimulated also the intellects of its citizens. If for no other reason, self-interest demanded an increase in knowledge, and utilitarian considerations prompted a new search after information. It was profitable to be informed. Nimbler wits than the countryman needed in his struggle with the forces of nature or in his wrangling on market days were required of the city dweller by the exigencies of urban competition. The cunning of the peasant gave way to the shrewdness of the business man. By constant association with his fellows, the citizen's mind was sharpened until he was able to penetrate new mysteries and grasp new ideas. As the goodliness of the world seized him, his ambition was magnified, and he acquired new desires and a way of life which led him to think in concrete terms of practical matters, to become a utilitarian. But getting and spending, establishing a reputation, founding a name respected in the community, and becoming perchance an alderman or even lord mayor, were not the sole preoccupations of worthy citizens, for some of the infinite curiosity that characterizes the intellectual Renaissance filtered down even to tradesmen; and unlettered men, more versed in the language of the market place than in that of the university, began to speculate about the universe and their relation to it. As a new physical world unfolded before their eyes, their own intellectual horizons widened, until it was no strange thing for plain citizens to think, talk, or read about everything from predestination to the motions of the planets. In the Renaissance, for the first time, books were useful to the rank and file of commoners, and as the literacy of Englishmen increased, ever more numerous became the books and pamphlets prepared for the intelligence of the "mean sort of men." Even stubborn learning gradually let down its bars of Latin until at length stores of erudition were available in English, and an Elizabethan apprentice might speak with more clerkly wisdom than a scholar in a previous age. And it was in this period that education came to be a goal desired of the generality of men. So potent was the ferment which set the minds of the middle class working that from their ranks came many of the writers, good and bad, who contributed to Elizabethan literature. Doubtless many a tradesman who sent his son to the university was not too pleased when the youth turned out to be a Bohemian, who rioted and wrote in London, but however that may be, many a tradesman's son sought to make his way with his pen. George Peele's father was a salter; Christopher Marlowe's, a cobbler; Anthony Munday's, a draper; John Webster's, a merchant tailor; Henry Chettle's, a dyer; Robert Herrick's, a goldsmith; Gabriel Harvey's, a ropemaker; Joshua Sylvester's, a clothier; John Donne's, an ironmonger; Thomas Browne's, a mercer; and many another had some connection with trade. A few skilled artisans like Thomas Deloney, the silk weaver, plied their pens in addition to the tools of their crafts. The busy world of trade, especially in London, woke men from the easy provincialism of the past and helped to set in motion the currents of activity that stimulated the desire, not merely for more and finer material possessions, but for better things in literature and learning.

Poverty and Social Regulation in Elizabethan England

Paul Slack

One of the most significant achievements during Elizabeth's reign was the enactment of the 1601 Poor Law. Perhaps the most important piece of social legislation prior to the nineteenth century, the poor law established a tax to finance relief for the deserving poor, specified punishment for vagrants and beggars, and authorized work plans for the unemployed but able poor. In this article, Paul Slack describes the legislation passed earlier in Elizabeth's reign that shaped the 1601 Poor Law, the causes of poverty that made such legislation necessary, and the responses of Elizabethans to such government intervention. In addition, Slack explains both why the material results of such legislation were negligible and why the impact of the poor laws on Elizabethan attitudes was substantial. As Tutor in Modern History at Exeter College, Oxford, author of several other articles on social issues in sixteenth and seventeenth century England, and co-author of the book *English Towns in Transition*, Paul Slack brings significant breadth and depth of knowledge to bear on this central piece of Elizabethan legislation. Paul Slack has also edited two other books, *Crisis and Order in English Towns* and *Rebellion, Popular Protest and the Social Order*.

After the Anglican Church, the English poor-law was the most long-lasting of Elizabethan achievements. As finally codified in the legislation of 1601, it persisted without fundamental alteration until 1834. That is one reason why we should pay some attention to its origins. The poor-laws also

Excerpted from "Poverty and Social Regulation in Elizabethan England," by Paul Slack, in *The Reign of Elizabeth I*, edited by Christopher Haigh (Athens: University of Georgia Press, 1985). Reprinted by permission of the author.

played a major part in Elizabethan government. Any list of the 'stacks of statutes' which the Tudors imposed on the shoulders of justices of the peace will include the acts of 1563, 1572, 1576 and 1598 which were concerned with the relief of the destitute and the punishment of vagabonds, along with related legislation aiming to regulate the lives and behaviour of the 'commons', such as the Statute of Artificers of 1563. Social welfare and social regulation were matters of increasing public concern between 1558 and 1603.

So much is familiar historical ground. What is less clear is the reason for this development. Was it that poverty and the social disorders to which it was thought to be related were in fact increasing in the course of the reign? Most historians would think that they were, although they would disagree about the degree of change, some taking a much more optimistic view than others. On the other hand, it might be argued that a change in perceptions of social problems, rather than in the nature of the problems themselves, provoked new government initiatives. Again, most historians would probably agree that attitudes did change, to some extent independently of social and economic conditions. But there is as yet no consensus on whether these shifts of view were connected with other intellectual changes, in religion for example. This essay will explore these uncertain and controversial areas in order to try to throw some light on the relationship between social circumstances and people's reactions to them.

The 1601 Poor Law

We ought to start by describing the developments which seem to require explanation. To begin with there was the poor-law itself, gradually shaped by successive statutes up to the great enactment of 1601. It had three essential features. The first, and ultimately the most important, was the poor-rate, the compulsory assessment in each parish which financed outdoor relief to deserving indigent households. In 1563 secular sanctions were threatened against those who refused to contribute to collections for the poor. In 1572 justices of the peace were empowered to determine the size of contributions, thus turning them into an imposed tax: they were to assess richer parishioners after surveys of the poor had been made to see what money was needed. Finally, in 1598, the ground was prepared for the widespread adoption of rates, when the main responsibility for levying them was transferred from overworked justices to the churchwardens and overseers of every parish.

The second feature of the poor-law, the *quid pro quo* [one thing in return for another] in return for public taxation and outdoor relief, was a sustained but unsuccessful campaign against vagrants and beggars. Begging and casual almsgiving were prohibited unless licensed by authority, and successive poor-laws viciously attacked wandering paupers with a variety of penalties. In the end, under a second act of 1598, vagrants were to be summarily whipped and returned to their place of settlement by parish constables. Once again the execution of the law was made quicker and easier than before by placing it in the hands of parish authorities; it did not require the cumbersome intervention of justices in every case, as the Act of 1572 had done.

The third feature of the law was complementary to the others: an effort to provide work for the poor so that they would neither wander abroad nor needlessly claim relief. By an act of 1576 justices of the peace were authorised to provide any town which needed it with a stock of flax, hemp or other materials on which paupers could be employed, and to erect a house of correction in every county for the punishment of those who refused to work. In practice little was done before 1603. Although some of the larger towns had houses of correction, workhouses, or work stocks, they were always small, they rarely lasted long and they were often mismanaged. Nevertheless, the imposition of labour discipline was from the start as fundamental an ambition of legislators as the provision of public doles for the deserving poor and public whippings for vagrants. . . .

Earlier Government Responses to Poverty

At first sight the concerns of the central government appear almost entirely negative, for the Council's most frequent declarations of social policy, in proclamations, concentrated on one simple target, rogues and vagabonds. There was a more positive side to government policy, however, and that appeared in a major Elizabethan innovation: the printed Books of Orders circulated to all justices of the peace. There were two series of these, one describing actions to be taken during epidemics of plague, the other directing local responses to dearth and harvest failure. Each codified earlier practices and imposed a new uniformity on local authorities. According to the plague orders, published for the first time in 1578, infected houses were to be strictly quarantined; the sick and their families should be supported from special rates and guarded in order to prevent fresh contacts. The dearth orders, first published in 1586, kept justices and parish officers equally busy. They had to take local surveys of grain when the harvest failed, to arrange for surpluses to be brought regularly to market, and to see that they were sold there in small quantities to the poor. Both books were reprinted whenever plague or dearth recurred, and they were enforced, haphazardly but widely. Scores of towns were isolating and supporting large numbers of infected households in the plague epidemics of 1592–6 and 1603–9, and lists of grain stocks were drawn up in the hundreds and divisions of several counties in 1586–7 and 1597–8.

Elaborate responses to poverty, dearth and disease were perhaps the most striking elements of Elizabethan social policy, but they were not the only symptoms of contemporary interest in social regulation and control. The Council tried to get at some of the roots of these problems in its prolonged battle against the growth of London: prohibiting new building and the subdivision of houses, at first through a proclamation of 1580 and then with the help of a statute passed in 1593. An act of 1589 against the erection of cottages on commons and wastes was directed against the same phenomenon in the countryside: rapid population growth which went hand in hand with impoverishment, disease and disorder. Statutes against enclosure and in favour of tillage in 1563 and 1598 exhibited a similar desire to prevent disruptive social and economic change. The Statute of Artificers of 1563 showed, among other things, that MPs [members of Parliament] wished the disciplines of apprenticeship to be widely enforced for the same purpose, in agriculture as well as in industry. Throughout the reign, proclamations enforcing sumptuary legislation [laws regulating expenditure on food and dress to perpetuate distinctions in social class] were intended to perpetuate existing social distinctions in styles of dress.

Much of this activity—apprenticeship restrictions, enclosure laws and sumptuary regulations in particular—had, of course, a long history behind it. But there was a change in emphasis in the course of the reign. Some old concerns fell into the background and others came to the fore. If we look at proclamations, for example, it is notable that six of the nine Elizabethan proclamations on apparel were issued before 1581, while ten out of thirteen proclamations concerning vagrants were issued after 1581. Parliamentary interest in the condition and conduct of the poor also increased in the last two decades of the reign. Sumptuary regulations were still debated, but government interference with the behaviour of the social élite now aroused opposition, and existing legislation on the subject was repealed in 1604. A warmer parliamentary welcome was given to proposals for stricter regulation of other matters: poverty, on which there were at least seventeen bills in the 1597–8 session alone; drunkenness, inns and alehouses, on which there were thirteen bills between 1576 and 1601; profanation of the sabbath, giving rise to six bills between 1584 and 1601; and bastardy and swearing, on which there were bills in 1597 and 1601 respectively. The manners and behaviour of the lower orders rather than of their betters seemed urgently to require reformation at the end of the reign.

Similar anxieties can be found at the local level, in the bylaws passed by town councils and in the orders made by quarter sessions. By the turn of the century urban magistrates all over the country were trying to control lodgers and inmates, the subdivision of houses, the number of alehouses, and popular recreations, especially on the sabbath. Country justices were spending an increasing amount of time dealing with bastardy, alehouses, unlawful games, cottages, vagrants and the settlement of the poor. Whether one looks at the records of the Council, of Parliament, or of local authorities, there can be no doubt that in the latter half of Elizabeth's reign people in authority felt threatened by rising populations, large numbers of vagrants and paupers, and the disorders they provoked. In the following section we must ask whether the realities were in fact as critical as contemporaries supposed.

Causes of Poverty

The most obvious circumstantial explanation for some of the developments considered above lies not in general economic trends but in the temporary crises which occurred in Elizabeth's reign. The Rising in the North[1] appears to have been a particularly formative event. Although there was no justification for the view that vagabonds caused rebellion, the myth was a potent force in the years immediately after 1569. It stimulated searches for vagrants throughout the country, and probably led directly to the legislation of 1572. An associated political conspiracy in Norwich was followed by the remodelling of social welfare there in 1570, and fears for political stability may have inspired the revision of poor-relief machinery in Bristol in the same year. The 1570s were also a decade of considerable activity in London, with the Council [Elizabeth's Privy Council] prodding the corporation [the local London authorities] to produce new schemes for the relief and employment of the poor, for grain provision and plague control, especially after a sudden rise in food prices in 1573 and an epidemic in 1577–8.

For the nation as a whole, the disasters of disease and dearth were much more serious in the last two decades of the reign. Plague spread to many towns after devastating outbreaks in London in 1593 and 1603, disrupting economic activity and throwing hundreds of victims onto parish relief. Harvest failures in 1586, and in 1595, 1596 and 1597, brought malnutrition, disease and further surges in mortality to the poorer suburbs of towns and to more isolated rural

---

1. a pro-Catholic, anti-government rebellion led by a conservative faction of earls in the north of England, 1569

areas, such as the uplands of Cumbria, where cases of starvation were reported. Food prices rose everywhere, however, and the later 1590s in particular were years of social stress over much of the country. Widespread distress was accompanied by a peak in crimes against property, by a similar high point in illegitimacy rates, and by food and enclosure riots. The comprehensive poor-relief legislation of 1598 was clearly prompted by critical circumstances.

It is much more difficult to judge the extent to which economic conditions were deteriorating in the longer term and producing a gradual increase in the number of the poor. There is no doubt that the standard of living of wage-earners and labourers declined. Population increased at a greater rate than productivity in the sixteenth century; prices rose faster than wages; and the purchasing-power of the latter dropped, to reach its nadir in the years around 1620. According to the available indices, the real value of wages fell by about a quarter in the course of Elizabeth's reign. . . .

It is plausible to argue from the evidence that conditions were getting worse: there were more vagrants and more paupers with valid claim to public assistance, and both were the result, not just of frequent temporary crises such as dearth and plague, but of long-term economic trends which produced heavy mobility and underemployment. Whether one describes these realities as 'critical' is perhaps a question of semantics. We can readily appreciate why contemporaries thought them so. Even though they failed fully to appreciate its causes, 'the great plenty of poverty in all the cities, great towns and other inferior market towns in England and Wales' was obvious. To understand the full nature of the contemporary response, however, why it was so energetic in some directions and so misconceived in others, we must turn from the circumstances which made it necessary to the attitudes which equally helped to shape it.

Reactions to Poor Law Legislation

It might seem that the natural conservatism of any social élite is sufficient to explain Elizabethan reactions to the conditions described above. An instinctive desire to maintain degree, order and place would set all sixteenth-century authorities against mobility, idleness, urban growth and the disorderly consequences of poverty. That this is not the whole story, however, is suggested by the opposition which some of the measures taken aroused at the time. However conservative its inspiration, public action in the interests of social welfare and social discipline had radical implications.

Part of the opposition to the poor-laws was, of course, self-interested. Taxation for poor-relief was vehemently resisted, in Warwick and elsewhere, because it was taxation. Those who were the victims or beneficiaries of public action had equally good reason to object to its regulatory aspects, to abuse the magistrates who, in the words of a Thetford man in 1577, 'did more than they might do . . . dealing with the poor but not with the rich'. But there were also issues of greater principle involved. In the parliamentary debates of the poor-law in 1571 and 1572, several members questioned whether the definition of a vagrant should be drawn so broadly that it encompassed such representatives of traditional wayfaring-life as minstrels. Miles Sandys thought the whole law 'oversharp and bloody': vagrancy could easily be eliminated if the justices worked to 'relieve every [poor] man at his own house'. On the other hand, Thomas Wilson urged harsh penalties because of the 'looseness and lewdness' of the times: 'he said it was no charity to give to such a one as we know not, being a stranger unto us'.

Behind such controversy lay two related questions. The first was whether the relief of the poor was a matter for government intervention at all. Should it not be left to the old practices of neighbourly, and largely informal, charity? The parishioners of part of the West Riding adopted this view when they opposed the prohibition of begging and the introduction of rates in 1598 on the grounds that 'many are able to give relief which are not able to give money'; neighbours would support their neighbours with help in kind. The second question was how much discrimination there should be in the giving of alms, whether public or private. Should minstrels or strangers be treated generously, as traditional ideals of hospitality might seem to imply?

These issues were never starkly articulated in this period, but they were tacitly present in much of the literature on charity and hospitality published in Elizabeth's reign. No English writers took as hard a line in favour of public intervention and discrimination as Martin Bucer and some continental reformers; still less did any of them openly oppose these innovations. While some stressed their necessity, however, others expressed reservations and insisted on qualifications. Robert Allen [in his *A Treatise of Christian Beneficence* (1600)], for example, warned his readers against being too scrupulous in their giving: in the end it was better 'that alms should be cast away, than any creature should perish for want of relief.' The tension between old ideals of private hospitality and the newer emphasis on public discrimination may even have been felt at the village level. It has been argued that it helps to explain many of the witchcraft accusations of the period, which had their roots in the local antagonisms and feelings of guilt aroused when neighbourly charity was denied.

There was certainly a good deal of confusion in practice. Informal and indiscriminate almsgiving continued, on an unquantifiable but probably large scale. [As stated in *The Book of John Fisher 1580–88*, edited by T. Kemp] vagrants went on calling 'at many gentlemen's and honest men's houses to have their charity'. Although poor-rates became more common after the Act of 1572, it was only in the generation after the 1598 statute that they spread to a majority of rural parishes. It is unlikely that they raised anything like the sums given in alms in the streets or in voluntary contributions in parish churches before the end of the reign; just as they certainly did not match the sums available for poor relief from privately endowed charities. The government itself was often forced to pay more than lip-service to old ideals while advocating the new. In years of dearth the Church was called upon to publicise the traditional virtues of neighbourly hospitality, with scarcely a hint of discrimination.

Yet the trend throughout the reign was plainly towards more government intervention and direction of welfare activity. The Books of Orders for dearth assumed that public regulation of markets would replace neighbourly charity as a more efficient and effective use of scarce resources when the harvest failed. The Books of Orders for plague imposed on infected households quarantine restrictions which prevented the visiting of sick neighbours, and thus, as some contemporaries complained, flew in the face of traditional charitable obligations. The campaign against vagrants and beggars and against indiscriminate almsgiving grew in vigour. By 1603 some old ideals were in retreat. . . .

Puritan Social Activism

There is considerable evidence that Puritans made a powerful contribution to the developments we have been seeking to explain. This lay first and foremost in what has been termed their 'social activism'. Their determination to shape a godly commonwealth led them to undertake practical reforms in pursuit of what were fundamentally commonplace social ideals, while their less committed colleagues did nothing. Again and again we find godly ministers and magistrates, often in close alliance, initiating new regulations and new institutions. It was the presbyterian divine, Thomas Cartwright, acting, it has been said, like a Calvinist deacon, who inspired the listings of the poor in Warwick in the 1580s and who helped to reform poor-relief there. The result was certainly closer discrimination in the giving of relief, but also a large increase in the sums spent on poor households. The consequences were similar in Norwich a decade earlier, where new orders for the poor specifically provided for a deacon in every ward. The wholesale reform of social welfare there between 1570 and 1572 occurred under a mayor, John Aldrich, who had Puritan leanings, and on the eve of the city's greatest fame as a Puritan citadel guided by its 'apostle', John More. As an MP Aldrich may well have influenced the poor-relief legislation of the 1570s, just as later Puritans, such as Robert Wroth and George More, took a notable part on committees on the poor-law in the last parliaments of the reign.

Energetic Calvinist paternalism had a further consequence. Directed as it was against a multitude of social and moral ills, it strengthened and multiplied the existing links between poor-relief and other forms of social regulation. In the 1570s some of the Norfolk justices had regular divisional meetings at the Acle Bridewell, where, after prayers, they punished rogues, bastard-bearers, drunkards and other unruly people. [Francis] Walsingham reported to [William] Cecil that it was work which was both 'necessary and . . . full of piety'. In 1578 the Puritan justices of Bury St Edmunds similarly drew up a list of orders against offences from idleness and fornication to usury and witchcraft. In Parliament men such as Wroth and More were active on committees on a whole range of subjects concerning the conduct of the rude masses. The relief and regulation of the poor was conceived as one part of a wider campaign for the reformation of popular manners.

Hardening Prejudices

The result could only be a hardening of established prejudices about the disorderly poor. Despite new generosity in the provision of outdoor relief, despite the facts which the censuses revealed about virtuous, inescapable poverty, the effect of much Puritan rhetoric was to associate the poor with social threats of all kinds. Puritan preachers and writers might admit the existence of the respectable pauper, but in their by-laws and orders Puritan magistrates spoke a different language, stressing the infectious vices which indigence bred. A proclamation in Norwich in 1571 pictured a society in which the lower orders slid inexorably 'from idleness to drunkenness to whoredom to shameful incest and abominable life, greatly to the dishonour of God and ruin of the commonwealth'. The overseers must therefore search the houses of the poor 'several times in every week' to identify men who broke down hedges for firewood, girls who wished 'to keep house by themselves', drunkards and those who absented 'themselves from their own houses at unseasonable times in the night'. Such orders display what Professor [Patrick] Collinson has called 'collective paranoia'; and it was a paranoia which prevented any cool appraisal of social and economic realities and which encouraged their misinterpretation.

Not everyone took so committed or extreme a view, of

course. Puritan magistrates and ministers were a distinct minority. But they were simply in the vanguard in the growing use of poor-relief as a means of social control, and their approach, in modified tone, was often widely adopted. While Puritans in Ipswich denied poor-relief to those who did not attend church, other local authorities refused it to those who broke hedges or 'unreverently abused any that is a contributor to the poor'. By the 1590s several towns had orders against the disorderly poor associating them, as in Colchester, with 'thefts, pilfering and other lewd and ill vices'. It was a less strident indictment than that in Norwich in 1571, but its message was the same; and it had the effect of branding as disorderly, with labels once applied only to a small and marginal group, that larger class of the poor which we have seen emerging in Elizabeth's reign. That was a major and lasting achievement, contributing to the closer definition of the respectable and unruly segments of society and to the growing gap between them.

A final caveat should be entered here. Much of the reaction to social problems described above was indeed rhetoric. Even laws and proclamations were often not enforced: they too were propaganda as much as prescriptions of viable solutions for real problems. The most burdensome provisions of social legislation, those relating to apprenticeship or work stocks, for example, were never fully implemented. Quarter sessions dealt more readily with symptoms, attacking bastardy, alehouses, unlawful games and, of course, vagrants; and even this campaign was only just beginning in the 1590s and was to acquire greater momentum in the early decades of the seventeenth century. We have seen that rhetoric and propaganda influenced contemporary ways of thinking, but we must ask in conclusion whether the efforts surveyed in this essay had any more positive impact, in the alleviation of poverty or the imposition of social control.

Results of Poor Law Legislation

As far as poverty is concerned, enough has perhaps been said already to indicate that the effects of contemporary remedies were probably marginal. The deliberate redistribution of wealth from rich to poor by 1603 was minimal. For example, the total yield of endowed charities for poor-relief amounted to less than 0.25 per cent of the national income; and the amount raised by poor-rates was much smaller than that. At the margin of subsistence and in crisis years public measures probably had a greater effect: control of markets, subsidised sales of grain, and increases in outdoor relief must have done something to save some people from starvation, especially in towns—though the effects of these enterprises have never been quantified. But the impact on poverty more generally was slight. It was to be economic growth not public welfare which alleviated social problems in the seventeenth century.

Much the same may be said about efforts to impose social control. Although the English welfare system might seem at first sight one reason why England had less internal disorder than some other countries at the time, it is difficult to substantiate the case. Against it we might point to the small numbers actually relieved, to the lack of effective police activity against vagrants, and above all, perhaps, to the fact that poor-relief was largely confined to social groups who would not have been major threats to public order anyway: orphans, widows, broken families and a few of the labouring poor. Again, the situation may have been different in crisis years. Grain policies, for example, were intended to prevent food riots and the threat or reality of disorder often prompted their use. They were implemented in Northampton in 1586–7 because [as stated in the Northamptonshire leutenancy papers 1580–1614] 'our poor people are so hardly distressed that we stand in great doubt of some mutiny or unlawful attempt to arise amongst them'. On the other hand, the frequency of food riots in the later 1590s hardly suggests that efforts to prevent them were wholly successful.

The issue is not quite as simple as that, however. Elizabethan social policies may have had a real effect, not through direct alleviation of poverty or disorder, but through their impact on attitudes. We return, in fact, to their role as propaganda. One function of the paternalism explicit in Elizabethan grain policies, for example, was to persuade poor consumers that the government shared their view of the social order and identified the same enemies of the common weal as they did: middlemen above all. The persuasion probably worked to some degree, and on this argument there would have been more disorder than there was in years of dearth if social policies had not existed. Even if scarcely successful in practice, welfare activities did something to encourage and to justify deference.

Social policies also had a propaganda effect on those who were not their objects. One reason for the absence of popular rebellion and serious public disorder after 1569, it has been argued, was the reluctance of the 'middling sort'—prosperous farmers and artisans—to lead it as they had once done. There were economic reasons for that, as local communities were increasingly polarised between the relatively rich and the poor. But there was also an attitudinal shift as the middling ranks of society adopted the view of their superiors that popular behaviour was deviant, disorderly and dangerous. They became agents of social control themselves and, in some cases, enthusiasts for a reformation of manners. Some of the policies we have described were an expression of that social distancing; but they also contributed to its formation.

The sticks as well as the carrots present in Elizabethan social policies thus helped to satisfy contemporary expectations and so to maintain social stability, even if the promise was greater than the performance in both cases. The ambivalent combination of charitable generosity and social discipline which we have seen in the vagrancy and poor-rate provisions of the law, in the ambitions of Puritan activists and in the efforts of local authorities, served a purpose. It was an uneasy combination, but regulation and relief, social control and provision for the poor, went hand in hand—as in social policies they always do.

Chapter 2

The Elizabethan Theater

Turning Points
IN WORLD HISTORY

The Birth of Professional Theater

Thomas Marc Parrott and Robert Hamilton Ball

The flowering of Elizabethan drama in the 1580s is often attributed to a group of young university-educated playwrights with training in the drama of classical writers, familiarity with English medieval drama and continental romances, and unique powers of innovation. The success of these writers, however, depended centrally on professional actors, public theaters, and an audience willing to pay for the pleasure of seeing theatrical performances.

The drama of the later Middle Ages had already created a large popular audience for theater, but the performers were primarily amateurs and the plays were religious and didactic. Although the rise of the professional actor occurred gradually during the fifteenth and early sixteenth centuries, the convergence of established professional acting companies, actual buildings for performances, and a willing audience made possible the distinctive drama which appeared in the last two decades of Elizabeth's reign.

In this selection from their book *A Short View of Elizabethan Drama*, Thomas Marc Parrott and Robert Hamilton Ball trace the emergence of organized theater companies and the establishment of public playhouses. Parrott and Ball also describe how the conditions of the companies and the theaters influenced the type of drama being produced.

Parrott has edited and introduced several collections of Shakespeare's plays, and he has written a handbook to Shakespeare. Ball has written a book on theater language and a history of the theater entitled *The Amazing Career of Sir Giles Overreach*.

Medieval drama was essentially an amateur affair presented first by the clergy and later by trade guilds. Elizabethan drama, while it retained its amateur standing in academic performances at schools and colleges and Inns of Court, and in the participation of lords and ladies in masques and entertainments, was, in its public aspects, almost wholly professional. In [poet Geoffrey] Chaucer's time [the fourteenth century], while large sums of money were spent on pageant performances and one craft vied with another in sumptuous expenditure, there was no direct charge to the audience for witnessing the performance. Actors, it is true, were paid for their exertions, but the performer was really a fisherman or a butcher, a tailor or a goldsmith, not a professional entertainer. By Shakespeare's time, audiences paid to witness plays in public theatres which earned ample incomes for managers and share-holders, and the business and art of acting had become a profession providing an adequate livelihood. . . .

The Rise of the Professional Actor

The transition from amateur to professional may most easily be marked by considering the rise of the professional actor. Local players of Miracles [cycles of plays dramatizing central events in the Bible, often called "mystery play cycles"], as in the case of the late *Ludus Coventriae* [plays of coventry], sometimes presented their cycle away from home and became thereby an embryonic stock company, amateur but paid for their services. When it grew apparent to them that there was a conflict between their acting and their local trade duties, that it was possible to earn a living wage and in a new and uncrowded activity, the step to professionalism was easy [members of trade guilds performed these plays]. Moreover, once a general interest had been aroused in the drama and the presentation of plays became profitable, the ever-present minstrels, mountebanks, and acrobats were quick to turn from juggling, jesting, and gymnastics to acting. Rivalry between amateur and paid entertainers or combinations for mutual assistance stimulated the process of professionalism. *The Castle of Perseverance*, ca. 1450 [a "morality play" tracing the temptations and decisions of a representative human character], was carried from place to place by a troupe of travelling players who drummed up trade by announcing performances a week in advance. A little later the actors of *Mankind* [another "morality play"] felt no compunction in interrupting their play to pass the hat, and professional comedians were assisting in the banquet-interlude, *Fulgens and Lucres, ca.* 1497.

Players Acquire Patrons

This development of acting nevertheless exposed the early groups of players to a new danger, as is shown by an Act of 1545. Since the strollers had deserted their regular trades and were no longer members of craft guilds, they were listed as vagabonds and masterless men and hence were subject to arrest and imprisonment. The more fortunate escaped this precarious position by putting themselves like the minstrels under the patronage of important personages, which made them automatically "servants" and freed them from the stigma and the perils of vagabondage. This process was accelerated by later statutes of 1572 and 1596. It had begun a century earlier, for we hear of companies protected by the Earl of Essex, and Richard, Duke of Gloucester, later Richard III, in 1482; and the earls of Northumberland, Oxford, Derby, Shrewsbury, and Lord Arundel had actors in their service before the fifteenth century closed. Henry VI had "pleyars of the Kyngs enterluds" at his Court as early as 1494 and paid them an annual wage, and similar royal patronage was granted by his successors as late as the reign of Elizabeth.

Since the connection between patron and company was partly nominal, it was natural that the acting groups when they were not on duty as members of a household should eke out their income by travelling. In 1559 Robert Dudley, later the Earl of Leicester, wrote a fellow-nobleman requesting his friend's license for "my servants" to play in Yorkshire, and fifteen years later he secured from the Queen permission for them to act in London and elsewhere, despite local rules to the contrary, so long as their plays met the approval of the Master of the Revels. Other noblemen who had companies followed suit, so that by the end of the century there were always two or three groups playing in London and a number of less distinguished companies touring through the country. They presented their plays in great halls and banquet chambers, on village greens, and, most important of all, in inn-yards.

Performances in Inn-Yards

The inn-yard had proved from early times a most satisfactory place for the presentation of plays. The restrictions of a room were absent; there was no chance for the audience to scatter when it came time to levy contributions. It is interesting, for example, that *Mankind*, which includes in its dialogue directions for gathering money, had its stage set in the courtyard of an inn. It is hardly necessary to point out that since the inn was a center of social life as well as a haven for travellers, it made its own contribution to the audience and the festive atmosphere of the theatre. As time went on, certain inns—in London, the Bell, the Cross Keys, the Bull, the Bel Savage, and the Boar's Head (not, however, Falstaff's Boar's Head in Eastcheap)—were specifically dedicated to dramatic purposes, partially reconstructed, and even, somewhat misleadingly, referred to as theatres. Three were destroyed in the London fire of 1666, but in 1668 Samuel Pepys visited the Bull, and the Boar's Head Yard may still be reviewed by the curious in Whitechapel.

Those Elizabethan inns in which actors' companies presented plays were usually made up of a collection of buildings grouped around a hollow square, which formed the courtyard, entered from the street by a single archway. Inside around the yard ran a series of galleries opening on the adjacent rooms of the inn. Opposite the entrance the players set up a scaffold projecting from the building into the yard, and backed by a curtain hung from the gallery immediately over it, which could be utilized for balcony scenes or the walls of a beleaguered city. Behind the curtain was "behind-the-scenes"; in other words, actors came on stage through the curtains from their dressing and property room in the inn. At the entering archway stood a "gatherer" who collected the admission fee, usually a penny, to the flagged quadrangle where the "groundlings" stood. No doubt other "gatherers" within the court pointed out the advantage of paying further pennies for particularly desirable positions. Members of the audience who had the money for more commodious arrangements hired rooms in the inn and sat on benches or stools in the galleries, whence they could look down on groundlings and the stage. The Elizabethan theatre was anything but aristocratic. Class distinctions were certainly important, but all classes were there from nobles and sober citizens and their wives to prentices, pickpockets, and harlots; and the wide scope and variety of Elizabethan drama is mainly due to the heterogeneity of the enthusiastic playgoers at these professional performances in inn-yard or theatre.

The First Public Theatres

In 1575 London had no regular theatres, that is, no buildings designed and constructed primarily for the presentation of plays. Nothing shows more clearly the growth of the professional drama than the fact that eight playhouses rose within the next thirty years, some of them so large and handsome as to evoke the unqualified admiration of travellers from the Continent. The first was built by James Burbage for his fellow actors of Leicester's company in 1576, and was called simply the Theatre; the site chosen was in Shoreditch, outside the city limits to the north, advantageous because of its proximity to the public playground, Finsbury Fields, yet not within the jurisdiction of the Common Council. The city officials from the beginning, unlike the Queen and her court, were chary of public play-acting, partly on moral grounds, more definitely for fear of three menaces: fire, sedition, and the plague. These were no idle fears. Fire was a constant danger to old London, which was at last almost wiped out by the great fire of 1666. The two largest theatres, the Globe and the Fortune, were burnt to the ground in 1613 and 1621. Plague was endemic in London; the deaths from this source averaged forty to fifty a week. When they rose above this number, the theatres were closed until it seemed safe to reopen them. The disorderly groundlings sometimes stormed the stage or indulged in rioting among

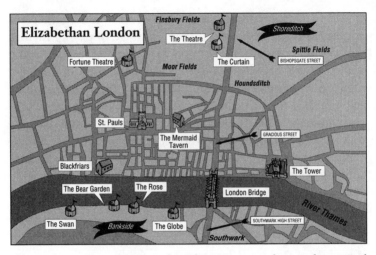

themselves. One theatre, the Phoenix, was almost destroyed by rioting apprentices in 1617. The Curtain, so called from the estate on which it was erected close to the Theatre, was built in 1577. Soon after another structure was opened at Newington Butts, marking a shift of locality to the south of the Thames; but this was never a popular theatre, since it was an uncomfortable mile beyond the river. The Rose, built in 1587 by Philip Henslowe, who became the most important theatrical proprietor of the age; the Swan, 1595, of whose stage we have a somewhat puzzling picture; and the Globe, erected in 1599 from the timbers of the demolished Theatre by the sons of James Burbage, Cuthbert and the famous actor, Richard, with five members of their company—Shakespeare among them—as share-holders, were all situated on the south side of the Thames in the district known as the Bankside, also beyond city jurisdiction. Later public theatres were the Fortune, 1600, and the Red Bull, *ca.*1605, north of the city limits, and the Hope, 1613, once more on the Bankside.

"Private" Theatres

Besides the public theatres, there were so-called private theatres, a somewhat misleading designation since they housed professional actors and were open to the public. The term was apparently chosen mainly to appease the London authorities, for some of these theatres, unlike the public ones, were within the city limits. Moreover, the distinction attached to the word "private" no doubt attracted a more select and higher paying clientele. Used first by children, they came to serve as winter quarters for adult actors. In 1596, for example, James Burbage purchased certain rooms in a building in Blackfriars, once the property of the Dominican monks, and made them over into a theatre. The Privy Council promptly forbade the public use of Blackfriars, but, after the death of James, Richard Burbage leased it to the manager of the Children of the Chapel. It was not until 1608 that Burbage's company was able to use it as a winter home. Other important indoor theatres were in a building near St. Paul's Cathedral, another at Whitefriars, the Cockpit or Phoenix in Drury Lane, and the Salisbury Court Playhouse; all but the first were west of the city walls and north of the Thames.

The Important Theatre Companies

The companies who played in the Elizabethan theatres are too many and various to discuss in detail, but it will be useful to sketch briefly the development and organization of two of them, and the names of the Burbages and Henslowe suggest the delimitation. With the Burbages we naturally associate Shakespeare; with Henslowe, Christopher Marlowe and a large group of later playwrights. The company of which Shakespeare was a member bore various names at different times as the patron, his rank, or his office changed. It may have begun as the Earl of Leicester's Men; after his death in 1588 its principal actors joined a group under the patronage of Lord Strange and for a time acted at Henslowe's theatre, the Rose. In 1593 Lord Strange became the Earl of Derby, and for a short time the company took over the new title, but he died the next year, and another patron had to be found. This was Elizabeth's cousin, the Lord Chamberlain, Henry Carey, and it is as the Lord Chamberlain's Company that until 1603 it is best known, for though Carey died in 1596, his son, Lord Hunsdon, shortly succeeded to his office. In 1603 the theatrical companies came under the direct patronage of the royal family, and the Lord Chamberlain's Men became the

King's Majesty's Servants, a title which they retained until the closing of the theatres in 1642. The principal playwrights associated with this company were Shakespeare, [Ben] Jonson, [Francis] Beaumont and [John] Fletcher, [Philip] Massinger, and [Sir William] Davenant; its best known actor was Richard Burbage, who interpreted the principal roles in Shakespeare's plays, both comedies and tragedies.

The other major group was that controlled by Philip Henslowe, in association with his son-in-law, Edward Alleyn, who rivalled Burbage as the star of the day. Besides the Rose, built and leased out by Henslowe, they controlled the Fortune and the Hope, and managed the companies under the patronage of the Lord Admiral and the Earl of Worcester; these became respectively after 1603 Prince Henry's and Queen Anne's Men. Alleyn played the principal characters in Marlowe's tragedies, and later dramatists associated with Henslowe's companies included [George] Chapman, [Thomas] Dekker, [Thomas] Middleton, and Thomas Heywood. Much of our knowledge of Elizabethan theatrical conditions derives from the valuable records kept by Philip Henslowe.

The Elizabethan theatrical company, especially such a group as the Lord Chamberlain's, was co-operative, self-governing, and self-perpetuating. It consisted of a certain number of full members who owned shares and divided profits, and leased, or, as in the case of the Globe, built a theatre; hired men paid a fixed salary to play minor parts; and apprentices, notably the boys who played all the female roles on the Elizabethan stage—there were no professional actresses until Restoration times—trained in the routine, as they would be in trade, by their individual masters, who hired them out to the company. The important members of the company played more or less definite "lines." Burbage, as a star, interpreted, we know, such roles as Richard III and the title-parts of Shakespeare's great tragedies; Shakespeare, as an actor, we principally associate with old men or kingly parts; Will Kemp and Armin were comedians. Playwrights were, as a rule, much more definitely associated with particular companies than is the case today. Plays were written for a particular troupe and frequently at their direction. A play-

wright often read the first acts of a projected play to the leading members of a company at a supper after their afternoon
performance. He would listen to their criticism, accept sug-
gestions, and promise to complete his work at a certain date.
Surviving manuscripts show that plays were often revised in
or after production. All in all, the major adult companies
were strong organizations, which so long as they submitted
to the rigorous restrictions by which the Master of the Revels forbade plays meddling with matters of Church and State,
were free to produce what they pleased as they pleased.

Children's Companies

With the children's companies who presented plays at Paul's
or Blackfriars it was an entirely different matter. These companies grew out of the choir-schools of the Chapel Royal, of
Windsor, and of St. Paul's, and were under the direct control
of a master who had the right to impress children for singing
and acting. The master supported and trained them, produced the plays, and received the money from performances.
For a time the "little eyases," as Shakespeare makes plain in
Hamlet, acting largely at the private theatres and at Court,
vied in popularity with their elders; they must have been unusually competent, for they elicited the charming courtly
comedies of [John] Lyly, and performed such tragedies as
[George] Chapman's *Bussy* and [John] Marston's *Sophonisba*.
Some of these children, Nat. Field for instance, later became
leading actors in adult companies.

The Physical Structure of Theatres

We may now turn to a consideration of the physical structure of the theatre itself. The public playhouses were by no
means alike in size or shape; yet there is substantial agreement about the basic plan of a typical public theatre. Since it
is vastly different from anything we have today, since the
methods of staging vary substantially from ours, and since
both theatre and staging exerted a strong influence on the
art of the playwright, it is essential to have a clear picture of
the most important features.

The Elizabethan theatre evolved from those structures

which had previously served most often and conveniently for the presentation of plays, the inns. Except for the Fortune, however, they did not retain the square or rectangular court-yard or pit, but were roughly circular or polygonal. The alteration was no doubt suggested by the bear- and bull-baiting rings on the Bankside, and assisted the hearing and vision of spectators in pit and gallery by bringing them nearer to the stage. As pictured in contemporary London maps the typical theatre justifies Shakespeare's description (*Henry V,* Prologue) of "this wooden O." Around the inside were three tiers of galleries, roofed over with thatch or tile; the center was uncovered and open to the weather. As in the inn court-yard, the audience entered through a door opposite the stage, except, perhaps, for a few especially favored who might use the players' entrance to the tiring-house or dressing rooms at the rear. A penny to a "gatherer" allowed the groundling to stand in the pit; and an additional charge of a penny or two permitted the more select spectator to climb stairs and sit on stool or bench in one of the galleries.

Halfway into the pit there projected a platform upon which most of the action of the play was presented. It is important to realize that the spectators were not only in front of the stage as in a modern theatre but actually on three sides of it. At the rear of the platform was an inner, or alcove, stage separated from the front by a traverse, or draw-curtain, and flanked by doors which allowed the actors to enter directly onto the platform from the tiring-house. Over the alcove-stage was an upper stage; it also had a curtain which could cut it off from the view of the audience when it was not in use, and in front of the curtain a balcony or "tarras" projected slightly over the platform. Occasionally it may have served as a music room, or for spectators presumably more interested in being seen than in seeing what went on in all sections of the playing space. Other spectators were sometimes allowed to sit on the platform-stage itself and must have been an unholy nuisance both to actors and audience. It is a pity there is no evidence that they ever fell through the various traps in the floors of all the stages. The upper stage, including curtained space and balcony windows on each side of it, over the doors to the main stage, was reached by interior stairs. Projecting from above the balcony-stage over a large part of the platform was a roof variously called the "heavens" or the "shadow" and on part of it a garret or "hut," which extended back over the third story of the tiring-house. The "shadow," usually supported by pillars, served in part to protect from the elements actors on the main stage. Moreover, through it heavy properties or even an actor impersonating a god—the ancient *deus ex machina*—might be let down to the platform. From the "hut" flew a flag on fair days to indicate, along with frequent trumpet blasts, that a play was to be given that afternoon. Sunday performances, though intermittently prohibited, continued till 1603.

The earliest private playhouses were apparently mere adaptations of rooms for the presentation of plays by the Children of the Royal Chapel or by Paul's Boys; there was a platform-stage backed by a curtain and artificially lighted, and seats in the hall, rather than standing-room, accommodated the more luxurious auditors. Beginning with Burbage's Blackfriars, however, the reconstruction included galleries, and no doubt alcove and balcony-stages not essentially different from those in the public theatres, though the galleries may have been less in number and the "interior" stages larger. The ceiling, of course, supplied the function of the "shadow," and an upper room that of the "hut." The public and the later private stages were therefore not essentially different; after 1608 the same plays were frequently given both outdoors and in, and there does not seem to be evidence of necessary adaptation because of the transfer. Performances at Court, of course, were given indoors. There dramatic entertainment was of two kinds: elaborate disguisings and pageantry emphasizing music, dancing, and spectacle for which special settings and properties were devised for the amateur participants; and more regular plays presented by professionals ranging from simple Interludes on simple platforms to more complicated drama with ornate multiple settings. After about 1580, when the regular theatres and their practices had become established, theatricals at Court were more and more dominated by professionals called in to give special performances on variable temporary stages much resembling those in the private playhouses though with more expensive decoration, furnishings, and properties. . . .

Stage Fosters Love of Language

It is not remarkable that Elizabethan drama is on the whole a poetic drama. Elizabethans—it is typical of the Renaissance everywhere—had fallen in love with language, with words, with speech of all kinds, homely and conceited, old words and new words, short words and long words, poor words and rich words. The young student of Elizabethan drama, having learned that the pun is the lowest form of humor, is often bothered by the plays on words he discovers there. The pun to an Elizabethan was not merely a joke; it was a rhetorical device by which he managed to say two or three things at once. Wit combats, badinage, thrust and parry are everywhere in Elizabethan drama. So are orations, elaborate descriptions, delicate sentiments, philosophical discussions. But if love of words and of their rhythms is a part of the inheritance of the English Renaissance, it was also fostered by the stage. Here were actors not cut off from the audience by orchestra-pit and proscenium-arch, but in the midst of a word-loving audience. All eyes were on them; all ears strained to hear. They were not puppets seen through a picture-frame but in intimate physical contact. Words accompanied by easily visible gestures and expression went home with extraordinary force and directness, whether they were high astounding terms or mere gags. And so Elizabethan drama is in its best sense a wordy drama. The playwright was not afraid of soliloquies; soliloquies properly used told the audience what was going on inside of a character, what he would not or could not say to anyone else. This was not a realistic stage; an aside was perfectly acceptable. Moreover, a speaker might very well be nearer to his audience than to the actor who was supposed not to overhear him. The variety and scope of the language, the emotional rhythms of poetic speech of the Elizabethan drama were partly the result of the Elizabethan theatre.

One other point may well be made. The Elizabethans loved stories, and their stage was ideally equipped to tell them in action. Since the scene could be shifted at will, and action was swift and continuous, it was not necessary to stick to one story. The playwright could tell two or three. If he was a poor craftsman, he could amuse his audience even if his method was entirely episodic. If he was an artist, he would carefully preserve cause and effect in his handling of multiple plots, and connect the stories to each other by the inter-relationship of characters, and by parallel and contrast. This was a stage which cried out for the narrative method, and the stories became the more real and effective because the characters were seen literally in the round.

Plays Written for Specific Acting Companies

If the stage played a vital part in determining the dramatic method of the playwright, he was also strongly influenced by the company for which he was writing. We shall never know how widely this influence operated, but there is no doubt of its force. A dramatist working for a definite group cannot compose in a vacuum; his play must fit his actors. The lovely lyrics scattered through Lyly's plays were written for singing children. How much are Marlowe's supermen due to the titanic Alleyn? Certainly Shakespeare knew his tragic heroes were to be played by Burbage. It is important to remember that while Will Kemp was a member of the company, Shakespeare created for him such parts as Costard, Bottom, and Dogberry; rustic, blundering, unlearned characters at which Kemp was adept. When Robert Armin took his place, however, the comedy role changed. Armin was brilliant, witty, himself a man of letters; as a result we have Touchstone and Feste, court jesters, "not altogether fool." Do we owe the Fool in *Lear* to Armin's expressed dissatisfaction with the very minor Clown in *Othello?* Moreover, these companies were fairly stable in size; the number of characters in a play was in part determined by the number of actors in the company. No doubt many characters in Elizabethan plays, absent in the sources, owe their origin to the need for utilizing the full talents of the company. The personnel may well have forced the playwright into minor stories and plot complications which structurally seem unnecessary or superfluous, simply to provide them all with opportunities.

All these forces interact. The companies produced the theatre; the kind of stage affects the work of the playwright. The playwright, conditioned by both theatre and company, may by the nature of his art modify both stage and acting. The Elizabethan audience played its part in creating Elizabethan drama. It is a complex problem. Unless we bear in mind these interactions; unless, more specifically, we understand the theatrical conditions under which Elizabethan playwrights worked, we have no basis for the assumption that we understand their plays. The freedom, the swift variety, the boundless scope in matter and manner, the universality of thought and expression which characterize the dramatic art of the English Renaissance and make it vital, vivid, and moving today stem alike from actor and theatre and poet-playwright.

Elizabethan Drama Reflects the Richness of the Age

John Gassner

The late John Gassner was a prolific scholar of theater. He edited and introduced numerous collections of plays, including *Medieval and Tudor Drama, Elizabethan Drama, Best American Plays, Masters of the Drama,* and *A Treasury of the Theater.* He also wrote *Form and Idea in Modern Theatre* and the *Reader's Encyclopedia of World Drama.* In this selection from his book *Elizabethan Drama*, Gassner defines the distinctive character of Elizabethan drama as "a fusion of popular and learned elements" in conjunction with a "romantic" spirit. Elements of medieval drama persist in Elizabethan drama, Gassner explains, but they are combined with a distinctively English assimilation of humanist learning from continental Europe and a contemporary spirit of ambition and enterprise. Gassner explains that Elizabethan dramatists also responded to the diverse interests of their audiences, who enjoyed foreign tales of adventure, English history, and courtly pageantry, as well as folk festivities, clowning, and vulgar humor. The plays reflect these various interests with a lively and distinctively Elizabethan "blending of styles, plots, and character types."

No one with even the slightest interest in English literature needs to be told that its greatest period is the Elizabethan Age, and no one familiar with that period is likely to depart from the consensus that its major literary achievement is the drama.

Although the term "Elizabethan drama" has often been used loosely to cover the dramatic literature of the second half of the sixteenth century and the first third of the seven-

Excerpted from *Elizabethan Drama*, edited by John Gassner (New York: Bantam, 1967). Copyright © 1967 by Bantam Books, Inc.

teenth, it is here applied only to the productions of Queen Elizabeth's reign, from her accession to the throne of England in 1558 to her death in 1603. Even when strictly—and somewhat arbitrarily—confined to the reign of Henry VIII's celebrated daughter, the Virgin Queen, the Elizabethan Age defies simple definition. It is said with some justice that it marks the high point of the Renaissance in England; but the Middle Ages were not miraculously abolished by the coronation of Elizabeth, and it is a mistake to overlook the persistence of strong medieval elements in Elizabethan culture and theatre. A residue is observable, for instance, in the popularity of the *De Casibus* "Fall of Princes" theme in tragedy, as in [Christopher] Marlowe's *Edward VI* and [William] Shakespeare's *Richard II* ("For God's sake, let us sit upon the ground / And tell sad stories of the death of kings," says Richard II), and the persistence of medieval morality-play figures, such as the prankish devil or "Vice," the struggles of the Good and the Bad Angel for the soul of the hero, and the presence of the Seven Deadly Sins in Marlowe's *Doctor Faustus*. Memories of feudal warfare abound in the "chronicle plays," or "histories," of Shakespeare and his colleagues. Fancy and superstition color the comedies and tragedies; the Middle Ages account for the elves and witches in Shakespeare's otherwise sophisticated artistry. The very playhouses of England, like its domestic architecture, retained medieval features.

The Renaissance, blended with vestigial medievalism, was itself no novelty during Elizabeth's reign but was already almost a century old in England by the time she became queen. By the 1550's it was no longer a question of introducing the "learning" or humanism of the Italian Renaissance into England but of giving it wider dissemination, of assimilating it, and of translating Renaissance learning into English creativeness. . . .

Continental Learning from University Playwrights

Courtly writing helped to refine popular playwriting by enriching its language and adding grace of manner and expression to its vigor of feeling and action. Professor [Alfred]

Harbage plausibly surmises that Shakespeare owed a portion of his literary education to the coterie writers ("he may have owed something to [John] Marston as he certainly owed something to [John] Lyly"). And it is noteworthy that university-bred Elizabethan playwrights were by no means content to be coterie writers; the most effective of them, led by Christopher Marlowe, were responsible for many triumphs of the popular stage—triumphs achieved without renouncing the pretensions to learning, triumphs which called attention to them as university men. In fact, Elizabethan writers in general liked to associate themselves with humanistic learning and embellish their writings with classical allusions.

The best Elizabethan plays therefore represent a fusion of popular and learned elements, producing both theatre and literature. In the best work of the age theatrical élan does not banish the literary flair, and the authors' literary ambitions do not inhibit theatrical vivacity and dramatic action. This rare entente cordiale between dramatic literature and "theatre" is apparent in the very structure and texture of the plays; most thoroughly in the work of Shakespeare . . . but conspicuously enough in much of the work of his fellow playwrights. The progress of Elizabethan drama from the courtly ventures of Lyly to the sturdier labors of [Thomas] Kyd, [Robert] Greene, Marlowe, [Thomas] Dekker, [Thomas] Heywood, and [Ben] Jonson is essentially a movement toward this synthesis of nonliterary and literary constituents of drama and is reflected in Elizabethan drama's characteristic mingling of prose and verse (and in the growing dramatic flexibility and expressiveness of the latter), action and reflection, refined sensibility and raw experience, tragedy and horseplay.

Romantic Elements

To these qualities we must add one more attribute: the relatively free form or loose structure of most of the plays. Their most obvious structural feature is their freedom of movement. In this respect they were still medieval, following the episodic organization of the passion plays or "mystery play" cycles. Efforts to restrict the action and to tighten the structure of Elizabethan plays were made in the name of the unities of time, place, and action, for which Renaissance scholars on the Continent had invoked the sanction of Aristotle, but the attempt was frustrated by the exuberance of the Elizabethan age as reflected in the theatre by its playwrights, performers, and audiences. Despite some lip service to classic example, the ruling spirit of the Elizabethan stage was notably romantic, manifesting itself in a flair for action, adventure, and violence even in the midst of the highest literary intentions. In supplying plays for the popular theatre the playwrights did not shrink from showing even the most savage actions (the gouging out of Gloucester's eyes in *King Lear* is an example) instead of merely reporting them, as was the custom in classic drama. Thus they activated the rhetorical turbulence of Seneca, whom the Elizabethans acclaimed as the exemplary classic playwright and whom they presumably followed in favoring themes of revenge, sententious comment, and the agency of ghosts. This same tendency toward histrionic extravagance appeared in the dramatic posture and dialogue of typical Elizabethan characters.

Within a century the Elizabethan period in theatre was viewed with mixed feelings of admiration and dismay as an age of genius and poor taste. Even Shakespeare was not exempted from such censure, and it was considered essential to tamper with his dramatic action as well as his language for the benefit of presumably more refined audiences than he had been obliged to please in his day.

Plays Reflect the Spirit of the Age

The content of Elizabethan plays conformed to the spirit of the age. Playwrights and their audiences were attracted to tales of comic or tragicomic adventure drawn from foreign literature; these were often folksy manners and beliefs, racy realistic speech, and vivid character drawing. The Elizabethans were also partial to chronicles of the English nation such as Holinshed's, replete with accounts of feudal warfare, national pacification, and the fatal course of lords and monarchs. The "history play," as exemplified by Marlowe's *Edward II* and Shakespeare's *Henry IV,* became a major genre. Parallel situations derived mainly from Roman history and recent events across the English Channel also occupied the theatre. The high tragedies of the age often had a context of history or legend that passed for history. This is true of Shakespeare's tragedies, with the exception of *Othello*— which, unlike *Hamlet, Macbeth, King Lear*, and *Antony and Cleopatra*, derives from an Italian *novella*, or tale, published in 1565. A strong pulse was provided by the vogue of revenge tragedies abounding in fury, intrigue, and bloodshed, in the manner of the first and greatest popular success in this genre, *The Spanish Tragedy*, and culminating in *Hamlet*, which for all its profundity contains more violence of passion and action (and more corpses) than most great tragedies of any other period. The more mundane substance of middle-class dramas such as *Arden of Feversham* was also far from placid, and the London life exhibited in such plays as *The Shoemaker's Holiday* reveled in the confident heartiness of the ordinary man.

Elizabethan Values and Aspirations

A commonly entertained set of values provided a stimulus to Elizabethan drama and an explicit or implicit rationale for its action. A political and moral principle of proportion—or, in Elizabethan parlance, "degree"—was official doctrine. Everybody was to have, and keep, his place in the human world ruled by kings as well as in the universe ruled by God to ensure the stability and civil order of England. This principle of "degree" received its clearest formulation from Shakespeare in *Troilus and Cressida* when Ulysses undertakes to heal the rift in the ranks of the Greek chieftains besieging Troy. In that famous long speech (Act I, Scene 3, lines 81–137) the best remembered lines define the ideal of "degree" as divinely ordained:

> The heavens themselves, the planets, and this centre
> Observe degree, priority, and place,
> Insisture, course, proportion, season, form,
> Office and custom, in all line of order . . . but when the planets
> In evil mixture to disorder wander,
> What plagues and what portents! what mutiny!
> What raging of the sea! shaking of earth!
> Commotion in the winds! frights, changes, horrors,

Divert and crack, rend and deracinate
The unity and married calm of states
Quite from their fixture. O, when degree is shaked,
Which is the ladder to all high designs,
Then enterprise is sick! How could communities,
Degrees in Schools and brotherhoods in cities
Peaceful commerce from dividable shores,
The primogenitive and due of birth,
Prerogative of age, crowns, sceptres, laurels,
But by degree, stand in authentic place?
Take but degree away, untune that string,
And hark, what discord follows. Each thing meets
In mere oppugnancy. The bounded waters
Should lift their bosoms higher than the shores
And make a sop of all this solid globe.

Shakespeare was saying poetically not only what the English humanist Sir Thomas Elyot had maintained much earlier in prose in the first chapter of his influential *Book of the Governor*—"Take away order from all things, what should then remain"—but also what nearly everyone supposedly believed.

Exemplified in many a history play and many a tragedy too (crudely in the early *Gorboduc* and superbly in *Macbeth* and *King Lear*), "degree" was good monarchical dogma and gave an ethical, as well as a metaphysical, coloring to Tudor absolutism. An entire nation, weary of civil strife and still mindful of the fifteenth-century Wars of the Roses before the Tudor dynasty ascended the throne of England, could assent to the doctrine. Encapsulated in it, moreover, was the worth and self-respect of individuals on the lower rungs of the social ladder.

At the same time, with God's will, or as a result of a favorable turn of "Fortune's wheel," the doctrine of degree did not, and indeed could not, inhibit lawful ambition. Although the place occupied by man was justified as part of the world order known as the "great chain of being," Elizabethan man was constantly striving to leave *his* place in that chain—and succeeding. He could derive encouragement from the familiar spectacle of common men acquiring great wealth and social status even as poor farmers were simultaneously being reduced to beggary and vagabondage because the landed gentry was enclosing the common pasture land to satisfy the increasing market for wool. Enterprise in trade, augmented by profitable piracy called privateering and underwritten by sound businessmen, spoliation of the land, and land grabbing, exploitation of monopolies, rivalries at court for patronage and political appointments, social climbing, and lavish displays of wealth and power characterized England as it moved out of the Middle Ages.

Elizabethan drama could not but reflect the dynamism of Elizabethan society. In it the sense of individual worth possessed even by the lowly characters we meet in the plays of Shakespeare and his contemporaries often translates itself into ambition, the will to self-realization, or the "will to power." Normal self-regard constitutes the vitality of the common man and the charm of romantic heroines in the comedies; over-weening egotism or unlawful ambition is the *hamartia*, or tragic flaw, in the tragedies. Since Greek drama has been called "tragedy of fate," serious Elizabethan drama may, with as much warrant, be called "tragedy of the will." In many an Elizabethan play the action of an energetic will to a considerable degree accounts for the presence of protagonists who, for better or worse, are among the most arresting characters in all dramatic literature.

"A Marriage of Tastes, Subject, and Genres"

The dramatic interest of the age appeared, moreover, in the dual content of aristocratic and popular, literary and nonliterary, entertainment. On the one hand the age luxuriated in courtly pageantry wherever the Queen resided or was entertained during her excursions to the country seat of some great nobleman. On the other hand the villages and country towns abounded in folk festivities, May-games, morris dancers, mummings, and other seasonal festivities not yet extirpated, although already severely deplored, by the Puritan sects which also frowned upon the theatrical profession. The passion for literary expression provoked the refined sonneteering of the age and the preciosity—known as euphuism and Arcadianism—of much of its prose and verse, as well as the vulgarity of humor and language.

For the theatre the ultimate result of regard for literary expression was the development of blank verse (unrhymed iambic pentameter verse with a shifting pause or "caesura") into the most distinguished and effective instrument of dramatic speech. At the same time a common penchant for traditional merrymaking, festivities, dances, jigs, popular ballads, jest books, folklore, buffoonery or clowning, sports, and pranks undoubtedly enlivened both dramatic action and dialogue and peopled the plays with the rustics or clowns who counterpoint the romantic sentiments of upper-class characters. Commoners also supplied farcical subplots to the exalted literary matter of Elizabethan comedies and tragedies.

This marriage of tastes, subject, and genres became an accepted convention in the courtliest of entertainments, approved by the Queen herself and by her "Master of Revels"; that Elizabeth should have had such an official in her menage is itself characteristic of the age. And characteristic, too, was the fact that in courtly revels such as those with which Elizabeth was entertained by her favorite, the Earl of Leicester, at his country seat Kenilworth, hearty rustic pastimes commingled with the mythological pageants. If a carefree blending of styles, plots, and character types could cause considerable confusion or inchoateness in Elizabethan drama, it also accounted for the variety and liveliness associated with the theatre of the age. A general spirit of holiday was one of the Elizabethan theatre's most characteristic features, as pleasing to its patrons as it was dismaying to its Puritan censors.

The Dramatic and Political Significance of Thomas Kyd's *The Spanish Tragedy*

J.R. Mulryne

Of the group of young, well-educated playwrights to whom the flowering of Elizabethan drama in the 1580s has been attributed, Thomas Kyd stands second only to Christopher Marlowe in popularity and influence. His reputation rests on one play, *The Spanish Tragedy*, which was perhaps the most enthusiastically greeted and most widely parodied of any early Elizabethan tragedy. Although the date of the play is disputed, it may be the first modern revenge tragedy, the first play that contains a play-within-a-play, and the first play that uses a Machiavellian villain (a double-crossing character who shares his plots and plans with the audience and believes that the end justifies the means). The influence of Kyd's play on Shakespeare's *Hamlet*, which is also a revenge tragedy with a significant play-within-the-play, and on *Othello*, which focuses on the vengeful machinations of the most famous of machiavellian characters, Iago, is commonly noted by literary historians.

In this selection J.R. Mulryne, Professor of English at the University of Warwick, provides a brief biography of Thomas Kyd, including comment on his classical education and his personal relationship with Christopher Marlowe. Mulryne then explores Kyd's use of his classical education in the construction of *The Spanish Tragedy*. Kyd adapts the structure and style of the classical Roman writer Seneca, and he alludes to the *Aeneid* of the Roman writer Virgil to convey his vision of political collapse and human waste. Mulryne concludes his essay by focusing on the significance of the play's contribution to the anti-Spanish Protestant polemic of the 1580s and 1590s.

In addition to editing and introducing Thomas Kyd's *The Spanish Tragedy*, William Shakespeare's *Much Ado About Nothing*, and John Webster's *The White Devil*, J.R. Mulryne has written a book-length study of Thomas Middleton and his works.

Thomas Kyd belongs to the first generation of Elizabethan playwrights. He was born in 1558, six years before Shakespeare and [Christopher] Marlowe, fifteen years before [Ben] Jonson, and more than twenty years before [Thomas] Middleton and [John] Webster. His death in 1594, at the age of thirty-six, preceded the staging of almost all the Elizabethan masterpieces, save his own *Spanish Tragedy* and the plays of Marlowe.

Biographical Information

Kyd was baptised at the Church of St Mary Woolnoth in London on 6 November 1558, the child of a prosperous middle-class family. His father, Francis Kyd, achieved some distinction as a scrivener, serving as Warden of the Company of Scriveners in 1580. He was a member of an affluent but often disliked profession, with duties in the field of document-copying, and with some importance therefore in the complicated world of Elizabethan law. As a well-educated man, Francis sought a good education for his son, sending Thomas in 1565 at the age of seven to Merchant Taylors' School, a new foundation under the care of Richard Mulcaster, the noted educationalist, whose pupils at this time included Edmund Spenser, Lancelot Andrewes and Thomas Lodge. Here, it seems probable, Kyd became familiar with Latin, French and Italian, and may have had some Greek. Merchant Taylors' may also have first introduced him to the stage, for plays formed part of the boys' training, some even being acted before Queen Elizabeth at Court.

We know virtually nothing of Kyd's early manhood, and

can only speculate that he followed his father's profession of scrivener—his handwriting in the few scraps that remain is markedly neat and formal. Certainly he seems not to have attended either university. By 1585, at the age of twenty-seven, he was writing plays for the Queen's Company, the leading London players, though none of his work for this company survives. During 1587–8 he entered the service of a lord, variously identified as Henry, fourth earl of Sussex, or Ferdinando Stanley, Lord Strange, either of whom he may have served as secretary or tutor. His patron was patron also, we know, to a company of players.

Information about Kyd's later life comes almost entirely from writings connected with a single incident: his detention and probable torture at the hands of the Privy Council. Details of the affair are in parts uncertain, but it seems that Kyd was arrested during an investigation ordered by the Privy Council on 11 May 1593, to discover the source of certain 'libels'. These were writings directed in all probability against foreigners resident in London. Among Kyd's papers the officers came upon what were described as 'vile heretical Conceiptes denyinge the deity of Jhesus Christe or Savior', and on suspicion of having written blasphemy Kyd was imprisoned. Kyd apparently claimed that the writings were not his but Marlowe's. After Marlowe's death on 30 May 1593, Kyd wrote to Sir John Puckering, asking for release from prison and explaining how Marlowe's papers came to be in his possession. The two authors, he said, were 'wrytinge in one chamber twoe yeares synce' and their papers were shuffled together. He added that Marlowe's known sentiments dovetailed perfectly with those of the 'hereticall Conceiptes'. Both in this letter and in another Kyd amplified the charge; Marlowe is accused, with vivid and sometimes forced illustration, of being blasphemous, disorderly, of treasonous opinions, an irreligious reprobate, 'intemp[er]ate & of a cruel hart'. The morality of the affair has been much disputed, some scholars thinking that Kyd acted disgracefully. He may, however, have suspected that Marlowe informed on him, he may have guessed or known that Marlowe was a spy for [Elizabeth's principal secretary Francis] Walsingham (and therefore deserved what accusations came his way), or he may in his anxiety to escape prison and torture have slandered his former acquaintance only when he knew he was dead. It is doubtful whether the truth will ever be known. In any case Kyd was himself dead little more than a year later, his death hastened, it seems probable, by his experiences in prison. He was buried at St Mary Colchurch in London on 15 August 1594.

The Spanish Tragedy

Kyd's writings may well have been much more extensive than those that have come down to us as his. Besides *The Spanish Tragedy* we have on good authority only a translation of Tasso's *Padre di Famiglia* (published in 1588 under the title *The Householder's Philosophy*). Kyd may have written *Soliman and Perseda*, a play that shares its main source with Hieronimo's last-act play-within-the-play in *The Spanish Tragedy*; but the evidence is not conclusive. A play known as *I Hieronimo* may, in one form or another, be Kyd's; a kind of fore-piece to *The Spanish Tragedy*, it was perhaps written after the major play, to capitalise on its success. The text we have, published in 1605 by Thomas Pavier, is written in a style rather unlike Kyd's and may derive from a revision of the play by another hand. Notoriously, Kyd may also be the author of an early version of *Hamlet*, now lost. Although the evidence rests, in the first instance, on little more than widely disputed allusions in Thomas Nashe's preface for Robert Greene's *Menaphon*, the balance of probabilities seems to incline towards Kyd's having in fact written such a play. Altogether, the skills apparent in *The Spanish Tragedy*, taken together with early references to Kyd as a dramatist of some note, strongly suggest that much more of his work than now survives found its way on to the sixteenth-century stage. . . .

The date of *The Spanish Tragedy* has long been a matter of dispute. The point is significant to literary historians, for a good deal in their account of the development of English tragedy depends on accurate dating of this play. Arthur Freeman writes:

If the play precedes [Christopher Marlowe's] *The Jew of Malta* and *The Massacre at Paris* it contains the first Machiavellian villain; if it precedes [Anthony Munday's] *John a Kent and John a Cumber* it contains the earliest modern play-within-play; and if it precedes [Shakespeare's] *Titus Andronicus* it may also be styled the first modern revenge tragedy. Given a date before 1587 and [Marlowe's] *Tamburlaine*, one might incontrovertibly call Kyd's play the first extant modern tragedy, without qualification.

But despite the attractions of a firm date no scholar has so far succeeded in establishing one. . . .

Adapting Seneca and Virgil

Kyd's debt to [classical Roman writer] Seneca and to Senecan imitators such as Giraldi Cinthio (1504–73) is a matter both of structure and of expression. The framing device of Andrea's Ghost and the use of the prologue are Senecan in origin, and revenge is a principal Senecan theme. Kyd quotes Seneca directly, makes use of Senecan tags in translation, and owes a general stylistic debt to Senecan rhetoric. His use of stichomythia (answering single lines of verse dialogue) repeats, for example, a Senecan technique. But more significant than the imitation of Senecan style is the recreation in *The Spanish Tragedy* of the emotional and political climate of a Senecan play. Eugene Hill, in an important article, shows how Kyd has appropriated for his own work some of Seneca's typifying interests. A Senecan play, as Hill puts it, conveys 'the texture of evil in a hopelessly corrupt polity'; characteristically, such a play depicts 'the bursting forth of malign forces . . . from the underworld, forces which in the course of the play infest and destroy a royal house.' Kyd's tragedy, that is, represents a genuine *translatio studii*, a work of cultural reclamation that re-makes for sixteenth-century audiences Seneca's horrifying vision of political collapse and personal waste. Moreover, an Elizabethan audience would have been aware of the implicit contrast between Seneca's dismal view of man and society and the optimistic vision expressed in the *Aeneid* of Virgil. The Induction scene of *The Spanish Tragedy* is directly reminiscent of book VI of the *Aeneid*. Its central figure, Andrea, is far, however, from being another Aeneas. Indeed, as Hill points out, Andrea's experience and outlook offer a systematic inversion of those of Aeneas. *Pius* (that is, dutiful) Aeneas becomes, in Kyd's play, proud Andrea; where Aeneas sets out to find his place in the world of the living, Andrea looks for a position among the dead; Virgil's Sybil (the guide of Aeneas) is ever alert, while Revenge, Andrea's mentor, behaves inconsequentially and falls asleep; Aeneas learns ultimately of the glorious destiny of Rome, Andrea of the destruction of Spain. Hovering behind the Virgilian allusions would be, for Elizabethans, the knowledge that England's future prosperity was becoming associated, in poetry and drama, with the happy fortunes predicted in the *Aeneid* for Rome. The *Aeneid* stands, in this regard, as an implicit ironic frame within which the Senecan landscape of *The Spanish Tragedy* may be viewed.

The Spanish Tragedy was written during the middle or later years of the 1580s, or the very first years of the 1590s. These were years of anxiety among Englishmen about the probability of Spanish invasion, leading to the Armada year of 1588, as well as of anxiety over the numerous plots, assumed to be Spanish in origin, hatched against Elizabeth throughout. Protestant polemic of the 1580s depicted Spain as a place of personal depravity and political corruption. An influential group within the court pursued a vigorous anti-Spanish policy both before and after the Armada. One way for Kyd's first audiences to respond to *The Spanish Tragedy* was to see the play as showing the merited collapse of a depraved enemy. Almost at the play's end the King of Spain, as he observes the carnage on the stage, cries out:

> What age hath ever heard such monstrous deeds?
> My brother, and the whole succeeding hope
> That Spain expected after my decease!   (IV, iv, 202-4)

Contemporaries would see Kyd as having employed the theatrical idiom of Seneca to enmesh modern Spain in the nightmarish world of political tragedy. The countervailing Virgilian myth of prosperous destiny is associated with England, at least implicitly, in Hieronimo's dumb show in Act I, scene iv. There, English warriors subdue both Spanish and Portuguese enemies. The complacency of the King of Spain in interpreting these shows would be understood by English audiences as a mark of Spanish blindness to the role England was called on to play in world politics.

The political significance of *The Spanish Tragedy* would shade easily for sixteenth-century audiences into its theological significance. Political success for England and destruction for Spain would be seen not merely as political in character, but as the expression in political terms of the divine management of human affairs. It is possible to interpret the play, as Ronald Broude does, as exemplifying the familiar commonplace *Veritas filia temporis* (truth the daughter of time). The text was a frequent one in anti-Spanish Protestant polemic of the 1580s and 1590s. Time brings *four* truths to birth in the course of *The Spanish Tragedy:* the revealing of innocence as Bel-Imperia is vindicated; the detection of calumny as Alexandro is cleared; the revelation of Horatio's murder; and the bringing to light and punishment of Spanish corruption. It is the last of these which draws together the personal and nationalistic interests of the play. 'The disaster which befalls Kyd's Spain,' Broude writes

> is thus representative of the doom awaiting all nations in which the laws of God are ignored. Viewed in this way, *The Spanish Tragedy* must have offered welcome comfort to Englishmen of the '80s, reassuring them that no matter how precarious their situation might seem, Divine Providence would punish their enemies' wickedness and Time would vindicate the truth and justice of the English cause.

Christopher Marlowe: Shakespeare's Most Accomplished Rival

Louis B. Wright and Virginia A. LaMar

Christopher Marlowe was born on February 6, 1564, just a few months before Shakespeare, but unlike Shakespeare, Marlowe was educated at Cambridge University, receiving both B.A. and M.A. degrees from Corpus Christi College, Cambridge. Because of his extensive university education, Marlowe is often considered one of "the University Wits," a label given by modern scholars to the group of Oxford and Cambridge educated playwrights credited with developing Elizabethan drama in the 1580s. During his very short life (he was killed at the age of 29), Marlowe far surpassed his contemporaries as a playwright. Although he wrote only six plays, his masterful use of "blank verse" and his creation of the Renaissance hero who aspires to infinite power influenced not only Shakespeare but also the development of English drama. (Blank verse is the term used for unrhymed ten-syllable lines of verse in which every other syllable is stressed.) In this selection from their essay "Christopher Marlowe and His Plays," Louis B. Wright and Virginia A. LaMar recount the dramatic story of Marlowe's life after college and mysterious murder in Deptford; they then concentrate on the aspiring heroes of Marlowe's plays, especially Doctor Faustus, and the powerful blank verse these heroes speak.

Louis B. Wright has written numerous books and essays on the history and literature of the Elizabethan period, including *Middle-Class Culture in Elizabethan England*, has taught at the Universities of North Carolina,

From Editors' Introduction to Christopher Marlowe's *The Tragedy of Doctor Faustus*, Louis B. Wright, gen. ed., Virginia A. LaMar, asst. ed. Copyright © 1959 by Washington Square Press, Inc. Reprinted with permission of Pocket Books, a division of Simon & Schuster, Inc.

California, Michigan, and Minnesota, and has served as director of the Folger Shakespeare Research Library in Washington, D.C. Virginia A. LaMar has written *English Dress in the Age of Shakespeare* and, with Louis B. Wright, has edited and introduced numerous Folger Shakespeare Library editions of Shakespeare plays as well as *Life and Letters in Tudor and Stuart England.*

Christopher Marlowe, whose life ended when he was twenty-nine, is one of the most significant of Elizabethan dramatists; he was a pioneer and innovator in addition to being a poet of genius. When he began to write for the stage, plays were still relatively crude and naive productions, frequently written in old-fashioned jog-trot verse. Marlowe introduced a powerful and flexible blank verse and centered interest in the portrayal of some strong character in each of his tragedies. The young Shakespeare was to observe Marlowe's practice and profit by imitation. Marlowe's plays represent a great step forward in literary skill and dramatic power.

Marlowe's Life

The son of a Canterbury shoemaker who was a substantial citizen of the community, Marlowe was born on February 6, 1564, a little over ten weeks before Shakespeare's birth. He attended the King's School, Canterbury, and in 1581 matriculated at Corpus Christi College, Cambridge, on a scholarship established by Archbishop Parker. He received his B.A. degree in 1584 and the M.A. in 1587. As the holder of one of the Parker scholarships, Marlowe was expected to take holy orders and to enter the clergy. At some point in his theological studies, however, he was diverted from orthodoxy and chose the stage instead of the pulpit for the expression of his ideas. . . .

Shortly after leaving the university, Marlowe took up residence in London. What he did for a livelihood is unknown to us, but that he turned his hand to dramatic writing is a certainty. The plays that have survived from his pen were not sufficient to support him, and he must have had some other source of income. He was part of a brilliant circle of young men who included Sir Walter Raleigh; Thomas Hariot, the mathematician and scientist; Thomas Nashe, the pamphleteer; and other writers. For a time he had as a roommate Thomas Kyd, playwright and author of *The Spanish Tragedy*, a sensational drama. . . .

In the spring of 1593, Marlowe appears to have taken up residence in the household of Sir Thomas Walsingham at Scadbury near Chislehurst in Kent. Plague was raging in London and Walsingham's country house made a pleasant retreat. But once more Marlowe found himself in difficulties, . . . with the Privy Council, which undertook to investigate a serious charge of atheism and blasphemy that had been made by Thomas Kyd, perhaps to excuse himself. On May 12, 1593, Kyd had been arrested on a charge of posting "lewd and mutinous libels" on a churchyard wall. When his room was searched, papers were found containing "atheistic" writings. Atheism in this period was a loose term that could cover almost any departure from orthodoxy. Kyd claimed that the papers had belonged to Marlowe and had become mixed with his own when the two shared a room and both dramatists were writing for the acting company of a certain unidentified lord, probably Lord Strange. Kyd also charged that Marlowe "would persuade men of quality to go unto the King of Scots . . . where . . . he told me . . . he meant to be." King James VI of Scotland was already being talked of as the possible successor to Queen Elizabeth and some Englishmen were anxiously looking toward Scotland and, as an insurance for the future, were hoping for favor with the Scottish King. A few days after Kyd's statement, a professional informer, one Richard Baines, came forward with a whole battery of "the most horrible blasphemes and damnable opinions" attributed to Marlowe, including a statement that the Sacraments "would have been much better being administered in a tobacco pipe." The charges were sufficiently grave for the Privy Council on May 18 to issue a warrant to its messenger, Henry Maunder, "to repair to the house of Mr. Thomas Walsingham in Kent, or to any other place where he shall understand Christopher Marlowe to be remaining, and by virtue thereof to apprehend and bring him to the Court in his company." Twelve days after this warrant was issued, Fate intervened to prevent a hearing of the charges against Marlowe. On May 30, he was murdered in the tavern of Eleanor Bull in Deptford.

Marlowe's Death

The circumstances surrounding the death of Christopher Marlowe are related in the testimony at the coroner's inquest. Marlowe, who had accepted an invitation from one Ingram Friser to a "feast," had arrived at Eleanor Bull's house at about ten in the morning. Two others joined them, Nicholas Skeres and Robert Poley. All three of these men enjoyed unsavory reputations. Friser and Skeres had been mixed up in confidence games and various swindles, apparently with the connivance of one who ought to have been above such trickery, no other than Sir Thomas Walsingham. Poley was a secret agent recently returned from some mission abroad. He too had been involved in shady transactions. Clearly, Marlowe was in bad company, but we have only conjecture to explain his friendship with sharpers and spies. They dined in the middle of the day and, after a walk in the garden, about six o'clock they returned to the private room that they were occupying and had supper together. After supper, Marlowe lay down on a bed while the other three sat on a bench at the table in front of him and played backgammon. Friser sat between Skeres and Poley with his back to Marlowe. Hanging from his belt was a dagger. Marlowe, who had begun to quarrel with Friser over the tavern bill, seized the dagger from his belt and struck him in the head with it. Friser, with his legs under the table, wedged between Poley and Skeres, was about to be slain by Marlowe, he swore before the coroner, but he managed to twist around, grab Marlowe's hand, and thrust the dagger back upon him in such a manner that it entered his forehead and gave him "then and there a mortal wound over his right eye of the depth of two inches and the width of one inch, of which mortal wound the aforesaid Christopher Morley [Marlowe] then and there instantly died."

This is the stark account at the inquest proceedings which

Professor Leslie Hotson discovered in 1925. Marlowe was buried on June 1 in the churchyard of St. Nicholas, Deptford, and the parish register incorrectly noted that he was slain by "ffrancis ffrezer." On June 28, Ingram Friser received a full pardon for the murder. He lived to a ripe old age and died a churchwarden.

Since the discovery of the inquest papers, scholars have speculated upon Marlowe's end and have wondered whether the testimony is all that it purports to be. . . .

Marlowe's Plays and Poems

Fascinating as are surmises about Marlowe the victim of a mysterious murder, we are more concerned with Marlowe the poet and dramatist, who at the age of twenty-nine had set a new fashion in stage plays. He had begun to write before he left Cambridge, and by the end of 1587 the two parts of *Tamburlaine* had won the plaudits of London audiences. In quick succession came *Doctor Faustus* (1588), *The Jew of Malta* (1589), *Edward the Second* (*ca.* 1592), *The Massacre at Paris* (1593), and *Dido, Queen of Carthage*, written in collaboration with Thomas Nashe (*ca.* 1593). He may have had a hand in one or two other plays. The dates of composition and first acting cannot be given with certainty, but this appears to be the most plausible chronology. In addition to his dramas he made translations from Lucan's *Pharsalia* and Ovid's *Amores*, and from Musaeus he retold a famous classical story in his own *Hero and Leander*, an unfinished poem that George Chapman completed.

Marlowe's poetry is the work of a young man of the Renaissance rebellious against many traditions and yet strongly influenced by the literary heritage from the ancient world. . . . During his years at Cambridge he read widely in classical literature and ranged beyond into geography, history, and philosophy—wherever his inquiring mind took him. Upon this storehouse of material he drew when he sat down to write his plays and poetry. To his work he gave a pagan twist, for Marlowe is an example of the influence of the pagan Renaissance. He would have found himself at home among some of the Italian writers of a previous generation.

One of the characteristics of the Renaissance was its intellectual curiosity and its belief in the potentialities of the human mind. It was a youthful age to which nothing seemed impossible. The age also placed a new emphasis on the individual and men learned to cultivate their capacities and to develop all sides of their personalities. The resources of the mind seemed as limitless as the great world, which the discoveries beyond the seas had more than doubled. . . .

Doctor Faustus

In *Doctor Faustus*, the greatest of his poetic conceptions, [Marlowe] provides a study of the scholar in search of unlimited knowledge and the power that knowledge may confer. Even more than in *Tamburlaine*, we feel that Marlowe is thinking of himself in the role of Faustus, the rebel against conventional university learning, the rebel who was willing to sell his soul to the devil for knowledge that was forbidden to less daring philosophers.

The theme of the man who makes a compact with the devil is old in folklore. The particular version that took shape in the Faust legend appeared in print in Germany in 1587 as *Das Faustbuch* and was translated into English as *The Historie of the Damnable Life and Deserved Death of Dr. John Faustus*. . . .

Marlowe gave the legend an interpretation characteristic of his own taste and personality. When the play opens, we see Faustus in his study surveying the state of knowledge and trying to decide which of the learned disciplines he will follow. Logic, medicine, law, divinity: all of these are inadequate for his towering ambition. He wants all knowledge, the ability to plumb the mysteries yet withheld from man, and the superhuman power that such knowledge will bring. The only way to attain this ambition is by magic, and the acquisition of the power of magic can be achieved only through a bargain made with the devil. Faustus is willing to pay the price, and makes the required compact. . . .

In *Doctor Faustus* [Marlowe] reaches new lyrical heights in passages where he is concerned with the infinite reaches of the human mind. When he invokes "divine astrology". . . he means something more than the word connotes today. He is probing into the mysteries of the universe where he can find revelations worth the price of his immortal soul.

In another passage of lyric intensity when he calls up Helen of Troy, he transcends sensual delight and Helen becomes the symbol of intellectual pleasure as she was also the acme of physical delight:

> Was this the face that launched a thousand ships
> And burnt the topless towers of Ilium?
> Sweet Helen, make me immortal with a kiss.
> Her lips sucks forth my soul—see where it flies!
> Come, Helen, come, give me my soul again.
> Here will I dwell, for heaven is in these lips
> And all is dross that is not Helena. . . .

Although Marlowe lived to write only a handful of plays, the English stage would be the greater for them. His melodious verse, the "mighty line" that Ben Jonson described, would forever influence English poetic drama. One greater than he, William Shakespeare, would learn from him and bring the blank verse line to perfection as a medium for dramatic expression.

A Playwright for All Time: Shakespeare's Dramatic Art and Life

Robert F. Willson Jr.

The popularity of Shakespeare's plays in his own time and their continuing appeal to four centuries of audiences, readers, writers, and scholars have led numerous literary critics to attempt an explanation of Shakespeare's historical and cultural significance. In this selection, University of Missouri professor Robert F. Willson Jr. identifies four characteristics of Shakespeare's plays that contribute to the playwright's universal reputation: the new words and aphorisms he created that have since become embedded in the English language; his unique ability to blend material from the native English and classical traditions; memorable, life-like characters who epitomize the essence of human relationships; splendid poetry and sustained patterns of imagery that unify the action of the plot. Willson's brief biography of Shakespeare's growth as a dramatist and his analysis of the London stage in Shakespeare's time reveal the degree to which Shakespeare's art was influenced by the talents of his theatrical company and the physical conditions of the Elizabethan stage. Shakespeare's ability to transform this bare stage and mere actors (considered the social equals of jugglers and bearbaiters) into a world that captured and continues to capture the imaginations of people from various social classes, countries, and ideological perspectives attests to the dramatic power of this playwright who was not only "of an age, but for all time," as his rival Ben Jonson wrote.

Robert F. Willson has also written several books on

Reprinted from "The Dramatist," by Robert F. Willson Jr., in *Critical Survey of Drama*, English Language Series, vol. 5, rev. ed., Frank N. Magill, ed., pp. 2,104–10, by permission of the publisher, Salem Press, Inc. Copyright © 1994, Salem Press, Inc.

rhetoric including *The Macmillan Handbook of English* and *Writing, Analysis and Application*, and he has edited and introduced *Student Voices on Political Action, Culture, and the University*.

Few dramatists can lay claim to the universal reputation achieved by William Shakespeare. His plays have been translated into many languages and performed on amateur and professional stages throughout the world. Radio, television, and film versions of the plays in English, German, Russian, French, and Japanese have been heard and seen by millions of people. The plays have been revived and reworked by many prominent producers and playwrights, and they have directly influenced the work of others. Novelists and dramatists such as Charles Dickens, Bertolt Brecht, William Faulkner, and Tom Stoppard, inspired by Shakespeare's plots, characters, and poetry, have composed works that attempt to re-create the spirit and style of the originals and to interpret the plays in the light of their own ages. A large and flourishing Shakespeare industry exists in England, America, Japan, and Germany, giving evidence of the playwright's popularity among scholars and laypersons alike.

A Playwright for All Time

Evidence of the widespread and deep effect of Shakespeare's plays on English and American culture can be found in the number of words and phrases from them that have become embedded in everyday usage: Expressions such as "star-crossed lovers" are used by speakers of English with no consciousness of their Shakespearean source. It is difficult to imagine what the landscape of the English language would be like without the mountain of neologisms [new words, usages, or phrases] and aphorisms [short sayings that embody a general truth] contributed by the playwright. Writing at a time when English was quite pliable, Shakespeare's linguistic facility and poetic sense transformed English into a richly metaphoric tongue.

Working as a popular playwright, Shakespeare was also instrumental in fusing the materials of native and classical drama in his work. *Hamlet*, with its revenge theme, its ghost, and its bombastic set speeches, appears to be a tragedy based on the style of the Roman playwright Seneca, who lived in the first century A.D. Yet the hero's struggle with his conscience and his deep concern over the disposition of his soul reveal the play's roots in the native soil of English miracle and mystery dramas, which grew out of Christian rituals and depicted Christian legends. The product of this fusion is a tragedy that compels spectators and readers to examine their own deepest emotions as they ponder the effects of treacherous murder on individuals and the state. Except for Christopher Marlowe, the predecessor to whom Shakespeare owes a considerable debt, no other Elizabethan playwright was so successful in combining native and classical strains.

Shakespearean characters, many of whom are hybrids, are so vividly realized that they seem to have achieved a life independent of the worlds they inhabit. Hamlet stands as the symbol of a man who, in the words of the famous actor Sir Laurence Olivier, "could not make up his mind." Hamlet's name has become synonymous with excessive rationalizing and idealism. Othello's jealousy, Lear's madness, Macbeth's ambition, Romeo and Juliet's star-crossed love, Shylock's flinty heart—all of these psychic states and the characters who represent them have become familiar landmarks in Western culture. Their lifelikeness can be attributed to Shakespeare's talent for creating the illusion of reality in mannerisms and styles of speech. His use of the soliloquy [speech delivered while alone calculated to reveal the speaker's thoughts] is especially important in fashioning this illusion; the characters are made to seem fully rounded human beings in the representation of their inner as well as outer nature. Shakespeare's keen ear for conversational rhythms and his ability to reproduce believable speech between figures of high and low social rank also contribute to the liveliness of action and characters.

In addition, Shakespeare excels in the art of grasping the essence of relationships between husbands and wives, lovers, parents and children, and friends. Innocence and youthful exuberance are aptly represented in the fatal love of Romeo and Juliet; the destructive spirit of mature and intensely emotional love is caught in the affair between Antony and Cleopatra. Other relationships reveal the psychic control of one person by another (of Macbeth by Lady Macbeth), the corrupt soul of a seducer (Angelo in *Measure for Measure*), the twisted mind of a vengeful officer (Iago in *Othello*), and the warm fellowship of simple men (Bottom and his followers in *A Midsummer Night's Dream*). The range of emotional states manifested in Shakespeare's characters has never been equaled by succeeding dramatists.

These memorable characters have also been given memorable poetry to speak. In fact, one of the main strengths of Shakespearean drama is its synthesis of action and poetry. While Shakespeare's poetic style is marked by the bombast and hyperbole that characterize much of Elizabethan drama, it also has a richness and concreteness that make it memorable and quotable. One need think only of Hamlet's "sea of troubles" or Macbeth's daggers "unmannerly breech'd with gore" to substantiate the imagistic power of Shakespearean verse. Such images are also worked into compelling patterns in the major plays, giving them greater structural unity than the plots alone provide. Disease imagery in *Hamlet*, repeated references to blood in *Macbeth*, and allusions to myths of children devouring parents in *King Lear* represent only a few of the many instances of what has been called "reiterated imagery" in Shakespearean drama. Wordplay, puns, songs, and a variety of verse forms, from blank verse to tetrameter couplets—these features, too, contribute to the "movable feast" of Shakespeare's style.

In a more general sense, Shakespeare's achievement can be traced to the skill with which he used his medium—the stage. He created certain characters to fit the abilities of certain actors, as the role of Falstaff in the *Henry IV* and *Henry V* plays so vividly demonstrates. He made use of every facet of the physical stage—the trapdoor, the second level, the inner stage, the "heavens"—to create special effects or illusions. He kept always before him the purpose of entertaining his audience, staying one step ahead of changes in taste among theatergoers. That both kings and tinkers were able to find in a Shakespearean play something to delight and instruct them is testimony to the wide appeal of the playwright. No doubt the universality of his themes and his deep understanding of human nature combined to make his plays so popular. These same strengths generate the magnetic power that brings large audiences into theaters to see the plays today.

Growth of the Dramatist

William Shakespeare was born in Stratford-upon-Avon, England, probably on or near April 23, 1564. His father was John Shakespeare, a glovemaker and later bailiff (or mayor) of the town; his mother was Mary Arden, the daughter of a well-to-do landowner in nearby Wilmcote. His parents had eight children; William was the oldest. Although no records exist to prove the fact, Shakespeare probably began attending a Stratford grammar school at six or seven years of age. There, he studied Latin grammar, literature, rhetoric and logic for between eight and ten hours a day, six days a week. William Lily's largely Latin text, *A Short Introduction of Grammar* (1527), was the staple of the course, but Shakespeare also read Cicero, Plautus, Terence, Vergil, and Ovid. Many of these authors influenced the playwright's later work; Ovid in particular was a favorite source of material, used in such plays as *A Midsummer Night's Dream* and *Romeo and Juliet*. Shakespeare probably knew very little of other languages, although he does exhibit an understanding of French in such plays as *Henry V* and *All's Well That Ends Well*. (The sources for most, if not all, of the plays existed in English translations published during Shakespeare's lifetime.)

Shakespeare may have left school around 1577, the year in which his father fell on hard times. Legend says the young man worked as a butcher's apprentice, but there is no proof to support this notion. His marriage to Anne Hathaway of Shottery took place in 1582; she was eight years his senior and pregnant at the time of the wedding. Whether Shakespeare felt obliged to marry her or simply took pity on her unfortunate predicament is yet another matter for speculation. Their first child, Susanna, was born in May, 1583, and in 1585, twins named Hamnet and Judith were born to the young couple. (It is interesting to note that by 1670, the last of Susanna's descendants died, thereby ending the Shakespeare family line.)

There is no evidence concerning Shakespeare's activities between 1585 and 1592. Legend asserts that he was forced to leave Stratford in order to escape punishment for poaching deer on the estate of Sir Thomas Lucy, one of Stratford's leading citizens. Another popular story has Shakespeare taking a position as schoolmaster at the grammar school, where he supposedly improved his Latin. None of these accounts can be substantiated by fact, yet they continue to seduce modern readers and playgoers. One intriguing suggestion is that Shakespeare joined a troupe of professional actors that was passing through Stratford in 1587. This company, called the Queen's Men, may have been in need of a new performer, since one of their members, William Knell, had been murdered in a brawl with a fellow actor.

Shakespeare and the London Stage

In 1592, Robert Greene, a playwright and pamphleteer, attested Shakespeare's presence in London in a sneering remark about the young upstart whose "tiger's heart [is] wrapt in a player's hide." This reference is a parody of a line from one of Shakespeare's earliest plays, *Henry VI, Part III.* Greene's "Shake-scene in a country" is clearly Shakespeare, who by this date was identifiable as both an actor and a playwright. Greene's remark also implies that the uneducated upstart had probably served an apprenticeship of a few years revising old plays, a practice that was common in this period. By 1594, Shakespeare had become a member of the Lord Chamberlain's Men, who were then performing at the Theatre in Shoreditch, to the north of the city. He continued as a member of this essentially stable company, which constructed the Globe Theatre in 1599 and, in 1603, became the King's Men, until he retired from the stage in 1611 or 1612. In part because of the popularity of Shakespeare's plays and in part because of the strong support of Elizabeth and James

I, the company achieved considerable financial success. Shakespeare shared in that success by acquiring a one-tenth interest in the corporation. By 1596, he was able to purchase a coat of arms for his father, and in the next year, he acquired the second-best house in Stratford. This degree of prominence and success was unusual for someone in a profession that was not highly regarded in Renaissance England. Robert Greene, Shakespeare's harsh critic, died a pauper, a condition that was typical of many Elizabethan playwrights.

Actors and playwrights were in fact regarded as entertainers whose companions were bearbaiters, clowns, and jugglers. Confirmation of this fact comes from evidence that some public theaters were used both for plays and for bearbaiting and bullbaiting. After 1590, moreover, the playhouses had to be constructed in the Bankside district, across the Thames from London proper. City fathers afraid of plague and opposed to public entertainments felt that the Bankside, notorious for its boisterous inns and houses of prostitution, was the fitting locale for "playing" of all kinds. Indeed, theatrical productions were not regarded as high art; when plays were published, by the company or by individual actors, apparently no effort was made to correct or improve them. . . . Shakespeare himself never corrected or took to the printer any of the plays attributed to him. Poetry was valued as true literature, and there is considerable evidence that Shakespeare hoped to become a recognized and respected poet like Sir Philip Sidney or Edmund Spenser. His poems of the early 1590's (*Venus and Adonis* and *The Rape of Lucrece*) were immensely popular. Still, Shakespeare chose to become a public entertainer, a role that he played with convincing brilliance.

The company to which this best of the entertainers belonged was relatively small—fifteen or twenty players at most. The actors were generally well known to the audience, and their particular talents were exploited by the playwrights. Richard Burbage, the manager of Shakespeare's company for many years, was renowned for his skill in acting tragic parts, while William Kemp and Robert Armin were praised for their talents as comic actors. Shakespeare composed his plays with these actors in mind, a fact borne out by the many comedies featuring fat, drunken men such as Sir John Falstaff (of the *Henry IV* and *Henry V* plays) and Sir Toby Belch (of *Twelfth Night*). Shakespeare could not compose his works for an ideal company; he suited his style to the available talent.

Since his company was underwritten to some degree by the government, Shakespeare and his fellows were often called upon to perform at court: thirty-two times during Elizabeth's reign and 177 times under James I. The king and queen did not venture to the Theatre or the Globe to mingle with the lower classes, depending instead on the actors to bring their wares to them. *Macbeth* was written as a direct compliment to James I: Banquo, the brave general treacherously murdered by the villainous hero, was one of James's ancestors. Shakespeare had to change the facts of history to pay the compliment, but the aim of pleasing his and the company's benefactor justified the change.

There were no women actors on Shakespeare's stage; they made their appearance when Charles II returned to the throne in 1660. Young boys (eleven to fourteen years old) played the female parts, and Shakespeare manipulated this convention with considerable success in his comedies, where disguises created delightful complications and aided him in overcoming the problem of costuming. The lady-disguised-as-page device is worked with particular effect in such plays as *As You Like It*, *Twelfth Night*, and *Cymbeline*.

Since there were few actors and sometimes many parts, members of the company were required to double (and sometimes triple) their roles. The effect of this requirement becomes evident when one notes that certain principal characters do not appear in consecutive scenes. One should likewise remember that performance on the Elizabethan stage was continuous; there was no falling curtain or set change to interrupt the action. No scenery to speak of was employed, although signs may have been used to designate cities or countries and branches may have been tied around pillars to signify trees. The absence of scenery allowed for a peculiar imaginative effect. A place on the stage that had been a throne room could within a few seconds become a hovel hid-

Shakespeare's use of intricate characters, poetic speech, and vivid imagery enabled his works to convey universal truths that are still relevant today.

ing its inhabitants from a fierce storm. Shakespeare and his contemporaries could thereby demonstrate the slippery course of Fortune, whose wheel, onstage and in real life, might turn at any moment to transform kings into beggars.

The apronlike stage jutted out into an area called "the pit," where the "groundlings," or those who paid the lowest admission fee (a penny), could stand to watch heroes perform great deeds. The octagon-shaped building had benches on the two levels above the pit for customers willing to pay for the privilege of sitting. Although estimates vary, it is now generally believed that the Globe could accommodate approximately twenty-five hundred people. The design of the stage probably evolved from the model of innyards, where the traveling companies of actors performed before they took up residence in London in the 1570's. On either side of the stage were two doors for entrances and exits and, at the back, some kind of inner stage behind which actors could hide and be discovered at the right moment. A trapdoor was located in the middle of the apron stage, while above it was a cupola-like structure that housed a pulley and chair. This chair could be lowered to the stage level when a *deus ex machina* (literally, a "god from a machine") was required to resolve the action. This small house also contained devices for making sound effects and may have been the place from which the musicians, so much a part of Elizabethan drama, sent forth their special harmonies. The little house was called "the heavens" (stars may have been painted on its underside), while the trapdoor was often referred to as "hell." For Shakespeare's Globe audience, then, the stage was a world in which the great figures of history and imagination were represented doing and speaking momentous things.

In 1608, the King's Men purchased an indoor theater, the Blackfriars, which meant that the company could perform year-round. This theater was located within the city proper, which meant that a somewhat more sophisticated audience attended the plays. Seating capacity was approximately seven hundred; there was no pit to stand in, and there is some evidence that the stage machinery was more elaborate than the equipment at the Globe. Some historians therefore argue that the plays written after 1608—*Cymbeline, Pericles, Prince of Tyre, The Winter's Tale, The Tempest*—were composed especially for performance at the Blackfriars. These tragicomedies or romances teem with special effects and supernatural characters, and this emphasis on spectacle differentiates them from Shakespeare's earlier comedies. While such a theory is attractive, at least a few of these plays were also performed at the supposedly "primitive" Globe.

Shakespeare's Final Years

By 1608, Shakespeare had achieved the fame and recognition for which he had no doubt hoped. He was in a position to reduce his output to one or two plays per year, a schedule that probably allowed him to spend more time in Stratford with his family. In 1611, he left London for Stratford, returning from time to time to see plays performed at both theaters and possibly to engage in collaborative efforts with new playwrights such as John Fletcher. His last play, *Henry VIII*, was a collaboration with Fletcher; it was produced on June 29, 1613, a fateful day for the Globe. A spark from one of the cannon shot off during the performance set the thatched roof on fire and burned the building to the ground.

From 1613 until his death in 1616, Shakespeare led the life of a prosperous citizen in his native town. No doubt the happiest moment of this period came with the marriage of his daughter Judith in 1616. One of the persistent legends about the cause of the playwright's death is that he celebrated too vigorously at the reception with his friends Ben Jonson and Michael Drayton and contracted a fatal fever. Whatever the cause, Shakespeare died on April 23, 1616, and was buried in Holy Trinity Church. His epitaph gives no hint of the poetic strength that marked his plays, but it does express a concern common among men of his age:

> Good friend for Jesus sake forbear
> To dig the dust enclosed here.
> Blessed be the man that spares these stones
> And cursed be he that moves my bones.

Chapter 3

Cultural
Turning Points

Poetry, Patronage, and Power in Queen Elizabeth's Court

Gary Waller

Gary Waller, Professor of Literary Studies and head of the Department of English at Carnegie-Melon University, explains that the Court was the center of power and the creator of tastes, habits, beliefs, and allegiances during the Elizabethan Age. Like other European monarchs, Elizabeth welcomed to her Court the intellectuals, the artists, the poets, and the statesmen who would propagate the image she wished to project. "Patronage" was the social institution through which these courtiers were rewarded and by which they could in turn dispense favors to others. The monarch and her Court exerted considerable cultural control by rewarding politically useful courtiers with money and offices and by excluding from the seat of power those courtiers who held or developed politically incorrect opinions.

Waller explains that during Elizabeth's reign "the patronage system in England took on a distinctive pattern." Elizabeth herself spent little money on patronage, but instead demanded that her courtiers promote the writers who supported her own social and political goals: "civil order, obedience, and a patriotism focused on the crown." The greatest epic poem of the period, *The Faerie Queene*, written by a recipient of the queen's personal patronage, Edmund Spenser, clearly intends to celebrate and justify Elizabeth, her Court, and her socio-political goals. Waller contends, however, that the structure of the poem and the content of its later books reveal an unsettling truth about how power was actually exercised in Elizabeth's Court: Conflict was resolved by brute force.

Waller has edited and introduced *Shakespeare's Comedies* as well as collections of essays on Sir Philip Sidney and Mary Wroth.

Throughout the sixteenth century, 'Court' was a powerful word as well as a powerful institution; it accumulated round itself ideas and feelings that were often contradictory or confusing, but always compelling. Men and women 'swarmed' to the Court (the metaphor is a favourite one) for power, gain, gossip, titles, favours, rewards, and entertainment. The Court was more than merely the seat of government, or wherever the monarch happened to be. All across Europe the *idea* of the Court, as well as its concrete existence, excited an intensity that indicates a rare concentration of power and cultural dominance. It is Gabriel Harvey's 'only mart of preferment and honour'; it is Spenser's 'seat of Courtesy and civil conversation'; it is [poet John] Donne's 'bladder of Vanitie'. What powers, real or reputed, did the Court have over the destinies, tastes, and allegiances of men and women? What recurring anxieties or affirmations are associated with the Court? By whom are they voiced? With what special or covert interests? And with what degree of truth? What can they mediate to us of the Court's influence on the ongoing and deep-rooted cultural changes of the period—the complex struggles for political and social ascendency, the fundamental changes of ideology and sensibility?

The Court's Power

Such questions come, perhaps, down to this: how did the Court's power operate upon the particular details of life? How did the dominant ideology control the specifics of living, including the way poetry was thought of, written, and received? I stress the word 'detail' because, as [literary critic] Edward Said explains, 'for power to work it must be able to manage, control, even create detail: the more detail, the more real power'. Power is felt more intimately in detail—in the particulars of our everyday lives, in the particularities of poetry. It is on such domestic levels that we are deeply influenced by the dominant ideology. In the sixteenth century, the Court was one of the key places where, in the words of [literary theorist] Michel Foucault, 'power reaches into the very grain of individuals, touches their bodies and inserts itself into their actions and attitudes, their discourses, learning processes and everyday lives'. The Court produced, in all who came into contact with it, a set of expectations, anxieties, assumptions, and habits, sometimes very explicitly, sometimes by unstated but very concrete pressures. And as we read the period's writings, we can see how writers and artists provide a kind of early-warning system; they are our most trustworthy guides to the tensions we can now look back upon.

So, then: what can the poetry of the age tell us about how it was to be exposed to, fostered by, or exploited by the Court? As [social historian] Roy Strong and others have shown, throughout the Renaissance, all European Courts attempted to use the arts to control and in a very real sense create the tastes, habits, beliefs, and allegiances of their subjects. In some cases this attempt was carried out through overt state apparatuses—through control and censorship of the theatre, imprisonment of playwrights, and the patronage and protection of particular literary forms and opinions for example. 'Before the invention of the mechanical mass media of today', Strong writes, 'the creation of monarchs as an "image" to draw people's allegiance was the task of humanists, poets, writers and artists'. Profound alliances therefore grew up between the new art forms of the Renaissance and the monarch. Around the monarch was the Court, and all over Europe, it was to the Court that intellectuals, educators, artists, architects, and poets were drawn. No less than the building of palaces or great houses, official state portraits, medallions or court fêtes, poetry was part of what Strong terms 'the politics of spectacle'. It was part of the increasing attempt—culminating in England in the reigns of James I and Charles I—to propagate a belief in the sacredness of the monarchy and the role of the Court and mobility within a ritual of power. Just as, in Strong's words, 'the world of the court fete is an ideal one in which nature, ordered and controlled, has all dangerous potential removed', and in which the Court could celebrate its wisdom and control over the world, time, and change, so poetry too became, as John Donne's friend, Sir Henry Wotton, put it, 'an instrument of state'. . . .

The Patronage System

If the Court is the major cultural apparatus which controlled the creation of poetry, within its activities the particular apparatus that distributed or withheld approval was the system of patronage. However suspect in our time (the pejorative associations of 'patronizing' today registering the changes that have occurred), patronage was certainly one of the major apparatuses of cultural control in pre-industrial Europe. Patronage, specifically financial support, was what all authors sought— whether from monarch, lord, or rich man (or woman). By 'patronage', however, we should understand not simply reward of money or a position given to an author: the term covers a huge variety of activities. Much patronage, especially for poetry, operated rather in the way 'public relations' works today. A writer might be directly commissioned to produce a work. Or he might simply decide out of gratitude or in hope of advancement to dedicate a work to an influential nobleman or woman. A dedication might be initiated by the author in the hope of just getting noticed. Either way, patronage formed a network of pressure, encouragement, and exclusion, providing the powerful—and notably the monarch and the Court—with a system by which politically useful subjects could be either attached to or excluded from their presence and power.

Like today, poetry as such did not often command much reward. The cries often heard from poets about the scarcity of money and offices were numerous, poetry providing, in [poet] Ben Jonson's words, 'but a meane *Mistress*', her rewards being limited and unreliable. Directly utilitarian writing was what the sixteenth-century monarchs and Courts preferred to support. Still, there was, right through the period, even as far back as late-fifteenth-century Scotland, and, in England from the time of Henry VII and VIII, an increasingly tightly organized system of patronage that exercised power over artists, musicians, and writers, in an interaction of what Richard Green has termed 'patrons and prince pleasers'. Throughout the century, many of the poets' complaints were caused by their awareness that while support was forthcoming to writers immediately useful to patrons, it rarely seemed to percolate to poets as if, in Samuel Daniel's words, patrons did not realize 'how small/A portion' would 'turn the wheels . . . to make their glory last'.

Under Elizabeth, the patronage system in England took on a distinctive pattern. As in all late Renaissance Courts, control of the arts became increasingly oppressive—or attractive, according to one's place and achievements within the system. At the centre of the society was the Queen, around whom there was concentrated a cult of extraordinary power by which she was celebrated—as the embodiment of power, beauty, justice, the imperium, and, within the court circles, as the quintessential, unapproachable yet alluring, Petrarchan mistress. While she flirted and flaunted her sexual power among her courtiers, her portraits and personal mottoes asserted her vaunted chastity before all else. Her admirers likewise responded by praising her 'cruelty' to them in tropes [figures of speech] derived from Petrarchanism [elaborate comparisons derived from the Italian poet Petrarch] and its Neo-platonic trappings [idealistic aspiration from the philosophical doctrines of Plato (380 B.C.)]. But hers was not merely a convenient pose to encourage courtiers to turn graceful compliments or to spend huge proportions of their incomes in bedecking themselves to attract her approval, as [Sir Walter] Ralegh [explorer and writer] for one most certainly did. Rather, it had practical and direct political importance—and especially from the late 1570s until the end of the century. Interestingly enough, Elizabeth herself spent little on patronage—certainly less than either her father Henry VIII or her successor James I. Instead, she demanded that her nobles and courtiers themselves dispensed rewards, and she used her frequent progresses through the country and visits to their great houses to encourage them to do so. In such ways, she would gain the glory while being spared the expense of the favours and perquisites that would bind her subjects more closely to her regime.

In the first twenty-five years of Elizabeth's reign, such a system worked almost exclusively to promote writers of religious, political, and generally utilitarian works. Hers was a regime that was nervous, unsure of its stability, afraid of religious and political enemies inside and out. Thus the patronage system was part of a concentrated effort by the regime to mould opinions and to direct writers to socially or politically approved goals. The tough-minded courtiers who surrounded Elizabeth—particularly Leicester and Cecil—supported writers who could be, primarily, propagandists. . . .

Poetry as Propaganda

The bulk of the poetry extant from at least the first three-quarters of the sixteenth century is unremitting in the way it subordinated itself to the public needs of the regime. The poetry before 1580 is mainly such versified Protestant and civic propaganda—moral commonplaces, precepts, *encomia* [poems of praise], epitaphs, expostulations on patriotism, exposures of moral dangers, or on social evils, the dangers of life in Court, the shortness of life in general. It sets out the rules for responsible behaviour, usually reinforced by stern moralizations of theological commonplace, like [Barnabe] Googe's:

> Behold this fleeting world, how all things fade,
> How every thing doth pass and wear away;
> Each state of life, by common course and trade,
> Abides no time, but hath a passing day.

Such verse, as [literary critic] William E. Sheidley comments on Googe (one of its most indefatigable producers), was designed to advance the general programme of the new regime, which included 'purging the realm of vice, papistry, and dissension, while educating the populace to the need for civil order, obedience, and a patriotism focused on the crown'. Even the period's satiric verse, such as [George] Gascoigne's *The Steele Glas*, is designed to point out the social ills of the time, to purge them so that the Court might become more like the pattern given, so the assumption was, by the Queen herself. Typical targets are the frivolity of modern courtiers and the corruption of foreign, especially Italian, influences. It is poetry firmly in line with [Roger] Ascham's requirement in *The Scholemaster* that literature 'gather examples' and 'give light and understanding' to good precepts.

Most of the century is dominated by such utilitarian poetry, and it would be a mistake to see such lugubrious verse as being transcended, as [C.S.] Lewis for one was wont to do, by an upsurge of aureate [golden, splendid], sophisticated courtly lyrics from 1570 on. The utilitarian emphasis continues. Its most triumphant creation is unquestionably Spenser's *The Faerie Queene* (1590–96), which is perhaps the clearest and richest example of how the Elizabethan regime advanced its ideals through poetry. . . .

The Faerie Queene's Place in Elizabethan Culture

The Faerie Queene is the ultimate test case in Elizabethan poetry for the ways in which power seeks to control language. It is a poem expressly dedicated to the praise of the Queen, her Court, and the cultural practices by which the Elizabethan regime established and maintained its power. Spenser accepts his role as that of the Orphic bard, praising, warning, and celebrating the society that not only rewarded but in a real sense created him. Thus his poem's central figure is the Queen—as head of the Church as well as the State, triumphing over heresy on the one hand and political dissent on the other, and as the inspiration of the poem itself. The Queen's response to the poem, at least to the first part published, was to reward Spenser with a pension, and in 1598 she requested his appointment as Sheriff of Cork. To have even a self-styled laureate praising her regime so fulsomely was to acknowledge poetry's usefulness as part of its ideological underpinning. More consciously than any other poem in the last two decades of the century, *The Faerie Queene* is 'Art become a work of State', asserting that beneath the contingent world the values of the regime are without contradiction and that when its norms are transgressed, chaos will result. The poem is offered as a microcosm of this truth.

To speak of *The Faerie Queene* as the most magnificent articulation of the Elizabethan Court's dominant ideology is, however, a claim that is contradicted by the poem itself. The poem raises the question of how a deeply conservative poet can be surpassed by his own poem so that his readers see the ideological [doctrinal] contradictions, not just the ideological mystifications, of his society. If we submit *The Faerie Queene* to a symptomatic reading, and are alert to its contradictions, to what is absent or silent, then we can see how to construct the latent text which is struggling to emerge.

The very length of time Spenser spent on his poem, perhaps twenty years, helps us open up the poem to such a symptomatic reading. The poem may have started as a celebration, and even with some plan like that which Spenser outlined in a letter to Ralegh, where he spoke of twelve books, each with its own virtue and a culminating feast in the Court of Gloriana. But by 1596, the original design had been abandoned. Lewis suggests we speak not of a 'whole' poem, but rather of fragments A (1590, Books I–III), B (1596 IV–VI), and C (Mutability). Certainly, between the image of mutuality and confidence in the reconciliation of Amoret and Scudamour in the cancelled final stanzas of the 1590 edition and the darker late books there are too many contradictions to ignore. The poem encodes many of the real historical conflicts and tensions of its time, dealing with them not (as Shakespeare was already starting to do in the mid-1590s) by juxtaposing and so exploring their rival claims to truth and allegiance, but by trying arbitrarily to displace and condense them to maintain the power of the dominant ideology. The poet's desire is clear: to justify the cultural and ideological practices of the Elizabethan Court. And yet his poem is fragmented by potent ideological breaks and contradictions. Book V is particularly revealing: in the opening canto, for instance, Artegall dismisses chivalric reconciliation as ineffective in deciding the conflict between Sanglier and his opponent, asserting that 'doubtfull causes' can be decided only by force. Conflict is settled not by the knights acknowledging their places in a hierarchy but by brutal militarism. Ultimately, ideological domination is dependent on force.

What the poem attempts—in the early books buoyantly, in the later ones desperately—is a denial of historical change. *The Faerie Queene* yearns for stasis, to project truth as unalterable in the face of unpredictability and, in its manifestation in Elizabeth and her Court, as natural, given, and unassailable. It is built therefore on a poetic that tries to avoid debate, to efface all contradiction, and to reconcile all partial truths into a higher harmony or ruthlessly to exclude them as heretical or unnatural. It tries likewise to create a reader who is active but subservient—a loyal participant in the decipherment of emblem, hieroglyph, and allegory. He or she is interpellated as part of a great celebration of ideological plenitude, just as the Elizabethan courtier was encultured and socialized by accepting his or her proper place in the Court. But just as there was in the Court, so in Spenser's poem there is an anxiety that emerges as continual contradiction. . . .

The Faerie Queene Reveals the Aspirations and Failures of Elizabeth's Court

There is a deep longing for meaning and stasis in *The Faerie Queene* which is contradicted at the deepest level by its own being. It attempts to transform history into culture, culture into nature, and to fix that which inevitably changes in stasis. As such it epitomizes all that the Elizabethan Court itself likewise tried and failed to do. Spenser's poem may be described as 'great' on two main counts. First, like the society which produced it, it could not remain faithful to the desires which motivated it, and the more those were asserted to be natural and true, the more their falsity and the naked power on which they rested, is revealed. *The Faerie Queene* is thus a rich and fascinating articulation of a complex and fascinating cultural formation. Second, as text . . . , it remains intriguing, perplexing, rich, unmistakably a great work of poetry.

The Golden Age of English Poetry

James Reeves

James Reeves, a prominent English poet and critic, finds "nothing more remarkable in the whole history of English literature than the sudden flowering that took place during the last twenty years of Elizabeth's reign." In this selection from his book *A Short History of English Poetry, 1340–1940*, Reeves suggests four factors that may have promoted the development of poetry during these two decades: the exuberant spirit of an age that was celebrating the Queen, the nation, and exploration; the fashion for poetic drama in the theaters, which fostered audience appreciation of poetry as well as authorial experimentation with verse form; the growth of the printing industry, which satisfied an increasing popular demand for anthologies of poetry; and a new national school of musical composition, which rewarded the efforts of those writing lyrics. The body of poetry produced during this golden age ranges from Christopher Marlowe's speculative eloquence, Sir Walter Raleigh's satire, and Sir John Davies's serious morality, to the efforts of countless sonneteers to evoke all of the moods and fancies of lovers. Reeves illustrates the appeal of love lyrics, especially sonnets, by focusing on the popular poetry of Michael Drayton and the sonnet sequence by the greatest of all love poets, William Shakespeare.

James Reeves has edited and introduced numerous collections of poetry, including *The Idiom of the People, English Traditional Verse, The Cassell Book of English Poetry, Selected Poems of Thomas Hardy, The Poetry of Emily Dickinson*, and several collections of poetry for children. In addition to *A Short History of English Poetry, 1340–1940*, he has also written *The Modern Poets' World* and *The Reputation and Writing of Alexander Pope.*

Nothing is more remarkable in the whole history of English literature than the sudden flowering that took place during the last twenty years of Elizabeth's reign. It may be compared to the outburst of Romanticism between 1790 and 1820; but in the latter period what is remarkable is the work of a mere half-dozen men of genius, the minor verse of the age being of small interest. This is not so with the later Elizabethan period. Not less notable than the splendour of the best poetry is the excellence of the average. Men whose talents might have been of small account at any other time composed at least a few lyrics of lasting worth; and men who did in fact compose a mass of very ordinary verse might, in moments of inspiration, break into something of outstanding quality. There is no accounting for the appearance at this time of the greatest poetic genius of all time; but it can at least be said that if genius is in any way to be attributed to the spirit of the age, Shakespeare emerged at the moment when he might most confidently be expected. All our judgements of the Elizabethan poets are made under the shadow of Shakespeare, but if he had never lived, that age would still be of surpassing interest. . . .

Factors Promoting Poetry

The spirit of the later Elizabethan age is a combination of sheer joy, national self-confidence, and a new zeal for discovery. The tide of nationalism ran high: England seemed to have extricated herself finally from foreign domination, and the decisive defeat of Spain in 1588 confirmed this; the navigators had opened up new worlds for British merchant seamen; the release of men's minds from medieval scholasticism, and the influence of the Continental Renaissance, gave the poets and dramatists unexplored tracts of experience in the hearts and passions of men; the whole social and political structure was surmounted by the enigmatic and dazzling figure of the Queen, who was venerated by the poets as the Virgin Muse, and by the nation at large as the spiritual and temporal head of a vigorous, self-assertive and prosperous nation. This is not to say that the Elizabethan age had no intellectual, social and political problems; but during the eighties and nineties the atmosphere was buoyant and optimistic.

Apart from the spirit of the age, three other factors were influential in promoting the development of poetry. In part these must be regarded as being due to those intangible influences we call 'fashion'. The first was the fashion for stage plays which came in with the growing wealth and importance of London. We cannot here consider the history of drama, but we must acknowledge that during this period, as at no other time, the history of poetry is inescapably involved with the drama. No real dividing line can be drawn between dramatic and non-dramatic poetry. There were, it is true, lyrists and sonneteers who had no dealings with the stage, and playwrights whose work was exclusively dramatic; but the mere fact that Shakespeare was supreme in both dramatic and non-dramatic writing, and that a host of other playwrights made significant contributions to lyric poetry, means that there is no real distinction to be insisted upon.

The two other factors which have some bearing on the astonishing poetic flowering of the eighties are the growth of the printing industry, especially in the City of London, and the emergence of a national school of musical composition. Poetry was in fashion; the writing of sonnets and love-lyrics became an acknowledged pastime of courtiers; and the demand from city printers for modish anthologies and sonnet sequences to please the taste of the times was insatiable. Much, perhaps most, of the verse so produced was little better than the minor verse of any other period; but at least there was no lack of a market for the best as well as the mediocre.

The English school of lutanists and madrigalists, of whom [William] Byrd, [Thomas] Morley, and [John] Dowland were at this time supreme, also created a continuous demand for lyric verses. It is not known how many of the lutanists composed their own words. But it must be assumed that hundreds of the lyrics printed in the song-books were the work of anonymous poets of considerable inventive talent and frequent high inspiration. . . .

Perhaps, however, the prior impetus was given to lyric poetry, not by chamber music, but by the stage. The earlier dramatists—[John] Lyly, [Thomas] Lodge, [Robert] Greene and [Thomas] Nashe, known as the University Wits—were among the first to explore, for purposes of stage entertainment, the infinite varieties of verse pattern for which the Elizabethan lyric is remarkable. The great majority of the lyrics deal with love in all its moods—rapturous, despairing, triumphant, frivolous, tormented, playful, disillusioned. What is remarkable about the Elizabethan love lyric, however, is not its psychological depth or subtlety, but its formal variety and charm. It is a commonplace that the average Elizabethan must have had a marvellous ear; but it is probable that, despite the popularity of the printed word, the importance of the theatre and of music meant that poetry was still largely an oral art. To read aloud any dozen pages from an anthology of Elizabethan lyrics is to be aware of a rhythmical subtlety and delicacy never achieved before or since. . . .

Attributes of Elizabethan Lyrics

The lyrics of this period are frequently distinguished by the rhythmic subtlety which combines a hesitant with a flowing movement. A lyric from [George] Peele's *David and Bethsabe*, which has escaped the anthologists more than some which are no better, illustrates this rhythmic inventiveness to perfection.

> Hot sun, cool fire, tempered with sweet air,
> Black shade, fair nurse, shadow my white hair;
> Shine, sun; burn, fire; breathe, air, and ease me;
> Black shade, fair nurse, shroud me and please me:
> Shadow, my sweet nurse, keep me from burning,
> Make not my glad cause cause of mourning.
> > Let not my beauty's fire
> > Inflame unstaid desire,
> > Nor pierce any bright eye
> > That wandereth lightly.

Another distinguishing mark of the Elizabethan lyric is its delight in external nature. For all its concern with the moods and fancies of lovers, and the varying perfections of the mistress' outward form, we feel that its setting is a harmonious and charming natural scene, realised in concrete and sometimes homely terms. It is not the wild nature of some of the Romantic poets, nor does it insist on naturalistic detail; it is none the less real and pervasive, though generalised and humanised by comparison. Nature is celebrated not for itself, but as a setting for human activity. Professor C.S. Lewis speaks of the 'note of almost idiotic happiness' in [Thomas] Nashe's famous *Spring the sweet spring*—a note which I think can sometimes be detected also in [Romantic poet William] Blake. And the happiness is the happiness of innocence, a sense of harmony between man and nature, of sheer joy in country pleasures. Such a note cannot be faked; its spontaneity is self-evident.

Marlowe, Ralegh, and Davies

Among the longer non-dramatic poems written by playwrights, the best-known are Shakespeare's *Venus and Adonis* and the *Hero and Leander* of Marlowe and [George] Chapman. CHRISTOPHER MARLOWE (1564–1593) is famous chiefly for his plays, which are the work of a young man, sensual, passionate, and ambitious. Little is known for certain of the sudden and violent death which put an end to a dramatic career of unusual promise. At its best Marlowe's dramatic verse has a lofty and overflowing eloquence unrivalled even by Shakespeare. It abounds in daring metaphor and hyperbole. Marlowe raised dramatic blank verse to altogether new heights. *Hero and Leander*, written in rhymed pairs of iambic pentameters, tells the story of the tragic drowning of a young man of Abydos while swimming the Hellespont to woo the beautiful priestess of Aphrodite at Sestos. This subject gives Marlowe scope for his tragic sense, his passionate intensity, and above all, his almost obsessive interest in rich and sensuous detail. No poet has ever crowded his lines with more gorgeous and highly-coloured imagery. These qualities may be discovered almost anywhere in the part of *Hero and Leander* written by Marlowe. But he was not content with mere sensuous description. He was a man of restless intellectual curiosity, and at its best his verse has a speculative eloquence, a music of thought as well as of sound and imagery. . . .

Among the more rewarding of lesser known Elizabethan poets is SIR WALTER RALEGH (1552–1618), sometimes slighted by literary historians as an 'amateur': that is, he was careless of the fate of his work, he left many of his poems unfinished, and he did not dedicate his major energies to the Muse. In one respect he was typically Elizabethan: one feels that he may have been called to write poetry by virtue of the prevailing fashion. In another age he might have been no poet. At the same time his work, which is mainly lyrical and reflective, carries the stamp of an individual sensibility and deserves its share of recognition. His satirical attack on the age, entitled *The Lie*, has a certain trenchant economy of phrase; and several others of his reflective lyrics are worthy to be remembered. But his long, semi-autobiographical meditation on unrequited love, *The Ocean's Love to Cynthia* has a sardonic intensity of feeling and a tone of almost desperate bitterness which distinguish it from most of the lyrical verse of the time.

But in my mind so is her love enclosed,
And is thereof not only the best part,
But into it the essence is disposed:
O love! (the more my woe) to it thou art

Even as the moisture in each plant that grows;
Even as the sun unto the frozen ground;
Even as the sweetness to the incarnate rose;
Even as the centre in each perfect round. . . .

Thou art the soul of that unhappy mind
Which, being by nature made an idle thought,
Began even then to take immortal kind,
When first her virtues in thy spirits wrought.

A notable characteristic of the poetry of this period is its power to assimilate the most varied kinds of experience. The songwriters express an unreflecting joy in love and the natural world; Marlowe explores the possibilities of a classical legend; Ralegh's poems are the subjective expression of a personal malaise; elsewhere we find a more objective treatment of philosophical themes. The two long poems of SIR JOHN DAVIES (1569–1626) are perhaps the best of this kind. Their subjects do not sound promising. *Orchestra* (1596) is a long and discursive dissertation on dancing, and *Nosce Teipsum* (1599) is a reasoned assertion of the immortality of the soul. These poems were formerly regarded as merely 'fantastic'; but recently it has been recognised that their themes are integrally related to the most important aspects of Elizabethan thought. Davies was a grave and serious moralist, capable of sustaining a long argument gracefully and without flatness. . . .

Sonnets and Sonneteers

The attraction of the sonnet form to the Elizabethans lay no doubt partly in its difficulty: the mere technical ingenuity needed to write a sonnet acted as a check on the excesses of undisciplined emotion, and the frequency with which minor poets not otherwise very distinguished managed to bring off at least a few fine sonnets is a sign of the poetic vigour of the time.

Judged by his immense output and by the esteem in which he was held by his contemporaries, MICHAEL DRAYTON (1563–1631) was something more than a minor poet. Like Shakespeare, he was a Warwickshire man and, like other poets of no fortune, succeeded in obtaining the support of a noble patron. He was, he tells us, attracted to poetry at a tender age.

> In my small self I greatly marvelled then,
> Amongst all other, what strange kind of men
> These poets were; and pleased with the name,
> To my mild tutor merrily I came,
> (For I was then a proper goodly page,
> Much like a pygmy, scarce ten years of age)
> Clasping my slender arms about his thigh.
> O my dear master! cannot you (quoth I)
> Make me a poet? Do it if you can,
> And you shall see I'll quickly be a man.

He responded to the demand for historical writings which arose in the nineties not with stage plays, as in Shakespeare's case, but with long chronicle poems, and a few shorter ones, such as *Agincourt*, which is among the best battle poems in the language. Everyone has heard of, but no one reads, the enormous topographical survey of Britain, *Polyolbion*, written in smooth and soporific alexandrines [a line of verse with twelve syllables]. In short extracts it reads pleasantly enough, but like nearly everything Drayton wrote, it lacks fire. On the other hand, his best lyrics have the serene grace and clarity which have earned them a permanent place in the lyric heritage. Among these are the superb sonnet, *Since there's no help, come let us kiss and part*, the lines *To the Virginian Voyage*, the exquisite *Sirena* stanzas, and some of the songs in *Muses' Elizium*.

> Clear had the day been from the dawn,
> All chequered was the sky,
> Thin clouds like scarfs of cobweb lawn
> Veiled Heaven's most glorious eye.
> The wind had no more strength than this
> That leisurely it blew,
> To make one leaf the next to kiss
> That closely by it grew.

The rhythmic sweetness of this and the truth to nature of its imagery exemplify the kind of surprise which is always to be found by the reader of Elizabethan verse. We are apt to regard impressionism and naturalism as things which came into poetry at a much later date—say with [William] Collins in the 1740's—but it is one of the delights of Elizabethan poetry that almost everything which it looks forward to in later times is there to be found at least in embryo. Drayton was a dedicated poet who, when very young, consciously desired to be blessed by the Muse. Few have worked harder for this honour and, although no one would call him great, posterity has acknowledged that the Muse was generous to him. He may never arouse the fiercest passions of literary critics, but his place is secure in the affections of generations of ordinary readers. . . .

Shakespeare

Of all Shakespeare's lyrical writing . . . it is his sonnets that place him most securely among the greatest love poets in any language. Indeed, had he written nothing but the sonnets, he would still have to be accorded a very high position. Two thousand lines of good, often superb, poetry give ample proof of Shakespeare's scope and quality. Moreover, they are not the work of a young man, comparatively early though they are dated in the canon. Shakespeare developed late, and the available evidence suggests that they belong to his middle years. The earliest edition of the one hundred and fifty-four sonnets is the Quarto of 1609, issued by Thomas Thorpe. The mysterious dedication (by Thorpe, not Shakespeare) to 'Mr W.H.' has engendered a library of speculation, none of which has any foundation in fact. The whole question of the biographical background has indeed been the subject of long and exhaustive research, but no indisputable evidence has come to light. Scholars have found out very little more than what can be inferred from the sonnets themselves. The general situation is stated in Sonnet 144, which begins:

> Two loves I have of comfort and despair,
> Which like two spirits do suggest me still:[1]
> The better angel is a man right fair,
> The worser spirit a woman colour'd ill.
> To win me soon to hell, my female evil
> Tempteth my better angel from my side,
> And would corrupt my saint to be a devil,
> Wooing his purity with her foul pride.

Speculation about the identity of the noble young man and the dark lady, or of the other *personæ* of the sonnets, especially the rival poet, is fruitless, and perhaps pointless. It is enough that the relationship between Shakespeare and these others engaged his deepest feelings, and moved him to as passionately personal an utterance as had ever appeared in English poetry. There are reasons for thinking that the order

1. *suggest me still:* influence me continually

of the sonnets has been confused, and attempts have been made to rearrange them to make a consecutive 'story'; yet none is very convincing. The fact is that we must forego a connected story and be satisfied with separate sonnets or groups of sonnets. The first group, in which the young man is urged to beget children in order to defy the destructive power of Time, forms a fairly coherent sequence.

> But wherefore do not you a mightier way
> Make war upon this bloody tyrant, Time?

and

> Shall I compare thee to a summer's day?

and

> Devouring Time, blunt thou the lion's paws

magnificent as they are, are variations on common Elizabethan themes, and are comparatively formal in tone, raised by their qualities of imagery and rhetoric far above the common level. Many of the later sonnets, however, transcend accepted themes and reveal the ideas, moods and feelings of an intensely individual man. No aspect of the sonnets is more remarkable than their marvellous variety, and in this we can detect the creator of the almost infinite range of characters to be found in the plays. *Tired with all these, for restful death I cry* (66) is a profound, but essentially simple, statement of the necessity for love; *Let me not to the marriage of true minds* (116) and *The expense of spirit in a waste of shame* (129) are opposed expressions, both equally valid, of the extremes of idealism and revulsion in the mind of a lover. By their imagery, their reasoning and their rhythmic vitality they strike us, again and again, as the product of a man of equally keen senses and intellect, with an emotional range and a command of language exceeding anything found elsewhere except in the dramatic writings of the same poet.

Portraits and Miniatures in the Elizabethan Age

Eric Mercer

The dominant form of art during Elizabeth's reign was portraiture. In both easel-painting and "limning," the production of miniatures, the subject was predominantly a person. In this selection from his book *English Art, 1553–1625*, Eric Mercer accounts for this near-monopoly of portraiture in painting by explaining that the art reflected the ideas of the State: It glorified the powerful individuals of the day who served the State, and it envisioned history as a pageant of heroes. The style of easel-painting that emerged, called "Elizabethan costume-piece," was distinguished by a flat, linear, lifeless depiction of the face of the sitter and exaggerated emphasis on the clothing and symbols of social position. The portraits depicted the sitters as holders of offices or representatives of powerful families rather than as individuals, Mercer explains. In contrast to the formal, public, official nature of the paintings, the miniatures focused on a more private side of the sitter. In the miniatures, symbolism was still used, but the emblems of office and status were replaced with symbols of unrequited love or uninhibited fancies. The miniatures seem designed to reveal the "most charming or winning aspects of a personality," Mercer asserts, and they are distinguished by attention to lively facial expressions and depictions of individual mood.

In addition to his book *English Art, 1553–1625*, Eric Mercer has published two social histories with an emphasis on material culture: *Furniture, 700–1700* and *English Vernacular Houses: A Study of Traditional Farmhouses and Cottages*.

Excerpted from *English Art, 1553–1625*, by Eric Mercer (*Oxford History of English Art*, vol. 7, 1962). Copyright © Oxford University Press 1962. Reprinted by permission of Oxford University Press.

The most important form of easel-painting in England in the period, both in amount and in contemporary estimation, was portraiture. . . .

An understanding of this near-monopoly by portraiture must be sought in the peculiar circumstances in which English painting developed in the early and mid-sixteenth century. There appeared in England at that time, almost simultaneously and in more or less direct association, an absolute State based on a landowning class, the religious doctrines of the Reformation, and the intellectual changes of the Renaissance. The new type of landowner was not, in many cases, any wealthier than his predecessors, but unlike them he was debarred, as the subject of an absolute State, from spending his wealth upon armies of retainers to win or maintain for him a national or local power. He spent it, instead, upon keeping up a 'port' and in looking after his comforts. One such comfort was to place tapestries, generally imported, and other hangings upon the formerly bare or painted walls of many rooms; and, in consequence, to reduce the demand for domestic murals. At the same time there was practically no demand for church murals as the doctrines of the Reformers enforced a 'decent plainness' upon religious buildings. The results of this double blow were twofold. The painter was robbed of two of his most important opportunities and was placed, as a member of a now crowded and almost redundant craft, in a very weak position against his prospective customers and patrons. The major field for the display of large scale figure and narrative painting was closed and the tradition and prestige of such painting greatly weakened.

In this situation the Humanist ideas of the Renaissance presented the painter with almost his only opportunity, but with a very limited one. The stress on the individual that was the most revolutionary concept of the period entailed, for all its liberating influence, some severe restrictions. It considered 'an interest in mankind to be an interest in persons, history to be a pageant of heroes' [according to Barrows Dunham] and religion a matter of direct communication between a man and his Maker. It was this negative aspect that was eagerly seized on by the contemporary monarchies, who saw in the glorification of the individual a sanction of their absolute control of the State, and by their courtiers, who looked on the Sovereign's glory as the guarantee of their position and their position as the basis of his power. In England, where the dynasty's legal title was as dubious as its supporters' moral claim to much of their land, it was especially welcome. This ideology of the most important patrons of the time had a threefold effect on easel-painting. An interest in persons demanded that they should be subjects of painting, and portraits therefore multiplied. The view of history as a 'pageant of heroes' led to a demand for portraits, real or imagined, of the famous dead and the far-away living, and to a lack of demand for 'historical' paintings, of events in which no particular hero participated. The more private nature of religion and the consequent attitude towards 'idolatry' eliminated any great desire for paintings of biblical subjects or of individual saints and Madonnas. With the painters in too humble a position to express whatever objections they may have had, and with the narrative traditions of mural painting exerting no influence, the easel-painting of the period was, in essence, a reflection of the ideas of the absolute State and its creatures and creators. . . .

The Elizabethan Costume-Piece

The common name for . . . [the portrait] style, 'the Elizabethan costume-piece,' indicates its exaggerated emphasis on the details of the gorgeous dress of the sitter. The portaits of the Queen herself are notorious for their display of finery but the same intention is apparent in the less ostentatious pictures of lesser mortals. A good example is the *Sir Edward Hoby* of 1578, formerly at Bisham Abbey, which obtains considerable decorative effect by the rich colour contrasts of the white doublet trimmed with silver, the maroon ribbon about the neck, the black hat with gold ornament, and the pale green background broken by a brightly painted shield-of-arms. In an age when the apparel oft proclaimed the man such emphasis is not surprising, for it was with man in his social position that the portraiture of the time was concerned. There is, indeed, evidence in the *Portrait of a Lady* (1576) in the Tate Gallery, of the repainting and alteration in the sitter's lifetime of her costume but not of her features. The phenomenon was not confined to England; it has been noticed in contemporary French painting. Such an emphasis precluded any life or movement in the sitter and reinforced the tendency initiated by other factors, to paint in a flat and linear manner; indeed some of these pictures are more decorative patterns than portraits.

The lifelessness of this art is most apparent in the treatment of the only portions of the human body whose existence was recognized, the hands and face. The tenseness of some of [Haus] Eworth's women sitters is derived not only from the facial features but from the often clasped or moving hands. In later work the hands are invariably still, holding a wand of office, or some other symbol of the sitter's rank, or a pair of gloves, or dangling loosely at the sitter's side. Hands, of course, were merely an embarrassment to the painter of a costume-piece, but the face was of prime importance. Yet because it was the face not of a man but of the holder of an office or a founder or representative of a family it was denied individual expression, given a timeless air, and painted very much as a hard flat outline. By the middle of the seventies the conception of a portrait as a State or family record had almost ousted any individual approach. It is not accidental that some of the earliest paintings in which this effect is apparent are such family groups as those of Lords Cobham and Windsor (1567 and 1568), the Judd Memorial painting (1560) in the Dulwich Gallery, with its accessories of corpses, candles, and 'All that makes death a hideous show', and the Bacon family picture of 1578 at Raveningham, which is almost a painting of a funeral monument. Examples of individual portraits in the same manner are numerous; the half-length of Henry Cary, Lord Hunsdon, is typical. Cary is turned a quarter-left, his left hand at his waist, his right holding a white wand. He is dressed in a black doublet and cap, both trimmed with gold and silver lace, a white ruff and ruffles, and a gold jewelled chain, all set against a plain dark-grey background. The face is almost without modelling or expression and with no other mark of individuality than its physical features.

Hand in hand with this, the background accessories of earlier years—the furniture of a room, a landscape seen through a window, the tapestry or cloth-hung walls of Eworth—are often replaced by objects wholly unrelated to the space in which the subject is set but expressive of his rank: The most obvious and commonest of such symbols were coats-of-arms placed above the sitter's shoulders or around the edge of the picture. Their siting mattered little, for neither they nor the sitter were represented as in an actual space. An extreme example is the picture in the National Portrait Gallery of Christopher Hatton as Chancellor of Oxford University, a portrait in which the person is lost amidst a confusion of shields-of-arms, complimentary and punning verses, and symbolic animals. Rarely can any man have shown so much respect for an office and so little for its holder as the painter of this picture, yet he was merely taking the typical portraiture of the period to its ultimate conclusion. . . .

Miniatures

Miniature-painting, or limning as it was then called, was a highly esteemed art in England in this period, and its leading practitioners, Nicholas Hilliard and Isaac Oliver, had a great reputation not only among their own countrymen but even in France. Each has a corpus of work which, despite some uncertainty about the frontier territory between the two, is well-founded and long-established. Further, it is and always has been beyond dispute that their work is of great merit, and that they are at least the equals in their field of any foreign artist of the time. All these qualities distinguish them sharply from their contemporaries among the large-scale painters, and an explanation of this is essential to an understanding of the English miniature in the late sixteenth and early seventeenth centuries. It is possible, of course, to attribute the contrast solely to the greater artistic talents of Hilliard and Oliver, but such an explanation is inadequate. It must be pointed out that the difference lay not merely in inborn qualities—if it lay there at all—but also and more significantly in the opportunities of exercising and developing them. The restrictions that stultified the latent talents of the painters bound the limners less tightly; more, it was precisely because the painters were so restricted that the limners got their opportunities to produce works of merit. The stiff expressionless 'physiognomies' of the large-scale painters were the price that the Elizabethans paid for the exquisite productions of Hilliard.

The work of a Danish scholar, Dr. [T.H.] Colding, has greatly altered the general view of the development behind the English miniature. In particular, by emphasizing and illustrating far more concretely than any of his predecessors the miniature's origin in, and dependence upon, the art of the goldsmith Dr. Colding has enabled us to understand how well suited it was to fulfil the purpose demanded of it in England at the beginning of Elizabeth's reign. Miniature-painting, in the sense in which it is applied to works of this period, means working in water-colours or gouache upon a surface of calf skin or vellum. The method was perfected in medieval book illumination, and its intimate connexion with goldsmith's work is shown by the way in which the illumination is intended to enhance the lavishly applied gold leaf. The backgrounds of such illuminations were almost invariably of an ultramarine, and the colours most favoured were ruby reds, fresh yellows, and emerald greens. . . .

Miniatures' Subjects and Focus

It is noticeable that while both forms [oil paintings and miniatures] are largely confined to portraiture their subject matter within that field is vastly different. The usual limning is not a representation of a statesman, a soldier, a court-favourite in all his regalia, but of a lover, a mistress, a wife, an intimate friend. A very great proportion of them, far greater than among oil-paintings, are of young men and women shown in all the freshness of youth, and these, as Mr. Graham Reynolds says, are generally the best. Like the oil-painters, the limners used a great deal of symbolism, but of a very different kind. Instead of badges of rank and office, or references to worldly achievements, they filled their works with symbols of unrequited love, with uninhibited fancies, and with now unfathomable allusions. One of Hilliard's best known miniatures is of a man clad in a shirt against a background of flames and fingering a locket; another is of an elegant youth with more than his share of what was then regarded as beauty, leaning against a tree amidst conventionalized rose-briars, with a Latin inscription meaning 'My praised faith brings my pains'. There are, of course, 'State' miniatures to be found but, with the exception of those of Elizabeth, they are overwhelmingly of the years after 1590 by which time the Elizabethan miniature was changing into something else. Further, although the miniatures of Elizabeth are, in a sense, 'State' portraits they are far more expressions in art of the high-flown emotional relationships, real or pretended, that existed between Elizabeth and her courtiers and were well fitted to the prevailing concept of the miniature.

This gulf between limning and painting, the private nature of the one and official nature of the other, itself calls, however, for an explanation, for the patrons who called the tune to the painters called it as loudly to the limners; perhaps more loudly, for miniatures, often in a jewelled setting, were thereby much more expensive than paintings and were, in general, beyond the pocket of any but the wealthy or spendthrift. Hilliard . . . considered they were 'for the service of noble persons,' and that limning 'tendeth not to comon men's usse'. As Professor [Ellis] Waterhouse has said, 'Hilliard's miniatures were for the very rich only' and, at least until the death of Elizabeth, the 'very rich' meant, in practice, the nobility and courtiers. The explanation of these men's simultaneous patronage of restricted formalized large-scale painting and of the exquisite and sensitive works of Hilliard is to be found in the contradiction underlying the ideology of the Tudor State and its supporters. The positive and most immediately striking aspect of the age is the universality of talent of its greatest figures. This is the epoch of 'a host of authentic geniuses', of men who combined in one body the qualities of the courtier, soldier, scholar and of the poet, musician, and natural scientist as well. Such a flowering of human potentialities was not the happy result of genetic mutations in the preceding generation but was fostered by a deliberate State policy at a time when opportunities were almost limitless and knowledge and resources very scanty. Even so early it was impossible to maintain a modern State with medieval notions; to keep itself in being the absolute State of the sixteenth century had to nurture and employ a great number of men trained in and permeated with the New Learning and all its implications. Tudor courtiers were, and had to be, not only men of affairs but men abreast or ahead of contemporary thought in all its aspects, and this, because of the nature of the Tudor State, involved them in an aesthetic dilemma. As men of affairs, as buttresses and beneficiaries of the Tudor dynasty, they developed a public art in which the glorification of the individual as a servant of the State and monarch destroyed all individuality; but the interest in human personality and the individual that they acquired from their participation in the most advanced culture of the time was too strong and too genuine to be stifled, and what it could not express in a public art it had to express privately. For that expression it found the miniature ready to hand. . . .

Nicholas Hilliard's Personal Style

By about 1570 the development of State-influenced portraiture had established an almost complete monopoly for the Elizabethan costume-piece and it was at that time that [Nicholas] Hilliard burst into his personal style and, without altering its technique, in fact by limiting himself to its traditional technique, gave the miniature a new content. I think it is probable that Hilliard was quite well aware of what he was doing. He declared himself to be an imitator of [Hans] Holbein's 'maner of limning', and, although the phrase is vague, it is reasonably clear that he meant by it what we would call 'technique'. There is no reason to disagree with him on the point, but it must be stressed that in fact it was not merely Holbein's but the goldsmith-illuminators' technique that he was continuing: the blue background, the colour-scheme related to precious stones, the lavish use of gold, the light flesh colours, and the avoidance of shadowing. He did however employ some methods that were peculiar to Holbein and not general to all miniaturists, in particular the firm outline and the subtle modelling of the sitter's features by the use of deeper flesh tints. But he employed these to a totally different end, and thereby sundered his art from Holbein's and, for that matter, from [Simon] Benninck's and [Luke] Horenbout's. The aim of his art was not, like theirs, to portray an individual with all possible clarity nor, like that of his painter contemporaries, to record a visage and the status of its owner, but to reveal the most charming and winning aspects of a personality. He might well have taken for himself the motto on some old sundials—'I tell none but the pleasant hours'. There is a passage, unfortunately too long for quotation in full, in which he nearly says as much: 'The curious drawer' he says must 'catch thesse lovely graces, wittye smilings and thesse stolne glances which suddenly like lightning pass and another countenance taketh place' and must call 'thesse graces one by one to theire due places.' In such miniatures as his self-portrait of 1577, the portrait of his wife (1578), of Leonard Darr in 1591, of Mrs. Holland in 1593 and Mrs. Mole the effect of this method can best be seen. They are all idealized presentations of their subjects, catching, with a liveliness of facial expression, an individual mood and creating a sense of intimacy.

The Growth of Printing and Advances in Literacy

D.M. Palliser

D.M. Palliser, who is G.F. Grant Professor of History at the University of Hull in England, first published his highly influential social history of Elizabethan England, *The Age of Elizabeth*, in 1983. This selection from the revised and expanded second edition of the book, published in 1992, reviews the non-literary cultural achievements during Elizabeth's reign, then focuses on two revolutionary changes that affected both high and popular Elizabethan culture: "the growth of printing and the increase in books printed in English." Books and pamphlets on a wide range of subjects, as well as English translations of continental works, were made available to a growing audience of readers. In the process the language itself nearly "doubled in volume" as words from classical and modern languages became familiar to readers of printed English works. Palliser explains that significant advances in literacy occurred during Elizabeth's reign, though the limitations of the evidence make it difficult to tabulate exact percentages.

Elizabeth's reign is associated readily enough with a literary golden age, but other artistic and cultural achievements are less widely known. Furthermore, culture in the widest sense was both broader and narrower, both richer and poorer, than today. The earl of Leicester—no outstanding intellectual—was fluent in Italian, and in middle life started to learn Latin before abandoning it for geometry. Yet it was also an age when nobles and commoners alike delighted in cock-fighting and in baiting bulls and bears. Elizabeth spent her time

Excerpted from *The Age of Elizabeth: England Under the Later Tudors 1547–1603*, 2nd ed., by D.M. Palliser. Copyright © Longman Group UK Limited 1983, 1992. Reprinted by permission of Pearson Education Limited.

'watching bears and bulls fighting dogs', grumbled a Spanish envoy in 1576; but it was the same queen who read Greek daily with her old tutor [Roger] Ascham whenever he was at court. The Renaissance belief in the 'complete man' prevented any sharp separation between sports and pastimes and more sober pursuits. Ascham was as proud of his treatise on archery, *Toxophilus*, as of his other writings; and the queen admired skill in dancing as much as in languages or theology.

Sports and pastimes varied widely between different regions and social groups. Hawking and hunting (the deer rather than the fox) were passions with many gentlemen. Sir Thomas Cockaine, who succeeded to his Derbyshire estate in 1538, could write in his *Short Treatise of Hunting* (1591) that 'for this fiftie two yeres . . . I have hunted the bucke in summer, and the hare in winter, two yeares onely excepted' when he was abroad on military service. Organised horseracing was started by gentlemen and urban corporations: York's in 1530 is the first known, and Carlisle still possesses two Elizabethan silver-gilt bells used as prizes for the winners. Fencing, tennis and bowls were becoming popular among the well-to-do; archery and fishing were popular at all levels; wrestling, footracing and football among ordinary people. [John] Leland noted of one Herefordshire hill-fort that 'the people of Leonminstar thereabout cum ons a yere to this place to sport and play', and the annual Cotswold Games which Robert Dover started about 1604 were probably a more organised form of a widespread community activity.

Popular Culture

Popular culture in Tudor England has been much less studied than learned culture; hence Peter Burke's wide-ranging *Popular Culture in Early Modern Europe* (1978) includes few English examples. The existence of a rich and varied repertoire of ballads, songs and stories is well-established, but these activities were in the main confined to the world of oral transmission and were either ignored or treated with contempt by literate observers. [Bishop Hugh] Latimer found that he could not preach in one village in 1549 because the parishioners were celebrating 'Robyn Hoode's day', and Nicholas Bownde observed in 1606 that many people knew more of Robin Hood than they did of the Bible: yet few printed ballads and plays of his deeds survive before the end of the sixteenth century, and many may never have been written down. There were many travelling players, entertainers and storytellers whose activities were noticed chiefly when the government took fright at the spread of seditious ideas. One of the few Tudor minstrels with an identifiable personality was Richard Sheale, a 'merry knave' (clown) whose version of the *Ballad of Chevy Chase* was preserved by Bishop [Thomas] Percy [an eighteenth-century antiquarian, scholar, and poet].

Any division of Tudor culture into 'literary' and 'popular' (the 'Great Tradition' and 'Little Tradition' of [Robert] Redfield's *Peasant Society and Culture*) is too simple. Gentry and clergy participated in popular festivals and rituals; a considerable minority of humble folk had access to books and could read if not write; and there were various levels of both literary and popular culture. For instance, there was a thriving market in ephemeral popular literature, which attracted the scorn of learned writers but which was defended by others as providing instruction or enjoyment. Such were the 'uncountable rabble' who, complained William Webbe, 'be most busy to stuffe every [book] stall full of grosse devises and unlearned pamphlets', while the witty scholar Thomas Nashe lamented that 'every grosse braind idiot is suffered to come into print'. But this was academic jealousy and snobbery. As one of Nashe's targets, Barnabe Rich, replied, 'such is the delicacie of our readers . . . that there are none may be alowed of to write, but such as have been trained at schoole with Pallas . . .' At another level, Martin Ingram has stressed that popular punishments of deviants at this period still involved shared attitudes between gentry and commoners; indeed, one of the best contemporary illustrations of a henpecked husband being publicly humiliated is on a plaster frieze in Montacute House.

High Culture

The high culture of the Tudor age was certainly learned, and it assumed a thorough grounding in the literature and history of Greece and Rome. It is often described as 'Renaissance', a term implying both a recognition of the values of Latin and Greek culture and a strong Italian influence. From the early years of the century foreign influences in the arts became fashionable, either directly from Italy, or indirectly via France and the Empire, and France, in particular, had an enormous influence on English culture throughout the century. The first arrival of the Renaissance style in England is usually dated from 1510, when Henry VIII summoned Torrigiano and other Italian artists to construct his father's tomb. [Humanist writer, Sir Thomas] Elyot grumbled in his *Governour* (1531) that Englishmen were compelled, 'if we wyll have any thinge well paynted, kerved, or embrawdred, to abandone our owne countraymen and resorte unto straungers', and Nicholas Carr, in a public oration at Cambridge (1556), bemoaned the tendency of the English to praise foreign arts and literature and to denigrate their own.

Yet artists and craftsmen under Elizabeth displayed a strong continuity with their medieval English past, absorbing only what suited them of new continental influences. . . .

Revolutionary Growth in Printing

Two massive and permanent changes did, however, affect both high and popular culture in a way that can fairly be described as revolutionary, the growth of printing and the increase in books printed in English. Far more books and pamphlets were published, and on a widening range of subjects. A little over 5,000 English books which survive were published between the 1470s and 1557, some 2,760 in the first half of Elizabeth's reign (1558–79), and 4,370 in the second (1580–1603). The number of books printed is a matter of guesswork. The size of an average edition of an Elizabethan book was apparently about 1,250, implying a total of some 9 million books published during the queen's reign. The figure sounds impressive, though it represents an average of only one or two books per head for a population of four million over a generation and a half.

Yet the impact of the printed word was incalculable, both among the minority of book-owners and the rest of the population. [John] Foxe the martyrologist gave thanks to God 'for the excellent art of printing', while [Francis] Bacon listed it (with gunpowder and the mariner's compass) among the three greatest inventions of the age. Foxe's own *Acts and Monuments*, despite its cost of over £6 [6 pounds], sold more than 10,000 copies by 1603; and such a publication was unusually expensive. Theological tracts could be produced for 2*d* [2 pence]—the Exeter Catholics branded their Protestant opponents as 'two penye booke men"—and ballads for 1*d*. Even these prices were beyond the poor; but many more could hear books and ballads read than could buy them, and of course they could hear the Bible which was placed in every parish church.

The well-to-do and educated had the opportunity to build up large private libraries. Sir William More of Loseley, a Surrey gentleman and JP, possessed some 140 printed books and manuscripts in 1556; one in three Canterbury men leaving wills by 1600 had books recorded in their inventories; and a Worcester vicar owned about 370 books at his death in 1610. Two peers—Lumley and Burghley—possessed over 1,000 books, while the largest collection of all, John Dee's at Mortlake, numbered over 4,000. Booksellers' stocks were becoming larger and more varied, not only in the capital but in towns of any size. Random survivals of stationers' inventories credit Roger Ward of Shrewsbury (1585) with nearly 2,500 volumes in stock, and John Foster of York (1616) with approaching 3,000.

Most major literary works were published in Latin in the first half of the century, and both Elyot and Ascham felt obliged to defend themselves for writing in English. As more and more writers followed their example and wrote for the wider readership of English readers, the language became enriched by a host of words from classical and modern languages; English vocabulary nearly doubled in volume during the century. Early Tudor writers apologised for the roughness and homeliness of the language; Elizabethans like Richard Carew (*The Excellencie of the English Tongue*, 1595–96) thought it not inferior to Greek or Latin in suppleness and beauty. Furthermore, although Elizabethan spelling seems today arbitrary and inconsistent, it represented a considerable improvement on early Tudor practice, thanks largely to the influence of books by John Hart (1551, 1569, 1570).

Many books published in English in the second half of the century were translations, including some of the most influential, like [Sir Thomas] Hoby's translation of Castiglione's *Il Cortegiano* as *The Courtyer* (1561), or [Thomas] North's *Plutarch's Lives* on which Shakespeare drew so heavily. . . .

Advances in Literacy

All could understand their mother tongue spoken, but reading and writing it was another matter. Evidence of literacy is patchy and ambiguous; indirect evidence of the extent of literacy—literary evidence, the volume of book publishing, and the extent of book ownership and of formal education—is often unsatisfactory. Inventories tend to omit books; the growing output of books could have been absorbed by a small fraction of the population; and statistics of schools are not able to include all the petty schools at which basic literacy was taught. [Historian D.] Cressy prefers to such indicators the 'direct' evidence of ability to write one's name. Many contemporary documents were attested by men and women with marks or signatures, usually taken to represent the illiterate and literate respectively. This assumption can also be questioned; many children appear to have mastered reading (which was taught first) but not writing, while a few illiterates at least could sign their names. Nevertheless, counts of signatures probably do correlate loosely with literacy; they furnish large samples on a uniform basis, and they reveal social, sexual and geographical variations which make sense.

All recent research on frequency of signatures concludes, not surprisingly, that literacy was higher among men than women, among clergy than laity, among nobles and gentry than commoners, in London than in the countryside, and in the South and East than the North and West. (Of the four dioceses sampled by Cressy, illiteracy proved far higher in Durham than in London, Norwich or Exeter, even among the gentry.) The pressure to acquire literacy depended on many things, including wealth, leisure, reputation, religious zeal, and the desire for social and economic advancement. Influential books like Elyot's *Governour* (1531) argued that nobles and gentlemen must be well educated if they were to share in government. Protestant theologians urged men and women to read so as to study the Bible; clergy, bureaucrats, merchants and professional men needed literacy for their occupations. Conversely, many poor could not afford either the time or the money needed for their children's education, requiring their labour or earnings from an early age; labourers had little need of literacy in their work; and the general attitude of society was also that women needed education less than men.

Nobles and gentlemen were almost all literate by mid-century. [Nineteenth-century historian John] Aubrey maintained that the first earl of Pembroke (1507–70), though a Privy Councillor, 'could neither write nor read', but Pembroke's signatures survive to cast doubt on the story. His fellow-councillor Norfolk, imprisoned in the Tower in 1547, asked for books so that he might read himself to sleep as was his habit. By that date all leading courtiers and officials needed to be literate, and even at the local level the skill was coming to be thought necessary, or at least socially desirable, for magistrates and town councillors. Of forty-seven Yarmouth councillors endorsing a document in 1577, thirty-seven signed their names. John Shakespeare, the poet's father, who was a Stratford alderman from 1565 to 1586, always marked documents, and was probably illiterate; but such a lack of accomplishment was becoming out of date. There was a defensive ring to the description of Robert Brerewood, mayor of Chester (1584), as one who 'could nether write nor read yet was . . . very brave and gentile otherwise'. In London, where the majority of craftsmen and tradesmen were literate (60% of Cressy's sample in the 1580s, 80% in the 1600s), not a single merchant, vintner or grocer sampled was illiterate.

In the countryside, the majority of yeomen sampled were illiterate at the start of Elizabeth's reign but literate by its end. [Historian M.] Spufford's work on Cambridgeshire suggests that it was the more prosperous yeomen who demanded education. At Willingham, for instance, where the inhabitants endowed a school by public subscription in 1593, most of the large donations came from half-yardlanders, who 'could afford to give sums which amounted to more than two years' rent in most cases'. Some well-to-do husbandmen were also willing to buy education; John Browne of Wigston Magna left 20*s* [20 shilling] to his young son, asking that he 'be kept to scoole tyll he cane wrytt and reade'. But of 558 Yorkshire tenants of the queen who subscribed to petitions in 1562—most of whom would have been husbandmen—only 6 made signatures rather than marks. And Cressy's samples for the later part of Elizabeth's reign indicate only 10 per cent literacy among husbandmen in the Durham and Exeter dioceses, rising to 20 per cent in the diocese of London with its proximity to the capital.

Literacy appears to have increased considerably in the second half of the sixteenth century. Cressy suggests, by

The Universities

In this excerpt from her book Understanding Shakespeare's England, *Jo McMurtry explains the organization, curriculum, and examination system of Oxford and Cambridge Universities during Elizabeth's reign.*

Universities were open to men only, a limitation that was to persist until the late nineteenth century. In the sixteenth century, entering students were not only male but were considerably younger than the age we associate with college, often matriculating at thirteen or fourteen, although some colleges tried to persuade parents not to send their sons until they were fifteen.

The two universities, Oxford and Cambridge, were roughly fifty miles from London in their respective directions, and while individuals and families might have strong loyalties to one or the other, there has never been a general consensus that either is superior. . . .

Each university consisted, as is still the case, of a number of separate and quite individual colleges. . . .

Then, as now, a student had more sense of belonging to his individual college than to the university as a whole. The uni-

plotting signatures against the age of the witnesses concerned, a sharp rise in literacy in the 1560s and 1570s, followed by a levelling off, or even a regression, between 1580 and 1610. There may have been a similar increase in numeracy, although in this field not even a rough quantification has yet been attempted. The impact of printing, of arabic numerals, and of arithmetical symbols allowed many administrators, architects, surveyors, sailors and others to handle figures more easily.

Formal Education

Formal education in sixteenth-century schools is still often described as a two-tier system, with elementary schools, largely unendowed, catering for reading and writing in English, and endowed grammar schools where teaching was ex-

---

versity, a rather vague entity, administered examinations and awarded degrees, but the college had a solid spatial presence and was populated by tangible friends and mentors.

What we would call classical studies, Latin and Greek, comprised the heart of most students' reading lists. Room could be made for individual pursuits, and the libraries got better and better. Sir Thomas Bodley, for example, restored Oxford's library in the late 1590s and did such a good job, giving generously himself and persuading his friends to follow suit, that the library now bears his name, the Bodleian.

Unlike today's American student, who takes a certain number of separate courses and earns a grade in each . . . the English student spent his college years preparing for the examinations which would determine at one fell swoop whether he got a degree or not. It must be added that many students did not aspire toward a degree and left without one, under no dire disgrace as far as public opinion was concerned, and presumably in possession of more knowledge than they had entered with.

Jo McMurtry, *Understanding Shakespeare's England: A Companion for the American Reader*. Hamden, Connecticut: Archon Book, 1989.

clusively in Latin; but this is a wild oversimplification. There were local and parish schools (often called song schools before the Reformation and petty schools after it) catering largely for reading, writing and simple arithmetic. There were grammar schools teaching exclusively in Latin and largely as a preparation for university, although most also included English teaching. But some grammar schools either included an elementary school or had one attached to them. A school list for Wolverhampton Grammar School in 1609—a rare survival—shows that the 69 pupils ranged from a petties class of 11 (mostly aged from 6 to 10) studying basic Latin or even basic English, to a 'head form' of 2 boys of 17 and 18 studying Greek and advanced Latin. Not all petty schools were unendowed, nor all grammar schools endowed. There were other, private, grammar schools which depended on pupils' fees; and there was a whole range of private schools and academies, including some which specialised in teaching letter-writing, accounts and business studies.

Almost certainly many who could read or write learned to do so in parish schools, which were often held in the church or in the master's house. Thomas Hobbes the philosopher 'went to schoole in Westport church' from the age of four to eight (c. 1592–96): 'by that time he could read well, and number four figures', [according to Aubrey]. Such schools far outnumbered the grammar schools, indeed, there may have been something like one elementary school for every parish or every two parishes at some time in the period, though not all had a continuous existence. Of the 266 towns and parishes in the Canterbury diocese, at least 113 (42%) had a schoolmaster at some time in the period 1561–1600, as against a total of 12 grammar schools. Of about 450 parishes in the diocese of Lichfield, at least 200 (44%) had a schoolmaster at some time between 1584 and 1642. South Cambridgeshire was apparently better off, with 23 parishes (21%) having a school in continuous existence between 1574 and 1628, and 87 (80%) having one at some time. And the city of York in Elizabeth's reign possessed at least 8 or 9 parish schools as well as 2 grammar schools. Most of these statistics are based on the evidence of licences to teach issued by the bishops, and are likely to be minimum figures: the licensing system seems to have been less effective with petty and private schools than with grammar schools.

Alternatives to Formal Schooling

Furthermore, much educational instruction was not given in schools at all. The children of nobles and gentlemen were often tutored privately in their own homes or in households which specialised in bringing up boys and girls, such as those of Lord Burghley and the earl of Huntingdon. And for many commoners, basic instruction in literacy and in craft skills was given in the home or the workshop. The practice has naturally left little record, but wills and inventories occasionally hint at it. In the 1570s, a York canon made a draper a guardian to his son, asking him 'to lerne hyme to write and to use hyme as hys owne', while a Gloucestershire man owed money to a yeoman 'for techinge of his sonne to wrytte and reade'. John Hart published in 1570 a simple method of learning to read English which, he said, any literate member of a household could teach to the others. Edmund Coote's *English Schoole-Master* could be used for home instruction as well as for the school; and he intended it also to be used for 'taylors, weavers, shoppe-keepers, seamsters' and others for teaching their apprentices. He promised the craftsman-teacher that 'thou mayest sit on thy shop boord, at thy loomes or at thy needle, and never hinder thy worke to heare thy schollers . . .' That it served a need is indicated by the fact that it went through twenty-five editions between 1596 and 1625.

The teaching of apprentices and servants by masters (which could include basic literacy as well as craft techniques) was a common alternative to formal schooling. Chester corporation ruled in 1539 that 'every chylde or chyldryn beinge of the age of vi yeres or above upon every wourkeday shalbe set to the schoule . . . or else to sum other good virtuus laboure, craft or occupacyon'. How many children actually profited from formal schooling, even at an elementary level, depended on whether they could be spared from home or work, and on whether they could take up free school places or could afford school fees. Relatively few schools had funds to aid poor boys to attend school, as was recognised by the corporation of Norwich in drawing up their regulations for the poor in 1571. 'Selecte women' were to be paid to teach letters to 'the most porest children whose parents are not hable to pay for theyr lear[n]inge'. Bequests for this purpose did multiply, however, in the late sixteenth century; typical was that of a Staffordshire yeoman who in 1603 left money for a schoolmaster to teach ten poor Wednesbury children free of charge.

Education for Girls

Girls generally enjoyed less education than boys, and female literacy as measured by signatures was considerably lower than that of males. Only the London diocese was exceptional, where 16 per cent of a sample of women in the 1580s could sign their names. Nevertheless, a significant minority of women at all social levels except the very poorest did acquire some education, and Richard Mulcaster, in his *Positions* (1581), implied that it was common for girls to learn to read and write. Humanist writers like [Sir Thomas] More and Elyot had argued for equal opportunities for both sexes, a movement which bore fruit in a group of distinguished women like the daughters of Sir Anthony Cooke (two of whom married Cecil and Sir Nicholas Bacon) and Queen Elizabeth herself. Lady Margaret Hoby, the daughter of a minor northern gentleman, learned to read, write, keep accounts and practise surgery, as her surviving diary makes clear.

Many village schools, such as that at Wigston Magna, were attended by girls as well as boys, and a few grammar schools are also known to have taken girls. Other girls, at least among the gentry, were privately taught by tutors or relatives. Grace Sharington of Lacock Abbey has left a picture in her journal of how she was educated by her aunt:

> When she did see me idly disposed she would set me to cypher with the pen and to cast up and prove great sums and accounts . . . and other times let me read in Dr. Turner's *Herball* and Bartholomew Vigoe . . . and other times set me to some curious work, for she was an excellent workwoman in all kinds of needlework.

Elizabeth Weston was by no means the only woman to have her work published. Margaret Tyler translated *The First Part of the Mirrour of Princely Deeds and Knighthood* (1578), defending in her preface the right of women to read and write, while Esther Sowernam wrote a spirited reply *(Ester hath hang'd Haman,* 1617) to Joseph Swetnam's *Arraignment of Idle, Froward and Unconstant Women* (1615). . . .

Taking the educational sector as a whole, there was clearly considerable expansion both at the elementary and higher levels. What is not clear, for lack of sufficient evidence, is how much effect the educational expansion had on social control and social mobility. It is scarcely surprising that educational opportunity increased with wealth and social status: more important is what proportion of poorer and humbler children acquired learning, and whether that proportion increased.

Chapter 4

Conquests and Discoveries

Elizabeth Had a Coherent Foreign Policy

F. Jeffrey Platt

F. Jeffrey Platt, associate professor of history at Northern Arizona University, argues against earlier historians' opinions of Elizabeth's confused foreign policy and capricious selection of foreign diplomats. Platt asserts, on the contrary, that Elizabeth had a definite foreign policy—to maintain a balance of power in Europe—and was the first monarch in English history to have a "significant corps of professional, non-ecclesiastical career diplomats." Furthermore, Platt explains, Elizabeth refused to enter a war for honor or dynastic ambitions, as earlier English monarchs had done; instead, she restricted armed combat to maintenance of England's national interests: "trade, religion, and territorial integrity." Platt argues that Elizabeth's foreign policy and her use of three principal secretaries (William Cecil, Francis Walsingham, and Robert Cecil) as chief officers of foreign affairs provides clear evidence of a significant step toward the creation of the modern bureaucratic state.

Although the British Foreign Office as it is known today was not established until 1782, a "foreign office" emerged in all but name at least two centuries earlier. The historian Garrett Mattingly maintains that "a first-rate diplomatic service" depends on the existence of a viable "foreign office," distinguished by a permanent staff, reliable archives, definite policies, and "the means of coordinating activities abroad." As late as the early seventeenth century, he argues, "it would be some time still" before European monarchies were able

Excerpted from "The Elizabethan 'Foreign Office,'" by F. Jeffrey Platt, *The Historian*, vol. 56, no. 4, Summer 1994. Reprinted by permission of the author.

to create and maintain such an office. The administration of foreign affairs under Queen Elizabeth I (1558–1603), however, shows that a professional, efficient, *de facto* foreign office thrived in Elizabethan England.

During Elizabeth's reign, the principal secretary of estate ran the large, multi-chambered office that supervised England's foreign and domestic security concerns. Like today's foreign secretary, the Elizabethan principal secretary sat on the Privy Council as the specialist on foreign affairs. He thus contributed significantly to the making of foreign policy, and was seen as the sole instrument for its execution. Elizabeth's three chief principal secretaries, Sir William Cecil (1558–72 and 1590–96), Sir Francis Walsingham (1573–90), and Sir Robert Cecil (1596–1612), found that their most arduous and time-consuming tasks were selecting, training, and directing the diplomatic corps, processing foreign correspondence and intelligence, accumulating and maintaining reliable archives, and safeguarding the territorial and religious integrity of an England whose interests they believed to be increasingly threatened by the Counter Reformation [the movement within the Roman Catholic Church which reacted against Protestant reforms of the church in England]. Foreign affairs were so important in the administration of Elizabethan England that its diplomatic corps, according to one historian [Charles Hughes], came to be seen as the country's "true first line of defense," serving as "the vital early warning and defense system of the realm.". . .

A Balance-of-Power Foreign Policy

Elizabeth . . . had a definite foreign policy evident in her unchanging, though seemingly confused, stance toward the Netherlands, and toward French interests and the Spanish military presence there. The queen desired a restoration of the historical status quo in those provinces. She always defended the rights of monarchs, whether her own or others'. Unwilling to accept as a legitimate policy the creation of a Protestant state in Scotland, France, or the Netherlands, she sought to support liberty of conscience and freedom from persecution. As an historian [Simon Adams] has noted, "The tortuous negotiations between Elizabeth and Spain over the Netherlands between 1572 and 1585 and her peculiar manner of assisting the Dutch between 1585 and 1603 only make sense if her desire to obtain toleration and home rule under Philip II's sovereignty are accepted." In the Netherlands, the focus of all west European diplomacy in the years after 1567, she sought security by risking the "wrath of a strong neighbor for the sake of a weak one."

From the start, Elizabeth and her principal secretaries recognized the value of applying diplomatic pressure at crucial points. Unable to match the power of Spain or France, they hoped to cut off Spain's lifeline to the Netherlands by controlling the English Channel, and to threaten France by pursuing contacts with Huguenots and Protestant German princes. Thus Elizabeth became the first to successfully practice a Continental balance-of-power policy made possible by "the perpetual rivalry between Spain and France, which had been the best guarantor of English safety in the past" [Wallace T. MacCaffrey]. Both nations had to pay serious attention to her maneuvers. Eventually the debilitating effects of religious civil war made it impossible for France to play its normal role in this European power balance. But Henri IV's 1593 "conversion and the consequent erosion of the Catholic League" led to "the re-establishment of a Continental balance of power," with France "once again a counter weight to Hapsburg power" [MacCaffrey claims]. Elizabeth was again freed to throw England's small but critical mass on the side of whichever power should become the weaker.

Diplomacy to Preserve Status Quo

Diplomacy became Elizabeth's chief weapon in this war of nerves. She knew instinctively that England's best policy lay [according to MacCaffrey] in "no serious foreign commitments and the cultivation of enough nuisance value on the continent to keep the greater powers at a respectful distance." She and Cecil harbored no "martial ambitions" and repeatedly expressed their "skepticism about the efficiency of affordable military operations." Unlike the French and Spanish, Elizabeth never went to war for motives of honor, or dynastic and territorial ambitions. She went to war for such vital issues of national interest as trade, religion, and territorial integrity—interests that were threatened by the presence of Philip II's army in the strategic Low Countries. "Secure behind its seas," one scholar [Simon Adams] states, "England could now take as much or as little of war as it liked. No commitment was more than tentative, no alliance irrevocable, and at each new shuffle in the diplomatic game the other players had to bid all over again for England's friendship or neutrality."

Elizabeth's policies emerged as the carefully considered products of compromise. The queen met almost daily with her principal secretary to discuss foreign correspondence and to formulate policy. Although she "kept ultimate decisions in her own hands, she rarely conceived, initiated, or shaped the specific policies to which she gave the force of her royal assent" [suggests MacCaffrey]. These were left to her council and secretariat. Despite the fact that decisions came only after a series of complicated and often confusing maneuvers, historians must not fail [says Adams] "to distinguish between the course she set and the track she had to follow." Organized to maintain the status quo, not to threaten it, her foreign office's strength lay in the extent of its influence, not the scope of its authority. That she never changed the direction of her foreign policy after 1572 is proof that Elizabeth had a definite foreign policy. For nearly thirty years, as a result of the mutual jealousies between France and Spain, the "politics of continuous tension," [Richard B. Wernham] and the sophistication of its diplomatic machinery, Elizabethan England enjoyed an uneasy peace. When war ultimately came, England, as "lord of the Channel," [Garrett Mattingly] was prepared for it.

The Elizabethan foreign office's means of "coordinating activities abroad" [as Mattingly phrases it] were surprisingly extensive. The long tenures of the queen's three great secretaries provided a continuity in foreign affairs that fostered success. England's gentrified diplomatic corps allowed the queen and her principal secretaries to maintain tight control over the actions of their diplomats. Rarely free to make significant on-the-spot decisions except within the parameters of their instructions, the queen's diplomats knew she would repudiate their unauthorized actions and even destroy their careers if they stepped out of line. Among the council clerks, a cadre of experienced ambassadors-at-large were ready at a moment's notice to rush off to Europe to defuse threatening international situations. Reliable post and courier services kept important information flowing to and from Westminster, while the keeper of the state papers worked steadily at collecting and organizing diplomatic correspondence.

Professional Diplomats

With an eye on the future, Elizabeth occasionally selected from lists of Oxford and Cambridge graduates for new diplomatic apprentices. Her secretariat kept updated rosters of potential appointees, divided between noblemen and gentlemen who had and had not served. The lists of those who served demonstrate the professionalism of the diplomatic corps. No churchmen appear on the lists, reflecting the new policy that such men were no longer the best diplomats in a religiously divided Europe. The absence of royal favorites and other courtiers also indicates that Tudor diplomacy had entered a more professional era. Most of the noblemen listed served only ceremonial missions, as their arrogance could be better employed for parade than for negotiation. Furthermore, the existence of such lists shows that Elizabeth's government recognized that the diplomatic corps represented not only a new class of professional civil servants, but also an extension of the foreign office.

The true workhorses of the Elizabethan foreign office were these experienced diplomats of gentry status, who set the tone of English diplomacy well into the seventeenth century. The Elizabethan foreign office consciously selected intelligent, highly educated, widely traveled men, exceptionally proficient in foreign languages, and rigorously apprenticed in the trains of England's finest diplomats. Their selection was not "capricious," nor did "their training for diplomacy only begin with their actual service" [according to Mattingly]. When not serving abroad they held complimentary domestic offices such as clerks of the council, Signet, and Privy Seal, or master of the posts, which kept them immersed in foreign-office affairs.

For the first time in English history the country had a significant corps of professional, non-ecclesiastical career diplomats, such as Sir Henry Cobham, Sir Thomas Wilkes, Robert Bowes, Thomas Randolph, Daniel Rogers, Sir Henry Killigrew, Sir William Davison, and Sir Edward Stafford. These men no longer divided their loyalties and responsibilities between church and state, and their government careers focused principally on foreign affairs. The Elizabethan secretariat thus reflected a rational and systematic approach to building and maintaining a professional diplomatic corps.

Intelligence Operations

Elizabeth's foreign office administered Europe's finest intelligence network. Official staff members, particularly the council clerks, were chosen with an eye to prior diplomatic experience and future overseas service. The office assisted departing English diplomats in choosing staffs and thoroughly briefed their envoys on the political and social background of the court to which they were sent. Diplomats read all recent correspondence and visited compatriots who had recently served at that court, and often helped draw up their own instructions. After receiving a letter of appointment, credences, written permission to go abroad, introductory letters, instructions, and cipher tables, the diplomat met with the queen for final words of instruction. For the principal secretary, a "huge amount of work was connected with foreign negotiations" [says historian Florence M.G. Evans]. As foreign affairs increasingly occupied the secretary's office in the second half of Elizabeth's reign, he farmed out more and more of the routine duties connected with foreign affairs to subordinates. [According to Charles Hughes] Nicholas Faunt's "Discourse" shows that the principal secretary's chief confidential clerk was to be "chiefly charged with Forraine matters . . . both to keepe his lettres of negotiacions that dayly come in from Forraine partes . . . to answere them when need shalbe . . . [and] to deliuer messages of greate importance to *Embassouders* or other forraine ministers that are sent hither." The clerk stood "in much the same relation to the principal secretary as the latter stood in relation to the crown" [Hughes says]. A second confidential clerk was used [in the words of Nicholas Faunt] "for the dispatch of ordinarie matters, and chiefly for Continuall attendant in the Chamber, where the papers are . . . to reduce them into a fewe heads."

Exchequer manuscripts and recent studies demonstrate that among all the diplomatic personnel of the European monarchies, Elizabethan diplomats alone were paid regular and adequate per diems and reimbursed for all expenses on officially sanctioned missions. By serving repeatedly and spending wisely they could even profit significantly from such royal perks as loans, cash gifts, duty-free export licenses, and cathedral deaneries. That diplomats customarily expected such gifts is compelling proof of Elizabeth's generosity to them. Foreign courts occasionally assumed a portion of the resident diplomat's living expenses and presented gifts such as gold chains, silver plate, or even a knighthood on a diplomat's departure. After returning home, the diplomat could expect offices, grants of wardship, leases on crown lands, and monopolies. Diplomats' frequent complaints of fiscal hardship constituted an accepted procedure for wrangling additional remuneration from England's frugal queen. Indeed, one scholar [Conyers Read] has shown that in numbers of diplomats appointed, time served abroad, and money expended, Elizabeth displayed a greater commitment to diplomacy than any other English monarch from Henry VIII to James II. This attention to diplomatic emoluments attests to the modernity of Elizabeth's foreign office. . . .

A Modern Bureaucratic State

Foreign office procedures became institutionalized during Elizabeth's reign. The Elizabethan secretariat was the headquarters of English diplomatic activity. The principal secretary's oversight of all foreign and some domestic matters was both more logical and more convenient than the later practice of dividing foreign affairs between two secretaries in separate northern and southern departments. Furthermore, Counter-Reformation politics did not reduce England's international contacts, but merely made them more complex. The issues between Protestants and Roman Catholics became so serious and the possibilities of unending religious war so frightening that England's international contacts actually expanded during the second half of the sixteenth century. Elizabeth understood from the beginning that, given her limited resources, she could accomplish more through diplomacy than with arms.

Elizabeth's foreign policy had a steadiness and consistency that would have done her cautious grandfather proud. Her government took a giant step away from the dynastic past, with its aggressive pursuit of royal ambitions, and toward the creation of an early modern bureaucratic state. Elizabeth established a rational, efficient, and highly bureaucratized secretariat that set England apart not only from its own past but from its royal neighbors, whose struggles for power were governed by the overpowering demands of honor and personal ambition.

The Sea-War with Spain, 1585–1603

Kenneth R. Andrews

Historian Kenneth R. Andrews asserts that the seemingly inconclusive eighteen year war between England and Spain in fact marked a turning-point in the fortunes of both nations. While Philip II of Spain and Elizabeth were able to maintain diplomatic relations for the first decade of Elizabeth's rule, Anglo-Spanish amity began to wear thin in the 1560s and erupted into war in 1585. Elizabeth did not want war, but her efforts to maintain a balance of power in Europe in fact provoked Philip's plan for a grand expedition against England. Elizabeth wished to limit Spanish power in the Netherlands and to play the two dominant powers in Europe, the French and the Spanish, against one another. Her strategy was essentially defensive, according to Andrews, but Philip construed her assistance of the Dutch resistance and her encouragement of Sir Francis Drake's missions to intercept the flow of treasure from the West Indies to Spain as convincing evidence of the need for a direct assault on interfering England.

In this excerpt from his book, *Trade, Plunder and Settlement*, Andrews explains the events which led to war, then examines the preparations for the famous 1588 battle in which the English defeated the Spanish Armada. As a result of this pivotal battle, Andrews argues, Spain was inspired to build up naval strength and continue its assault on England. Although the English failed to achieve a clear victory in the war, English privateering (officially licensed operations of privately-owned vessels against enemy shipping and goods in time of war) gave England a different form of victory. Privateering contributed to the decline in

Excerpted from *Trade, Plunder, and Settlement: Maritime Enterprise and the Genesis of the British Empire, 1480–1630*, by Kenneth R. Andrews. Copyright © Cambridge University Press 1984. Reprinted with permission of Cambridge University Press.

the Spanish economy, produced a considerable increase in English shipbuilding, and established England's reputation as an enterprising maritime power.

Kenneth R. Andrews, professor of history at the University of Hull in England, has also written *Drake's Voyages: A Re-Assessment of their Place in Elizabethan Maritime Expansion* and *Elizabethan Privateering During the Spanish War, 1585–1603*.

In 1585 England and Spain came into . . . open conflict. In August Elizabeth formally allied herself to the Dutch rebels and at the end of the year sent an army under the earl of Leicester to the Low Countries to engage the Spanish forces of occupation. Meanwhile at sea that summer English privateers began a campaign of reprisal against Spanish shipping in retaliation for the arrest of English ships, men and goods in Spanish harbours ordered by Philip II in May. In September [Sir Francis] Drake, with two of the queen's ships and twenty-three others, apart from pinnaces, set out from Plymouth to menace the coast of Spain and to ravage the West Indies. Thus began a war which was to last eighteen years, until the accession of James I in 1603 and the Treaty of London in 1604. Seemingly an inconclusive, even at times half-hearted, struggle, this war in fact marked a turning-point in the fortunes of both nations and above all in their oceanic fortunes. This is not to say that the war itself decided the course of empire overseas, much less that the protagonists recognized its imperial implications or attached more than marginal significance to its extra-European dimension. Indirectly and unintentionally, however, it had an important bearing upon the genesis of the British Empire.

English/Spanish/French Relations

The Tudor rulers before Elizabeth had maintained friendly relations with Spain most of the time. The two countries found a common enemy in France and, when Charles of Habsburg acquired the Spanish crown, a common interest in the Netherlands. France and Spain, the two great powers of

Europe, were continually in conflict, a conflict only aggravated by the growing dominance of the Habsburgs in Italy, Germany and the Low Countries as well as the Peninsula. England meanwhile, having lost all her former conquests in France save Calais, clung stubbornly to that and hankered yet to recover some other footholds to counter the growing menace of French power across the Channel. The great trade of the English at Antwerp prospered until the mid-century, strengthening the old bond between England and Burgundy. And when Elizabeth came to the throne the threat from France seemed greater than ever. Calais had fallen to the enemy, Mary of Guise ruled Scotland and her daughter, Mary Stuart, in Catholic eyes the rightful queen of England, was married to the French dauphin. In 1559 the latter became king and the treaty of Cateau-Cambrésis ended the long wars between France and Spain. The prospect of a Franco-British empire dominated by the Guise family, likely enough in 1560, receded with the death of Francis II and the success of the Lords of the Congregation, but the Guise remained a power to be reckoned with and Elizabeth had cause to fear the French and look to Spain for support. As for Philip II, he had no wish to alienate England in the years that followed Cateau-Cambrésis, for he needed an ally to hold France in check while he struggled to contain a more dangerous enemy—the Grand Turk.

Such were the circumstances that held Philip and Elizabeth in diplomatic accord for nearly a decade after her accession. But already the ground was shifting beneath their feet. France, torn by faction and religious hatred, was sinking into impotence; the Low Countries, deeply disturbed by the economic crisis of the fifties and by the spread of Protestant ideas, seethed with discontent and resistance to Spanish policy; and Anglo-Spanish amity itself was wearing thin. The cause of the reformed religion held no strong appeal for Elizabeth, who resisted pressure to become the champion of the Protestants against the Catholics. Nevertheless she was irrevocably a heretic in the eyes of Philip of Spain and his advisers, some of whom thought her overthrow necessary to secure the Catholic faith and Spanish rule in the Netherlands. . . .

Elizabeth's Efforts to Avoid War and Maintain a European Balance of Power

Elizabeth did not want war with Spain. All along it had been her policy to avoid the confrontation which ensued in 1585, to keep Philip at bay in the Low Countries and induce him by indirect pressure to accept a compromise there. She would lend the rebels money, allow English volunteers to fight alongside them, play the French against Spain and use every means short of war to embarrass and contain Spanish power. Her attitude in fact was fundamentally defensive and her main object was limited: a Netherlands settlement favourable to England's security. That security would not, in her view, gain by a demolition of Spain's power, nor did she dream, as [Sir Walter] Ralegh did, of beating that great empire in pieces and making their kings kings of figs and oranges as in old times. Apart from her well-justified fear that any great weakening of Spain would only strengthen France—potentially a more dangerous enemy, especially in possession of the Netherlands—she was far too realistic a statesman to imagine that such a total victory was possible. Unlike Ralegh and some others of her 'men of war', not to mention later pundits of the Dreadnought age, the queen fully appreciated the political, financial, organizational and logistic difficulties any ruler—and particularly any ruler of England—had to face in conducting warfare at that time.

Politically, at every juncture of this conflict both powers were entangled in a net of international relations which restricted their freedom to manoeuvre. Above all, neither could ignore the fate of France. Philip became increasingly committed to frustrating Henry of Navarre, who succeeded nominally to the throne in 1589, and to reducing France to a Spanish dependency, but the military resources this required had to be drawn mainly from the Netherlands, to the great relief of the insurgents and their English allies. Equally, however, Elizabeth was obliged continually to lend Henry money to keep an army in the field, to finance German and Swiss reinforcements for him and to send forces from England to his assistance, so that until he made a separate peace in 1598 France remained an important theatre of

Elizabeth's war. Beating Spain and Spain's allies in France had to take precedence over beating Spain's empire in pieces. And the same considerations applied with even greater force in the Low Countries, where the maintenance of a strong Dutch bulwark against the tide of Spanish aggression was always a prime concern of Elizabeth's government.

Moreover the mounting of campaigns or expeditions of war was so costly that even Philip of Spain, with all the riches of the Indies at his disposal, faced repeated army mutinies over pay, was driven into bankruptcy three times and so taxed the people of Castile that he left them severely afflicted by inflation, famine and plague. Yet Elizabeth's financial resources were far inferior to his. Her three million subjects amounted to less than half the population of Spain, let alone that of Philip's other dominions, and were lightly taxed. The ordinary revenue of the crown amounted, by dint of rigorous exploitation in this time of war, to some £300,000 a year, and the government managed to raise about two million by direct taxation over the war period, which together with other extraordinary revenue probably brought gross income to between £400,000 and half a million a year, out of which it had to pay the normal expenses of the Court and the administration. What remained was not enough to pay for a full-scale war: Elizabeth had to cut her coat according to her cloth and confined her military effort to supplying the French and the Dutch with auxiliary troops and raising small expeditionary forces for specific actions such as the assault on Cadiz in 1596. Even so, these modest efforts and the heavy burden of the Irish wars after 1595 increased military expenditure to such an extent that it represented a very large proportion of the total budget and could not have been raised without bankrupting the state: as it was, the crown's debts exceeded its assets in 1603.

Events Leading to the 1588 Battle

Campaigning was expensive partly because military administration was inefficient and corrupt and partly because great efforts were required to make relatively small gains in the field. England in the reign of Elizabeth lacked a regular army and depended on an antiquated system of recruitment which tended to produce troops of poor quality. Losses by desertion and disease were heavy, far exceeding losses in action; the survivors usually turned into hardened veterans and valued soldiers, but they were few; vast sums of money were embezzled by unscrupulous captains and victuallers. English forces on land might here and there make tactical gains, but they could never achieve a major victory and stood no chance of winning an important campaign. Indeed major victories and successful campaigns were rare in European warfare at this stage, chiefly because defence tended to prevail over attack. Open battles between armies seldom occurred; the fortification of towns and even villages became so effective that warfare consisted largely of sieges and associated skirmishes for control

Francis Drake and the *Golden Hind*

Francis Drake, who was later instrumental in the defeat of the Spanish Armada and the rescue of Sir Walter Raleigh's first Virginia colony, gained fame and knighthood in 1580 after he circumnavigated the globe.

Francis Drake, on his voyage in the late 1570s that was eventually to circumnavigate the globe, subscribed to [the general English] anti-Iberian [anti-Spanish] feeling, as did the financial backers of his expedition—investors who hoped for a large return on their money. When Drake sailed around the tip of South America and found himself on the Pacific coast—backstage, so to speak—the pickings were rich. The Spaniards expected no trouble from that direction and were going about their business of harvesting treasure. Gold and silver, newly mined or taken from the Indians, had been collected in storehouses; cargo ships, only lightly armed, shuttled along the coast picking up the stored treasure and taking it to a collection point on the Pacific side of what is now Panama. Here the treasure would be loaded on pack animals—the canal, of course, would not be dug for another 300 years—and carried to the Atlantic side, where well-guarded convoys would begin the final stage of

of tactical strongpoints, especially in densely populated areas like the Netherlands. Occupation of territory and sheer numbers of effectives were very important, strategy was reduced to a struggle of attrition, money was the arbiter more directly than it usually is in war.

These considerations perhaps sufficiently explain why Elizabeth [in the words of J.S. Corbett] 'never believed she could strike her enemy a fatal blow'. Such a blow was not only politically unnecessary, even undesirable; it was impossible to deliver. Consequently from the start she waged a limited war—limited in scale as in purpose. The intention in sending Leicester's army was to maintain Dutch resistance in order to bring Philip to terms; the essential mission of Drake in 1585 was to interrupt the flow of treasure to Philip's war

---

the journey home. But the Spanish warships were on the wrong side of the continent to deal with Drake, and after a few raids his ship, the *Golden Hind*, was loaded with as many ingots as she could carry.

Coming home the long way round, Drake and his men sailed across the Pacific for sixty-eight days without sight of land, arriving eventually at what is now called Indonesia. The *Golden Hind* picked her way among the islands, trading for spices. Then she crossed the Indian Ocean, rounded the tip of Africa, and sailed north into waters familiar to English sailors, so that captain and crew were fully aware of what they had done. It is true that the globe had been circumnavigated fifty years before by an expedition under Ferdinand Magellan, a Portuguese in the service of Spain, but Magellan had been killed on the voyage and did not get to enjoy the rewards of his achievement. Drake enjoyed his quite fully. The appearance of the *Golden Hind* in the autumn of 1580, almost three years after she had sailed away, delighted the English, especially those who had bought shares in the voyage, and the queen knighted Drake as he knelt on the deck.

Jo McMurtry, *Understanding Shakespeare's England*. Hamden, Connecticut: Archon Books, 1989.

machine, damaging thereby his immediate power and demonstrating to him the penalty he would pay if he refused to compromise. Unfortunately the effect of these measures was to convince Philip of the need to eliminate England from the struggle by a direct offensive. It was in 1586 that he approved plans for a grand expedition against England and set in motion the preparations for the Invincible Armada. Elizabeth continued to prevaricate, to negotiate, to limit the conflict; even though she found herself engaged in a *de facto* war, she could never regard this as more than a provisional state of affairs, necessitated by an emergency, which must pass when the European system resumed its normal shape. France in time would regain the strength to counter-balance Spain; the Dutch in time would become able to fend for themselves. Meanwhile she would do what she could to maintain their resistance to the domineering armies of Spain and to ward off Spain's offensive blows at England or Ireland.

At sea, therefore, the vital issue was control of the waters between the Strait of Gibraltar and the North Sea. That would enable Spain to send troops and supplies directly to Flanders instead of by the circuitous 'Spanish Road', which would mean immense logistic gains and all but certain victory, for it would solve her fundamental problem of finding the means to deploy her undoubtedly superior land forces effectively in northwest Europe, the only important theatre of operations. But in fact the English, in alliance with Dutch and Huguenot seamen, had dominated that north-south Atlantic route since the late sixties and could whenever they wished deny the Spaniards its use. So long as they retained this advantage, moreover, the islanders could continually reinforce their Dutch allies and hold the army of Flanders in perpetual check. Likewise they could maintain their French allies and frustrate Spanish attempts to seize or use bases on the French coast. They could also disrupt the mobilization of forces in the Peninsula ports by raiding down that coast. Command of the sea gave them, in effect, the power to negate Spain's main purposes and the logic of the situation demanded that if Philip could neither keep Elizabeth out of the war nor persuade her to withdraw, he must try to knock her out of it by a frontal assault.

In reality of course the issue was much less clear-cut and the king's intention to mount the Enterprise of England took many months to harden into an irrevocable decision. From the spring of 1586 the marquis of Santa Cruz was accumulating forces, but it was by no means certain that they would be used against England. Philip had good cause to hope that the threat alone might bring Elizabeth to reason, while on the other hand he had to take seriously the need to protect the treasure of the Indies against the enemy in the Atlantic. It was always possible that Santa Cruz would sail for the Azores instead of the Channel, and in the summer of 1587 he did so with a powerful detachment of the fleet and consequently delayed the launching of the attack upon England for a whole year. Both sides attached much importance to the American bullion because upon it depended Spain's entire credit structure and in particular her ability to transfer funds to the Netherlands, without which the army there would quickly grind to a halt. The contest in the Atlantic at large was thus relevant to the main issue and it remained so throughout the war. Conversely, as we shall see, the contest in Europe and European waters had implications for the oceanic fortunes of both parties. Spanish merchants, especially those with an interest in the Indies trade, supported the Armada and threw the ships and men of the Indies fleets into that battle because to them the defeat of England meant the safety and prosperity of the American trade. The Armada campaign was also a battle for the Atlantic. . . .

Spain and England Prepare for Battle

The mere launching of this expedition was a remarkable achievement for Spain, for until his acquisition of the Portuguese navy in 1580 Philip II had possessed no high-seas fleet (as distinct from galleys) of his own. Until then the crown had relied on requisitioning the ships of private owners, some of whom—naval entrepreneurs—built, manned and set forth ships for the crown at agreed rates for agreed periods of hire. When not required for royal service such ships were used for trade. By 1588 the crown had still done little to create a Spanish royal fleet, though it was then able to supplement the twelve Portuguese galleons with eight new galleons of the 'Indian Guard', built on private contract for service with the plate fleets, while the four galleasses provided for the Armada were royal ships. The rest of the expedition, consisting of about forty so-called great-ships and various other craft, were requisitioned merchantmen. The 130 vessels listed at Lisbon before departure were officially rated at 57,868 tons, a monstrous force the like of which no one had ever seen in those waters, set forth at the even more monstrous cost of some ten million ducats (equivalent to the total income of the English crown for five or six years). Yet the Armada was fatally deficient in several respects. The ships themselves were generally inferior to those of the English as sailers; the galleons, with their high freeboard and lofty castles, were less seaworthy and handy than the queen's ships, while the leading Spanish merchantmen, though large, did not share the strength and speed of their English counterparts. Many of the seamen had died of disease or deserted before the fleet sailed—the inevitable result of maintaining a state of mobilization for nearly two years on end—and had been replaced by unskilled men. Above all the Spanish fleet could not match the enemy in artillery, a fact which the king of Spain himself admitted in instructing his commander to come to close quarters and grapple with the English ships. Recent research has proved beyond doubt that [as I.A.A. Thompson suggests] 'the Spanish Armada was at such a disadvantage in fire-power, in both weight of shot and range, that it was probably incapable of winning the sea battle on whatever terms it was fought'. There is also evidence that its powder and shot were deficient in quality and quantity. As the admiral himself, the duke of Medina Sidonia, pointed out, success in such an offensive required superiority, but in fact the Armada was inferior to the English fleet in everything that mattered.

In terms of tonnage the shipping the English had available at the time in the area of the fighting was probably smaller. About 140 vessels appear to have been present—ninety under the Lord Admiral, Charles Howard, in the west, and fifty under Lord Henry Seymour in the east—but many of these were barks and pinnaces. The core of this force, however, was strong: the thirty-four queen's ships included eighteen powerful galleons of 300 to 1100 tons and seven lesser galleons of sufficient force to count in battle. The pride and confidence of the English commanders in these ships contrasts remarkably with the almost defeatist comments of Medina Sidonia on the quality of his. Since the late sixties and still more since 1580 the Navy Board had pursued a vigorous policy of building and rebuilding the queen's ships to produce by 1588 a fleet of remarkably efficient warships, not only more seaworthy, weatherly and faster than others, but better designed for fighting, longer in relation to beam and generally reduced in their top-hamper. These changes, though not radical, significantly improved the sailing qualities of the ships and made more room for battery guns at the expense of secondary armament, while the guns themselves and their mounting appear to have been improved. Nor should we dismiss all the private ships as mere auxiliaries. There were half a dozen of 300 tons and over—the *Galleon Leicester,* the *Edward Bonaventure,* the *Merchant Royal,* the *Roebuck,* the *Hercules* and the *Sampson*—which were substantial galleons, and at least another twenty in the 200 to 300-ton class were very useful fighters, as John Watts's *Margaret and John,* among others, proved herself to be in more than one engagement. The effective fighting ships on the English side thus numbered at least sixty—just about as many as those in the Armada—and the private ships, like the queen's, were unquestionably superior to their Spanish equivalents, as we know from the formidable record of many of them as privateers.

Circumstances moreover ensured that the defenders, both ships and men, were in better shape than the enemy when the moment of action arrived. The Armada had been two years and more in the making and as from month to month departure was delayed the ships deteriorated, victuals went bad, men sickened, died, disappeared. As Medina Sidonia set sail from Lisbon he was aware of a serious shortage of water and victuals, largely owing to defective cask, which was also spreading sickness throughout the fleet, and after he had decided to put into Corunna for fresh supplies a terrible storm broke, ruthlessly exposing the deficiencies of the ships and multiplying the sick. The respite at Corunna, which lasted a month, saved the Armada, but it could not make it sound. For the most part these difficulties of the attacking force resulted from the fundamental weakness of Spanish naval organization: the absence of royal dockyards, of a naval administration, indeed virtually of a royal navy, meant that the enormous task of preparing the Armada was carried out *ad hoc* and inadequately in spite of the efforts of Medina Sidonia to bring order out of chaos when he took over in March 1588. His problems and those of Santa Cruz before him were also due in part to Drake's forestalling and disrupting operations in Cadiz Bay and off Cape St Vincent in the spring of 1587, but those operations, conducted with quite a small force (four queen's ships and thirteen others with five pinnaces) were only possible because the Spaniards could not get a fleet to sea to drive him off, though they had been mobilizing for twelve months already.

English naval organization no doubt left much to be desired, but in comparison with Spanish administration the Navy Board was a model of efficiency. With royal dockyards at Deptford, Woolwich and Chatham, a victualling department and ordnance stores, apart from the resources of the outports and especially of Plymouth, now rapidly emerging as an important naval base, the means of mobilizing a fleet and maintaining it in readiness for service at short notice existed. This it was that enabled Elizabeth, having made no preparations for naval action throughout the autumn of 1587, to mobilize a major fleet within a fortnight in December and then, as the danger seemed to recede, to cut back the strength by half until the spring. Some naval historians have called this niggardly and deplored the risk, but in fact the queen saved men's lives thereby as well as the sinews of war, so that the fleet was fit in every sense when the enemy came to the Channel.

The Defeat of the Armada and Its Significance

Medina Sidonia left Corunna on 12/22 July with 131 vessels manned by approximately 7000 seamen and 17,000 soldiers.

His instructions were to proceed to the 'Cape of Margate' and to 'join hands' with Farnese (now duke of Parma) to ensure the safe crossing of his army from Dunkirk and Nieuport to England. Parma had an assault force of about 17,000 men, the cream of the army of Flanders, waiting to embark in barges and flyboats, and 6000 soldiers of the Armada were to reinforce him once he had established a bridgehead. How the two forces were to effect a junction was not explained. It would be difficult because Dutch flyboats commanded the banks and shoals of the Flanders coast and would sink Parma's army with the greatest of ease unless he or Medina Sidonia found the means to drive them off. Parma certainly lacked such means, nor could Medina Sidonia do much to help him without first destroying the English fleet. King Philip clearly expected the Armada to engage and defeat the English and thereby to obtain total and unchallenged control of the crossing, but in fact the Spaniards were unable to join battle in earnest until it was too late. Tactically Medina Sidonia lost the initiative very soon after entering the Channel, when Howard won the weather-gauge, for from that moment onwards the superior sailing qualities of the English ships and their superior artillery prevented the duke from precipitating the close general engagement in which his 17,000 soldiers with their arquebuses, muskets, pikes and swords might well have won the day. It was only after they had been driven from the Calais roadstead by fire-ships and when they were retreating in disarray that Medina Sidonia and his galleons turned at last to face the enemy at Gravelines and were there defeated by those same guns.

The failure of the Armada was by no means a matter of bad luck, bad leadership or lack of effort on the part of its officers and men: it was outsailed, outgunned and finally broken in battle. After that the Spaniards could not turn back. Already mauled by storm and enemy action, grievously short of victuals and water, they had no choice now but to brave the storms of the North Atlantic and the inhospitable shores of Ireland. So far they had lost only a few ships; now many more were wrecked—probably as many as twenty on the Irish coast alone—and thousands of men died by drowning, starved to death or were captured ashore and slaughtered. In all some fifty vessels of the original fleet failed to return, and many of those which made Spanish ports were beyond repair. The force which embodied the naval strength of Spain lay in ruins and Philip II's bid to win the war by a decisive victory had failed.

Yet this was rather the beginning than the end of the war and the beginning rather than the end of Spanish naval power. In fact the fighting capability of Spain at sea had suffered much less than her merchant marine. Only four galleons were lost, while no less than eighteen out of forty of the substantial merchantmen (Biscayners and Levanters especially) failed to return, in addition to a number of hulks and small craft. The nucleus of a state navy remained, but the maritime resources upon which the sea power of the country must in the long run depend were impoverished. Moreover the strategic situation created by the defeat of the Armada meant that for the rest of the war Spain's merchant fleet came under increasing pressure and continued to decline, while the crown made great efforts—and with some success—to develop a powerful navy. For on the one hand the defeat of the Spanish offensive returned the initiative at sea to the English, who could now once again range the Atlantic in search of prey, hounding Iberian shipping at will and forcing Spain to invest heavily in the protection of its most precious and vital trade, the Seville-Atlantic system. On the other hand the strategic position in northwest Europe was not essentially changed by the events of 1588: Spanish power there, still formidable, was still held in check by England. The way to win the war was to neutralize England first, but to do so by diplomacy and compromise now seemed less possible and less acceptable than ever. Would it not be preferable to build up the naval strength to do it by force? Philip II had the incentive and the will to try again, nor did he lack the means to launch more armadas against England. . . .

The War Continues

By 1595 Spain's naval revival was an obvious fact and Elizabeth was strongly impressed by reports of a new armada in the making, threatening Ireland or even England itself with invasion that year or the next. Nevertheless she was persuaded to allow Drake and [Richard] Hawkins to attempt an assault upon Panama, the original intention being to block the isthmus for some time in order to divert the bullion of Peru into her treasury. The queen's fear of the Spanish fleet, however, caused her to limit the expedition to a mere hit-and-run raid, the prospects of which were prejudiced by a last minute decision to attack San Juan de Puerto Rico first, where a great galleon of silver lay crippled. Bad leadership, bad luck and a Spanish response which was good in parts turned the last voyage of Drake and Hawkins into a disaster: both leaders, along with many men and some ships, were lost in what had been from the start a gamble for treasure, essentially a privateering venture in which the crown was the largest shareholder. It represents the nadir of Elizabethan strategy. . . .

Another armada threatened in 1599, but was diverted to the Azores, while England waited with bated breath. After that her men of war pursued carracks and treasure and blockading action by fits and starts with no more success than before. Some have blamed the civil power for this failure, some the commanders, and truly there is as much to blame as to admire in the conduct of either, but still more damaging was the conflict between them, which repeatedly reduced English strategy to compromises which achieved nothing of importance. Even so, the faults of over-cautious ministers and irresponsible men of war cannot alone explain why the English were unable to win the war by sea, for what they faced was objectively a very hard task. Time and again they were defeated by wind and weather, distance and disease, the intractable forces of nature and the inevitable limits of their own resources, technology and skills. The naval power at their disposal was small; the army available was scarcely adequate for the capture of a major sea-port, let alone its tenure as a base in the heart of enemy territory; expertise in the mounting and handling of large-scale amphibious operations took many decades to mature, as some disastrous expeditions of the next century were to show; men had still to work out the strategy and tactics of oceanic warfare and tended to underestimate the difficulties of a blockade, for example, or the seizure of an Atlantic island or a West Indian base.

And while the Atlantic thus posed new and typically modern problems, the naval means available to meet them were slow to change and the traditional conception, organization and methods of sea-warfare persisted. The queen's navy was still but a small part of the force the country could exert at sea, nor did it differ radically in character from the rest of that force. . . .

Privateering Contributes to English Sea Strength

Far from being a professional navy, distinct from the mass of private shipping, the royal navy was dominated by private interests deeply entrenched in every department of its organization and activity, from the building of the ships to the settling of accounts at the end of a cruise. Those interests were concerned above all with privateering, and the queen's policy encouraged the use of her ships in expeditions of plunder, for she expected them to pay their way when not employed in the defence of the realm or the necessary operations of the Continental and Irish wars. Other naval campaigns she would seldom finance without the assistance of noblemen, seamen and merchants willing to adventure ships, goods or money for profit. In some great naval enterprises of the war—the Islands voyages of 1592 and 1597, for example, in both of which [Sir Walter] Ralegh had a strong interest—public and private elements were so entangled as to become difficult to distinguish, and when all parties looked thus to their peculiar advantage it surprised no one that these semi-official expeditions, in which privateers outnumbered the queen's ships, filled every purse except the public one. Nor should it surprise us that forces thus constituted and directed failed to inflict decisive defeat upon a powerful enemy. Ralegh blamed the queen because he did not recognize the real weakness of the weapon she wielded, a weakness he, with his privateering interests and privateering approach to the war at sea, personified.

Thus the main naval war achieved nothing more positive

than the frustration of Spain's enormous efforts by land and sea to dominate the northwest. This meant, however, that in the little war which accompanied it the English were free to exercise and develop their maritime capability by the sort of private enterprise that suited them best.

Privateering consisted in the officially licensed operations of privately-owned vessels against enemy shipping and goods in time of war. It was customary for the crown thus to allow its subjects to wage war, as it were, on their own account, and in this war it did so by issuing letters of reprisal in the High Court of Admiralty to those who claimed damages by the confiscations of 1585, though before long proof of loss became little more than a legal fiction and ventures of reprisal were promoted by men who had never dreamed of trading in Spain. Thus in the summer of 1585 the first of a host of voluntaries took to the sea, and soon the reports of Drake's triumphs in the West Indies 'inflamed the whole country with a desire to adventure unto the seas, in the hope of the like good success, [so] that a great number prepared ships, mariners and soldiers and travelled every place where any profit might be had' [as John Hooker remarks]. It was natural for the English, not themselves possessed of a rich and vulnerable merchant marine, to take advantage of their initiative in the Atlantic to conduct an unceasing campaign against Iberian shipping. In the next eighteen years hundreds of private ventures were organized for plunder. Ships of reprisal normally accompanied the official and semi-official expeditions and many more sailed independently. John Hagthorpe's statement that in the 'queen's time' there were 'never less than 200 sail of voluntaries and others' on Spanish coasts may have been an exaggeration, but the number may well have reached that level in some years of the war and seldom if ever fell below a hundred. . . .

England's Emergence as a Sea Power

The sea-war in general and privateering in particular did much to associate English nationalism with militant maritime expansion. In attitudes at least the war marked a turning point, signalized by the publication, of [Richard] Hakluyt's *Principall Navigations* in the year after the Armada and of its extended edition in 1598–1600. Hakluyt's message of oceanic imperialism conquered the reading public with such triumphant ease because the public mind was now ready to accept it.

The material effect of privateering upon the balance of sea power between the nations was important for the future. Commerce-raiding, it is true, could not win the war. Nothing like an effective blockade was ever achieved, scarcely even attempted, and the amounts of treasure the English captured during the war were insignificant in comparison with those that reached Spain. It was only when they occasionally caused the postponement of the Havana sailings that the corsairs impeded the operation of the Spanish war machine. Yet the cumulative impact of continual shipping losses upon the Iberian marine was heavy. English sources suggest that the English captured well over a thousand Spanish and Portuguese prizes during the war, losses which must have contributed as much as any other factor to the catastrophic decline of Iberian shipping noted in 1608 by a Spanish shipbuilding expert. . . .

The Spanish economy suffered even more from the indirect consequences of the naval war. The replacement of ships lost, whether in the disastrous invasion attempts or in the ceaseless little war of Atlantic depredation, was increasingly costly; and so was the building of warships for the defence of the Atlantic, which now became a major concern and a major outlay alongside the growing burden of the military effort in France and the Netherlands. Inflation sent up the prices of war materials, such as timber, and of labour much more steeply in Spain than in England, so that the strain of defence upon that country's resources was proportionately greater, indeed in the long run crippling. An increasing supply of American treasure for the time being kept Philip's war afloat, but in the process it aggravated the financial difficulties of the state and hastened the onset of famine and plague before the end of the century. The contribution of the corsairs to the decline of Spain was of course one factor among many, but in the decimation of Iberian Atlantic commerce they played a leading part. Spain, it is true, responded by developing her naval power, but this served only to erode the maritime base on which lasting naval power must rest. The stock of skilled seafaring men, already gravely depleted by 1585, was nearly exhausted in the early seventeenth century in consequence of losses at sea, pestilence, low wages and ill-advised attempts at conscription. . . .

The success of privateering brought about a remarkable boom in shipbuilding—specifically in the production of the larger sort of private vessel, of 100 tons and over. The official survey of 1582 had shown about 250 of 80 tons and up, whereas in the sixteen years from 1581 to 1597 no less than 133 of 100 tons and over were built. Of these 106 were Londoners and 72 were rated at 200 tons and over—England had possessed fewer than twenty ships of that size in 1582. The boom was still accelerating in the mid nineties and appears to have continued until after the end of the war. Some of these new ships were intended primarily for privateering, like the *Neptune* of London, built by Francis Glanville, a leading London goldsmith, his son-in-law Christopher Newport, and his brother Richard Glanville, a warship Spaniards in the Caribbean came to know to their cost. Others worked in the Levant, Barbary or Muscovy trades. Many brought home prizes. England at the end of the war possessed a more powerful merchant marine than at the beginning of it, and it was better adapted to the conduct of long-distance and oceanic commerce. With the ships, moreover, there had grown up a rare of skippers who knew the ocean as their forefathers had known the Channel, men like Newport, Lancaster and hundreds more, trained in the school of reprisals not only to navigate and to fight, but to manage the whole course of an expedition from the fitting out to the safe delivery of the privateers and their prize. Elizabethan statesmen were right in seeing ships and seamen as the key to mercantile power and wealth. These two decades of maritime warfare brought no clear victory; uncertainty and depression prevailed in the nation's traditional trades abroad; hopes of eastern trade, western planting, a northwest passage, all running high in the years before the Armada, were deferred. But the English kept the initiative in the Atlantic and used their peculiar form of sea power, dilute and pervasive, to tilt the oceanic balance in their favour, developing at the same time the resources—not only in ships and men but in commercial capital and momentum—to produce the new wave of enterprise which broke with the new century upon the East and West Indies, North and South America. Spain would and could still resist the encroachment, especially in the Caribbean, her most sensitive region, but the war so weakened her maritime and imperial system and so strengthened the forces of expansion in England that projects which had stood little chance of succeeding in the eighties became actualities in the Jacobean era.

Sir Walter Raleigh and the First Virginia Colony

J.H. Adamson and H.F. Folland

Sir Walter Raleigh organized the first English colonizing expedition to America, and in 1584 captains Philip Amadas and Arthur Barlow, who landed on an island off the coast of present day North Carolina, took possession of the land for Raleigh in the name of Queen Elizabeth. Upon Captain Barlow's return to England, Raleigh asked the queen if she would allow the new land to be called Virginia, in honor of her, their virgin queen. Elizabeth agreed, and the coast from present day Florida to Newfoundland became Virginia. Although the first Virginia colony lasted only a year, and the second colony had disappeared by 1602, Raleigh succeeded in connecting Elizabeth's name with the New World.

In this excerpt from *The Shepherd of the Ocean*, J.H. Adamson and H.F. Folland examine Raleigh's first attempt to win the New World from Spain. While Captain Barlow and company were actually exploring Roanoke Island, Raleigh asked his friend Richard Hakluyt to write a treatise persuading Elizabeth that colonization of America was in England's national interest. Elizabeth supported the colonizing plan, but assigned official responsibility to Raleigh, not wishing to openly defy Spain's claim in the New World. Richard Grenville led the second Virginia voyage in 1585, established a colony of 107 men on Roanoke Island, and paid for the venture by overhauling a Spanish freighter. The colony sustained itself for over a year, largely due to the efforts of scientist Thomas Hariot; however, the disenchantment of the settlers, Chief Pemisapan's nearly successful plan to massacre the settlers, and

Excerpted from *The Shepherd of the Ocean: An Account of Sir Walter Ralegh and his Times*, by J.H. Adamson and H.F. Folland (Boston: Gambit, 1969). Copyright © 1969 by J.H. Adamson and H.F. Folland.

Grenville's failure to arrive at Easter with supplies, marked the end of this first effort. Sir Francis Drake's timely arrival allowed the settlers to return to England. Although the first colonizing effort had failed, and the surviving colonists spread rancorous stories about America, Hariot described a wonderful medicinal herb in America, tobacco, which prompted Raleigh's renewed efforts at settlement.

In addition to *The Shepherd of the Ocean*, Adamson and Folland have also jointly authored *Sir Harry Vane: His Life and Times (1613–1662)*.

None of [Sir Walter] Ralegh's labours can approach in significance his great unwearying efforts to colonize in America. From 1584 until he died, he spent his treasure and gave the full force of his feverish intellectual energy in various attempts to win the New World from Spain and make it part of an English empire. He had probably first become interested in the possibilities of the New World when he had served in France under Admired [Gaspard de] Coligny who had planted the first French colonies in America. And from members of the Admiral's expedition, he came to know the difficulties that had beset Coligny, and would beset him, in the founding of new colonies.

The first problem was that Spain and Portugal had arrived first and had established cities, roads, naval bases and army garrisons. Further, Pope Alexander VI, wishing to avoid a possible clash between the two Catholic powers in the New World had issued a bull of May 4, 1493, intended to prevent further difficulties. In this bull the Pope ceded to Spain

> all islands and lands found and to be found, discovered and to be discovered, to the west and south by making and drawing a line from the Arctic or North Pole to the Antarctic, or South Pole, which line shall be distant an hundred leagues west and south of any of the islands which are commonly called the Azores or Cape de Verde.

The Pope concluded this amazing document by saying that

if any man presumed to infringe the rights therein conferred he should incur the indignation of Almighty God and the apostles Peter and Paul. . . .

Ralegh knew that Spain and Portugal intended to keep the New World free from intruders, and that if he ventured out there he had better be prepared for rough play. More important, he knew that there was a limited future in defrauding the natives: colonists, in order to keep the friendship of the Indians, must carry or plant their own food. Further, he realized that there needed to be a systematized trade; the New World must yield something to the old. The old world, in turn, to win the new, must make a national effort backed with ample resources. That was the kind of effort Spain had made, and Spain had been richly repaid.

Seven months after [his half-brother Humphrey] Gilbert's death, one month after he received his Letters Patent from Parliament, on April 27, 1584, Ralegh despatched two barks from a Westcountry port. Their captains were Master Philip Amadas and Master Arthur Barlow; their pilot was the highly skilled Portuguese, Simon Fernandez, who had made a voyage of reconnaissance to the New World for Humphrey Gilbert in 1580. . . .

Exploration of Wokoken and Roanoke Islands

After touching at the Canaries the ships sailed to the West Indies and then north along the American coast. On July 2, the land breeze brought them the scent of a 'delicate garden abounding with all kind of odoriferous flowers'. Two days later they made landfall at Wokoken, an island which is part of a long sand reef off the coast of North Carolina. Immediately they lifted up turf and twig and took possession of the land for Ralegh in the name of Queen Elizabeth. He now owned the North American continent if he could hold it against the Spaniard.

After the ceremonies were completed, the explorers 'viewed the land'. The place was overrun with wild grapes. Arthur Barlow had never seen anything in the vineyards of Europe to compare with this. Grapes even grew down to the beach where 'the very beating and surge of the sea overflowed them'.

All this was propitious, for England imported so much wine from Spain as to cause an unfavourable balance of trade. Since claret and port could be profitably freighted a long distance, wines might be the commodity that could make the American venture a success financially.

For two days the little party lay at anchor; on the third a canoe with three Indians appeared. The three English leaders rowed out to meet the natives, exchanged greetings and invited them aboard. They were timid, but one Indian came. He was given a shirt and hat which pleased him, then a drink of wine which delighted him so much that he got in his canoe and soon returned with it full of fish. This, the captains thought, showed a disposition to trade.

The next day some forty or fifty Indian men came aboard. They were 'very handsome and goodly people and in their behaviour as mannerly and civil as any of Europe'. The leader, Granganimeo, made 'all signs of joy and welcome', and soon the English and the Indians began trading; the colonizers could not resist repeating the mistakes of Coligny's men by taking advantage of the natives. . . .

The expedition then sailed north some twenty miles to Roanoke Island where they saw their first Indian village. They were hospitably entertained by Granganimeo's wife, and Barlow was so impressed with the 'love and kindness' shown to his men that he concluded, as Parmenius had done before him, that the ancient myth of the golden age was already a reality in the New World.

> We found the people most gentle, loving and faithful, void of all guile and treason, and such as live after the manner of the golden age.

But the Indians gave the white men a friendly and hospitable reception not because their natures were unspoiled by a vicious society but because they believed—until they came to know their guests better—that they were supernatural beings. Marvelling at the whiteness of the skins, they thought their visitors were reincarnated men who had come from the pale world of shades. The fact that the visitors had no women with them and refrained from attempting to possess the bare brown flesh they saw all around them supported that theory. Besides, it was ripe and lush summer; fish were plentiful; crops were growing; food was easy to get. It was a pleasure to share it with visitors who brought excitement and wonder into their lives and offered tin plates and copper pots in exchange for the common objects of their routine lives. But amidst all this friendliness, Barlow maintained an unusual degree of caution. He never allowed his men to go unarmed among the Indians nor would he allow them to sleep in native houses.

Barlow carefully noted that the Indians had poor weapons: their breastplates were of wood, their swords of wood hardened in fire; they carried war clubs which had a staghorn in the end; and their arrows were small, barely powerful enough to kill a naked man, certainly not one who wore armour.

Barlow and his men sowed some peas into the ground. In ten days they were up fourteen inches. They had seen enough; the natives were friendly and a colony would be able to grow its own food on Roanoke Island. Barlow reported enthusiastically that the 'soil is the most plentiful, sweet, fruitful and wholesome of all the world'. . . .

Ralegh Engages Hakluyt to Advertise the Colonial Mission

While Barlow was in America Ralegh was making larger plans for his colonization. Always in his mind was the contrast between the effective efforts of Spain and the fumbling inadequacies of England and France. It was the small scale of Coligny's and Gilbert's enterprises that had foredoomed them. Ralegh had a friend in France, an English clergyman named Richard Hakluyt who, like Ralegh, had known personally a number of the French colonists from the Florida colonies. Like Ralegh also he had a passionate sense of mission about the New World, so Ralegh asked him to come to England and prepare a treatise which would persuade Elizabeth and her councillors that it was in England's vital interests to make a national effort in America. It was to be no proposal for an exotic trading post, for a little highly publicized adventuring, but for an empire that would match, and ultimately overmatch, that of Spain. Even before Amadas and Barlow had returned, Hakluyt had completed his *Discourse on Western Planting*, written 'at the request and direction' of Walter Ralegh.

Much of what he said had all been heard before about converting the heathen, employing idle men and finding the Northwest Passage. But in pursuit of Ralegh's larger aims, he asserted that an American colony might make England a self-sustaining nation. Wine, olive oil and silks, which were now imported, could be produced in America. Also gold, silver, copper and pearls are to be found there. He insisted that the people were gentle and obedient (both Barlow and Hakluyt probably had instructions from Ralegh to emphasize this point), but obedient or not, will they or nil they, the natural inhabitants, with whom England will make every effort to trade peaceably, will if necessary be forced to surrender the 'natural commodities of their lands' and Englishmen will become 'great gainers'.

Most important of all, Hakluyt mapped out a comprehensive attack on the Spanish empire which, if successful, would simply drive Spain from the New World. The black legend of Spanish cruelties ensured, he said, that the natives, given a chance, will revolt and willingly join their English liberators (all his life Ralegh thought of himself as the humane emancipator of the Indians). Once a good base has been established in the middle of North America, the English can raid northward against the fishing fleets and southward against the West Indies and the Spanish Main. Hakluyt boldly suggested that then the English may with impunity violate the Pope's line and Spanish territories.

> If you touch Philip [in the Indies], you touch the apple of his eye; for take away his treasure, which is *nervus belli* and which he hath almost [entirely] out of his West Indies, his old bands of soldiers will soon be dissolved, his purposes defeated, his powers and strength diminished, his pride abated, and his tyranny utterly suppressed.

But if England did not drive Spain from the New World, if she did not plant in North America immediately, Hakluyt was convinced that the Spanish would soon occupy all of the American territories.

Elizabeth had read Hakluyt's *Discourse* when Ralegh brought her the report by Barlow which so fully (and perhaps suspiciously) confirmed Hakluyt's arguments. Since the emoluments from the Crown had not yet started to flow into his pockets, Ralegh himself had no money, and so he urged Elizabeth to take a personal interest in the venture. He tempted her with a brilliant stroke. Would Her Majesty allow the new land to be called, after her, Virginia? Elizabeth, smiling, nodded approval. Immediately the northern boundary of Florida retreated from the Arctic Circle where Spain had placed it and came to rest around the 31st parallel where it is today. The North Atlantic coast, from Florida to Newfoundland, had a new name and Elizabeth was part of the New World forever.

While the new land bore the name of Elizabeth, the legal title to it remained with Ralegh if Parliament would confirm his claim. In February, 1585, that title was confirmed but hedged with a few restrictions: he could not take imprisoned debtors, wives, wards or apprentices to the new colony. Shipping and supplies must be paid for; they could not be requisitioned by the authority of the Crown. All of this Ralegh agreed to; shortly thereafter Elizabeth knighted him and he had a seal made of his coat of arms with an inscription, 'Lord and Governor of Virginia'.

Knowing that Ralegh desperately needed money to further the American enterprise, and believing that he was entitled to it, Elizabeth began to supply it through the farm of wines, the license to export cloths and other privileges. Ralegh knew that these gifts were to be used in the service of the nation and that is how he used them.

Elizabeth, then, would support the colonizing plan, but only indirectly and cautiously, for she was not ready to defy Spain openly. The official responsibility was to be Ralegh's. But his urgent duties in England demanded his presence there, even without Elizabeth's reluctance to expose her favourites to hazard. He was therefore forbidden to lead the expedition in person. He would set the goals and formulate the plans, but he must find a deputy to carry them out. He needed a man in whom he could place entire confidence, and he selected his cousin, Richard Grenville of Cornwall, who in certain ways resembled Sir Humphrey Gilbert, a man of unqualified, even fanatical courage. Although more self-assured than Gilbert, like him he had a tendency to near hysteria in moments of crisis. He was a most formidable captain. Ralegh approached his stern, combative cousin and asked him to take the general charge of the voyage. Out of 'the love he bare unto Sir Walter Ralegh, together with a disposition he had to attempt honourable actions', Grenville agreed to hazard himself in the second Virginia voyage.

Because Elizabeth had provided no money, although she did provide a ship, Grenville was expected to take enough from piracy to pay the costs of the voyage and, if possible, return a profit to the investors. Those accompanying Grenville were not given land grants; rather they were to be paid wages and given a share in any profits. This first colony was not an attempt to establish English homesteaders in a new land but to make enough money by piracy, trade, or by finding gold or pearls, to make future large-scale colonizing a possibility.

The Second Virginia Voyage

The ships left England on April 9, 1585, with Grenville as Admiral aboard the *Tyger*, the Queen's ship. . . .

The colonists decided that it would be safer to establish themselves on Roanoke Island than to attempt a village on the mainland, for the island offered a natural defence. There they settled and, in about two months, Grenville left them with a promise that reinforcements and supplies would reach them by the following Easter. He then returned to England by way of the West Indies. Off Bermuda he overhauled a large Spanish freighter of 300 tons, the *Santa Maria*. The ship's manifest indicated that she carried gold, silver, pearls, ginger, cochineal, and other cargo to the value of 120,000 ducats. Grenville himself, with a prize crew, took over the *Santa Maria* and brought her into Plymouth on September 18.

Ralegh, who had been nervously awaiting word, hurried

down to secure the cargo. Rumours had already reached London that it was worth half a million pounds, but, disappointingly it was not. Grenville said there was no gold or silver; the main cargo was sugar and ginger which he valued at only 50,000 ducats. However, that, along with the other booty he had taken, made it possible for Grenville to give each of the investors all of his money back, along with some gain; he had thus completely fulfilled the dual task Ralegh had assigned him. A colony of 107 men had been transported to America, and Ralegh's credit was good for future ventures. . . .

Hariot Sustains the Colony

The one unmistakable stroke of genius which Ralegh showed in this venture was his persuading Thomas Hariot to go to America as a kind of second in command, for Hariot played the most important role in the relations of the colonists with the natives. He began by showing the Indians some sea compasses, the loadstone, a perspective glass (precursor of the telescope), burning glasses, fireworks, clocks and so on. These were the instruments and inventions that were revolutionizing Elizabethan technology and when the Indians saw them, they thought they 'were rather the works of gods than of men', and Hariot said, it led the Indians to feel that God must especially love such people to have taught them so much. The Indian fear of Hariot's magic made it easier for him to teach religion to the natives and helped keep them in fearful wonder.

He set up his perspective glass in such a way that, by concentrating the rays of the sun, it would start a fire several yards away. One of his glasses was apparently so made that if the viewer stood close, he would see things in their usual size and appearance. If he stepped back, however, the image would suddenly be gigantic. While the *wiroan* was still shaking his head in disbelief, Hariot could shift the focus further outward until suddenly all images would be reversed, and people, trees, and animals would all be standing with their heads downward, their feet pointing up.

At these tricks, and similar ones performed with a loadstone, such as picking up iron with a magnetized sword, the

Indians were properly amazed, and it was a good thing; the survival of the colonists would soon depend on the superstitious awe which Hariot had engendered. For soon food became scarce. The coastal Indians were not good hunters; their weapons were poor and they took large animals only occasionally. Their diet was mainly fish caught in weirs, and crop foods which they had stored. Never having been taught Puritan thrift, they stored enough maize only to see them through the winter and to provide seed for the next spring. They had no provisions for long visits from pale visitors. Nothing except a fear more terrible than that of starvation could induce them to part with their seed corn.

Further, the Indians had little else to trade with; their supply of skins was small and they had already lost their taste for trinkets: copper utensils were what they wanted most. Before long they became shrewd bargainers: they demanded many utensils for a little food until they had all the utensils they wanted and the colonists were growing more desperate for food all the time. Then it occurred to the crafty and disillusioned mind of the chief of Roanoke Island, Pemisapan, that he should continue to accumulate copper, that the mainland Indians might want it as badly as his people had, that with it he might effect an alliance that would see the white interlopers destroyed through the agency of their own copper pots.

Meanwhile the colonists were not enjoying their journey into the golden age. Many who were city-bred longed for the taverns, the bull-baitings, the plays and other amusements of London. Not finding them they sulked and lazed, pampering their bellies, as Hariot said. Many of them had come hoping to find gold and silver; when the first explorations failed to find it, they lost interest and simply existed from day to day without any effort to learn the language, teach religion, or fulfill any of the high aims of Hakluyt's *Discourse*. . . .

Lane Leads Expedition for Gold

As the winter wore on and food for 104 men was increasingly difficult to find, frustrations grew on both sides. The Indians likely observed that those pale celibates, before many months had passed, were merely pale; and for men from the spirit world they had uncommonly large appetites which their god seemed incapable of satisfying. Among the colonists doubts about the New World were growing; even [Ralph] Lane was dubious. It read very well when Hakluyt wrote about establishing new industries, but when had Englishmen ever cultivated grapes and made wine from them? It was an art that took generations to learn; and there was no real hope of making silk or cultivating olives with inexperienced men; all of that was simply visionary. The conviction grew on Lane that there were only two practical hopes for his colony; he must find either a rich mine or a passage to the South Seas. Once he had arrived at this decision, he forgot agriculture and gambled the future of his colony on explorations. . . .

Lane prepared two boats, taking the little food he had been able to barter from the Indians, and with forty men, nearly half of his entire company, he set out on the expedition that would probably determine the success or failure of the colony. This was the opportunity Pemisapan had been waiting for, and he showed a certain primitive genius in the way he plotted the destruction of the colonists. First he travelled up the Roanoke River, along the route which Lane planned to take, telling the Indians that Lane intended to kill them. Their only hope, he said, was to abandon their towns immediately, taking all their food with them. Such a policy was disastrous for Lane, for he depended entirely on being able to secure food along the way. His expedition crossed Albemarle Sound and travelled up the Roanoke River a total distance of 160 miles from Roanoke Island. At that point he had two days' supply of food left. He therefore stopped and called his men into council. Lane said he thought that the Indians had probably enticed them into a trap with the intent of starving them; he believed, therefore, that it was wisest for them to return. Actually, he inwardly wished to continue, but thought it best, in case things went badly, to be on the record with the contrary opinion. The vote was 38 to 2 to continue up river; someone pointed out that there were two mastiffs which, if necessary, could be boiled with sassafras and eaten. This was the only time on the entire voyage that Lane's men showed enthusiasm. The scent of gold was in their nostrils.

Two days later all of their food was gone. They heard some savages calling, to Manteo they thought, who answered them. Soon they heard a song which they believed to be a song of welcome. Manteo, however, perceiving that it was a war chant, shouted a warning; immediately there was a volley of arrows. It is a commentary on the prowess of the Virginia Indians that not a single colonist was hurt. The voyagers replied with musket fire which drove the Indians into the woods. But it meant the end of the voyage. The colonists ate the mastiffs and hastened back down stream. On Easter eve, Lane said, 'they fasted very truly', one of his few essays into humour. Finally they found some weirs and helped themselves to the fish, just in time, too, for some of the light horsemen were 'far spent'. The next day they arrived home.

Pemisapan Plans War

In the meantime, Pemisapan, never expecting to see them again, had been engaging in psychological warfare on Roanoke Island. He told the remaining colonists that Lane and his men were all dead. He also denounced the god of the white men and blasphemed Christ, saying that a god who couldn't feed his worshippers wasn't a true god. Upon his return, Lane discovered all of this and more. Gradually he saw the outlines of the conspiracy. . . .

Under the guise of funeral obsequies for Ensenore, the Indians were to gather on the mainland across from the island. Then a score or so of braves, chosen for their courage and strength, would come over to Roanoke in the dead of night and set fire to the houses of Lane, Hariot, and the other leaders of the colony. When the sleepers awoke, they were supposed to run out of their houses 'of a sudden amazed', in their shirts and without arms. There each would be met by a destroying angel who was to knock out his brains with a stag-horn war club. When the leaders went down, a signal would be given and the war canoes from the mainland would ferry all the braves to the island where they would massacre the remaining colonists.

It was a good plan and should have worked. But there was one hitch: the young prince Skiko. Lane and his men had treated the young blood with consideration and respect and he had come to like them. Two weeks before the scheduled attack, he revealed the entire plot. . . .

Drake Rescues the Colony

One week later, twenty-three sail appeared off the island. No one knew whether they were friendly or whether the King of Spain, once again, had sent a force to clear the intruders from the kingdom the Pope had given him. It turned out to be Sir Francis Drake, who had been plundering the Spanish Main. Elizabeth had at last given her permission for a raid against the Spanish Empire in reprisal for Philip's seizure of some English merchant ships. Drake had sacked San Domingo and Cartagena, receiving ransom for both cities, and then, surprisingly, he sailed up the coast of Florida and attacked the Spanish colony at St. Augustine, burning the fort and driving the survivors into the interior. Since that attack promised no hope of booty, it was likely carried out at the request of Ralegh, in order to remove the threat to the flank of Virginia.

So Drake arrived in Virginia at the critical moment when the colony was shaken by the attempted massacre, its hopes disappointed, its incentive gone. Drake tried to save Ralegh's colony. He offered to leave enough supply to keep Lane until August when Lane had intended to return to England anyway. That would give him the summer in which to explore; to try once again for the *wassador* or to find a route to the sea. He also offered to leave ship captains who knew good harbours, who would help find one for the site of the next colony, and who could then bring them all back to England. He also volunteered guns, oarsmen, ammunition, and clothing, and finally he offered the *Francis*, a bark of 70 tons; she was small enough to avoid shoals and bars, but large enough to transport the colony north to Chesapeake Bay.

It was all agreed upon when, on June 13, a bad storm swept up the Carolina coast; there were waterspouts and hurricanes. Cables snapped, anchors were lost, the pinnaces and many of the small boats were driven into shore and beaten to pieces. Only by skill and good luck were the larger vessels saved. On June16, when the storm cleared, Lane saw, in disbelief and dismay, that the *Francis,* with all the stores which Drake had given him aboard, and a number of his colonists too, was crowding full sail eastward for England. It is surprising that a ship under Drake's command should have been guilty of such a breach of discipline. But the sea-captains were independent men; and when they had called a council and had the full voice of crew and passengers, no court in England would hold them guilty of malfeasance.

Drake still tried to save the colony. He offered another ship, but she was too big to be brought inside the reef at Albemarle Sound; she would have to lie at anchor in the road. Lane realized that she was also too large to use in exploring the coast; it would be difficult to load and unload her while she was lying out at sea. Besides, even to a moderate Puritan, the storm looked like the finger of an angry God. So Lane called an assembly, reminding the colonists that Ralegh had promised them relief by Easter; it was now past the middle of June. He suggested that with the increased hostilities against Spain it would be unlikely that England could spend much money or thought on the colonists. He therefore proposed returning to England with Drake. The company 'readily assented' and began to fetch their baggage off Roanoke Island in the small boats. The wind came up again, the ships began to pitch and roll, and the sailors, angered at the many risks they had already undergone for the colonists, threw overboard the chests, books, writings and valuables, including a string of pearls Lane had intended for the Queen. Then Drake's fleet, with all the colonists aboard, stood out at sea.

Seventy-two hours later, Ralegh's first relief ship appeared and dropped anchor. Two weeks later, Richard Grenville arrived in the *Tyger* accompanied by other vessels. Bad winds, sickness, any of the hundred reasons that inevitably delayed naval expeditions in the age of Elizabeth had delayed Ralegh's ships. Had they arrived a few hours earlier, the colony could have been removed to Chesapeake, founded on the shores of a good harbour, and given food for a year. Destiny had beaten Ralegh by the margin of three days and nights. . . .

Hariot's Report Inspires Another Colonizing Effort

Back in England, many of the returned colonists were bitter. They spread rancorous stories about the New World and scoffed at its potential. Ralegh, who was determined to send out a new colony and who still hoped for support from private or state sources, determined to counteract these libels against the land which he had never seen but in which he had so much confidence. And so he urged Thomas Hariot to write a comprehensive report that would inspire confidence in the new land and make a permanent addition to the nation's literature. That report was completed and published in 1588.

Hariot gave a survey in depth of the resources of Virginia; it has been called the first statistical survey on a large scale in the English language. Concerning precious metals he is very reserved. There is rich iron ore; he himself has seen copper plates and some silver, and that is all he will say. Clearly he did not share the fantasies about gold and pearls.

The most interesting section in his report is the one on 'The Nature and Manners of the People'. For the first time an Englishman wrote about the religion of the Indian without indignation. Because Hariot was neither shocked nor repelled, he saw beyond the savagery and superstition into what appeared to be the rudiments of a natural religion. For example, he said that they have 'one only chief and great God, which hath been from all eternity'. He also pointed out that the Indians believed in the immortality of the soul, including a kind of heaven and hell, and believed also that they would ultimately be sent to one or the other as a judgment for their life on earth. This belief, he said, made the common people respect their governors and also motivated them to take 'great care what they do, to avoid torment after death'. . . .

If there was to be profitable trade between the two nations, a commodity was needed which could be cheaply freighted and sold at a profit in England. Such a commodity existed and Hariot had described it.

There is an herb which is sowed apart by itself and is called by the inhabitants Uppowoc: . . . the Spaniards generally call it Tobacco. The leaves thereof being dried and brought into

powder, they use to take the fume or smoke thereof by suck-
ing it through pipes made of clay, into their stomach and head;
from whence it purges superfluous phlegm and other gross
humours, and openeth all the pores and passages of the body.

Through the use of this herb, Hariot says, the Indians have
avoided entirely many diseases which afflict the English. And
he explained how tobacco was used for sacrifice, to quiet
storms, and to pacify the gods. When the Indians wished to
dedicate a new fish weir, or when they had escaped from danger, they would throw some tobacco up into the air and always with 'strange gestures, stamping, sometimes dancing,
clapping of hands, holding up of hands, and staring up into
the heavens, uttering therewithal, and chattering strange
words and noises'. But when James of Scotland, the world's
leading authority on witchcraft, read that passage and realized that tobacco was a tool of the Devil, an agent of sorcery
and witchcraft, he hardened his mind against the man who
had been responsible for its popularity at Elizabeth's court.

But Ralegh himself loved all the strange new things that
came to him from America. The words intrigued him and
the people and the adventures. He would have liked pearl
and gold and a passage to the Orient. But he was still fasci-
nated with tobacco and the potato and other herbs. He knew
a place in Ireland, in the deep soil by the Blackwater River,
where they might grow. He would see. He had a silver pipe
cast for himself and, in his usual manner, made it into his
own personal symbol. When he lighted it, the ladies would
squeal and run away in pretended fright or annoyance; and
an old servant allegedly threw water on him when he saw
smoke pouring from his nostrils. But many others were
being soothed and then captivated by the Indian medicine
and soon they were willing to lay down an ounce of pure silver for a few dried leaves.

Three members of the expedition, it was said, had become
Americans: Lane, Hariot, and the artist, John White. But
even of those three only one, the artist, was willing to return.
In the other members of the expedition there had not yet
arisen that ambiguity of emotion that includes a willingness

to leave the English sky and taverns, the noise and bustle of the streets and ports, and live in the new land. It was still alien. Virginia was an inspired name for a beautiful land, but it awaited a people who would pay the price of exile for it.

Mastering his intense disappointment at the failure of his first great expedition, Ralegh began to lay plans for an entirely different kind of venture. He sent out a third colony, but shortly after it arrived in Virginia, the Spanish Armada sailed against England. The New World would now have to wait, while great matters were settled in the old.

Appendix of Documents

Document 1: A Private Letter to the Queen

Elizabeth saved several private letters from Robert Dudley, whom she had considered marrying. In August of 1563 Dudley traveled to Bagshot to meet his brother who had been wounded in France and whose troops were infected with the plague. In the letter Dudley explains his desire to avoid getting and passing the infection to his queen.

Lord Robert Dudley to Queen Elizabeth   7 August 1563
Bagshot

My most humble thanks, my most dear Lady, I must render as most bound for all, but in particular for this your gracious advertisement which I have received by your own handwriting . . . And yet ten hundred deaths would I more suffer rather than by my evil chance the fear of any such sickness should happen to that dear person. And albeit to my judgement all doubt had been past, for the later and more perilous passengers hath been lightlier by others accounted of repairing to your presence, notwithstanding the natural care and love toward my brother might well much sooner have provoked me to desire the sight of him, yet surely both care of your person for fear of such danger and the occasion thereby to be absent from it, which thereby must force me, had been enough the least of both to have made me fast from the dearest and best sight that this world could show me. Wherefore my own Lady pardon me, though otherwise it will be painful enough to be so long from you, that I should do anything that might seem to any others careless of so great care as I am bound to have more than any other in this case . . . So remaining your farther pleasure always, I humbly take leave. From Bagshot this Saturday.
    Most bounden for ever and ever,
    R.D.

Robert Dudley, letter to Queen Elizabeth, August 7, 1563. In *Rivals in Power, the Lives and Letters of the Great Tudor Dynasties*, ed. David Starkey. New York: Grove Weidenfeld, 1990.

Document 2: A Personal Letter from the Queen

While her favorite, Robert Dudley, earl of Leicester, was serving as governor-general in the Netherlands, Elizabeth drafted the letter which follows. The draft was found among her official papers on the English

campaign to aid the Dutch against the Spanish. It is the only personal let-
ter from the queen to Dudley which survives.

Elizabeth I to Earl of Leicester   19 July 1586

Rob: I am afraid you will suppose by my wandering writings that a
midsummer moon hath taken large possession of my brains this
month, but you must needs take things as they come in my head,
though order be left behind me . . . I have fraught this bearer full
of my conceits of those country matters and imparted what way I
mind to take and what is fit for you to use: I am sure you can credit
him and so I will be short with these few notes . . . If there be fault
in using soldiers or making of profit by them, let them hear of it
without open shame, and doubt not but I will well chasten them
therefor. It frets me not a little that the poor soldier that hourly
ventures life should want their due that well deserve rather reward
. . . And if the treasurer be found untrue or negligent, according to
desert he shall be used, though you know my old wont that love
not to discharge from office without desert, God forbid . . . Now
will I end that do imagine I talk still with you and therefore loathly
say farewell ô ô [i.e. 'Eyes'—his nickname] though ever I pray God
bless you from all harm and save you from all foes with my million
and legion of thanks for all your pains and cares.

As you know, ever the same, [Elizabeth's motto, *Semper Eadem*]
E.R.

Elizabeth I to Earl of Leicester, July 19, 1586, in *Rivals in Power, Lives and Letters of the Great
Tudor Dynasties*, ed. David Starkey. New York: Grove Weidenfeld, 1990.

Document 3: Marriage and the Succession

*When Elizabeth received a petition from Parliament urging her to
marry and declare a successor, she responded by asserting her authority as
both queen and prince. In the following excerpt from her 1566 response
to Parliament, Elizabeth acknowledges her femininity, but invokes the
traditional order of society: The monarch is the head of state who will not
be directed by the feet, the subjects.*

As for my own part, I care not for death; for all men are mortal. And
though I be a woman, yet I have as good a courage, answerable to
my place, as ever my father had. I am your anointed Queen. I will
never be by violence constrained to do anything. I thank God I am
endued with such qualities that if I were turned out of the realm in
my petticoat, I were able to live in any place in Christendom.

Your petition is to deal in the limitation of the succession. At
this present it is not convenient; . . . But as soon as there may be a

convenient time, and that it may be done with least peril unto you—although never without great danger unto me—I will deal therein for your safety, and offer it unto you as your Prince and head, without request; for it is monstrous that the feet should direct the head.

Quoted in J.E. Neale, *Elizabeth I and Her Parliaments, 1559–1581*. London: Jonathan Cape, 1957. Reprinted in Leah Marcus, "The Political Uses of Androgyny," *Women in the Middle Ages and the Renaissance*, ed. Mary Beth Rose. Syracuse: Syracuse University Press, 1986.

Document 4: The Problem of Mary, Queen of Scots

In 1567 Mary, Queen of Scots, was forced to abdicate her throne. Her husband, Lord Darnley, had killed her private secretary, David Riccio. Mary was perhaps responsible for arranging Lord Darnley's murder in revenge, and when she ran off with Darnley's murderer, James Hepburn, earl of Bothwell, she appalled her subjects and was forced to abdicate. Mary fled to England where the duke of Norfolk was rumored to be seeking her hand in marriage. In his 1569 letter to Elizabeth, Sir William Cecil, Elizabeth's principal secretary and chief of foreign affairs, explains the threat posed by Mary and the duke of Norfolk.

Sir William Cecil to Elizabeth I   16 October 1569

The Queen of Scots indeed is and shall always be a dangerous person to your estate. Yet there be degrees whereby the dangers may be more or less. If you would marry, it should be less; and whilst you do not, it will increase. If her person be restrained either here or at home in her own country, it will be less: if it be at liberty, it will be greater. If she be manifested to be unable by law to have any other husband than Bothwell whilst he liveth, the peril is the less: if she be esteemed free to marry, it is the greater. . . .

Now for the duke. Whilst he liveth unmarried the hope of matching will continue. And if he shall marry in any other place which of all other things in the end be necessary, all pernicious intents depending upon him shall cease. Again, if he be charged with the crime of treason and shall not be convicted, it shall not only serve, but increase his credit.

Sir William Cecil to Elizabeth, October 16, 1569. In *Rivals in Power, the Lives and Letters of the Great Tudor Dynasties*, ed. David Starkey. New York: Grove Weidenfeld, 1990.

Document 5: The Official Anglican Position on Predestination

In 1563 the Thirty-Nine Articles of the Church of England established the official Anglican position, and in 1571 the Articles were given statu-

tory authority. Predestination was one of the most controversial religious issues at the time. Radical Protestants, following John Calvin, argued that God had elected some for salvation and had reprobated others to damnation. Elizabeth was not a Calvinist, so Article Seventeen is phrased to suggest that Christ died for all men, and it allows the possibility that all men are eligible for salvation.

Article Seventeen: Of Predestination and Election

Predestination to life is the everlasting purpose of God, whereby (before the foundations of the world were laid) He hath constantly decreed, by His counsel secret to us, to deliver from curse and damnation those whom He hath chosen in Christ out of mankind, and to bring them by Christ to everlasting salvation, as vessels made to honor. Wherefore, they which be endued with so excellent a benefit of God be called according to God's purpose by His spirit working in due season; they through grace obey the calling; they be justified freely; they be made sons of God by adoption; they be made like the image of His only-begotten son Jesus Christ; they walk religiously in good works; and at length, by God's mercy, they attain to everlasting felicity.

As the godly consideration of predestination, and our election in Christ, is full of sweet, pleasant, and unspeakable comfort to godly persons and such as feel in themselves the working of the spirit of Christ, mortifying the works of the flesh and their earthly members and drawing up their mind to high and heavenly things, as well because it doth greatly establish and confirm their faith of eternal salvation to be enjoyed through Christ, as because it doth fervently kindle their love towards God: so, for curious and carnal persons, lacking the spirit of Christ, to have continually before their eyes the sentence of God's predestination, is a most dangerous downfall, whereby the Devil doth thrust them either into desperation, or into wretchlessness of most unclean living, no less perilous than desperation.

Furthermore, we must receive God's promises in such wise, as they be generally set forth to us in holy scripture; and, in our doings, that will of God is to be followed which we have expressly declared unto us in the word of God.

"Article Seventeen: Of Predestination and Election" in *Shakespeare's World, Background Readings in the English Renaissance*, eds. Gerald M. Pinciss and Roger Lockyer. New York: Continuum, 1989.

Document 6: The Homily Against Disobedience

The 1571 homily "Against Disobedience and Wilful Rebellion" was one of the most frequently reprinted documents during Elizabeth's reign. It

*restates familiar positions from sermons gathered and printed in 1547
and 1562, but it was a direct response to the rebellion of the Northern
Earls in 1569. The homily clarifies the importance of order and the horrors that follow rebellion.*

Against Disobedience and Wilful Rebellion

The First Part

As God the creator and lord of all things appointed His angels
and heavenly creatures in all obedience to serve and to honor His
majesty, so was it His will that man, His chief creature upon the
earth, should live under the obedience of His creator and lord. . . .
And as God would have man to be His obedient subject, so did He
make all earthly creatures subject unto man, who kept their due
obedience unto man so long as man remained in his obedience
unto God, in the which obedience if man had continued still, there
had been no poverty, no diseases, no sickness, no death nor other
miseries wherewith mankind is now infinitely and most miserably
afflicted and oppressed. . . . The first author of rebellion, the root
of all vices and mother of all mischiefs, was Lucifer. . . . Thus you
do see that neither heaven nor paradise could suffer any rebellion
in them, neither be places for any rebels to remain in. . . .

After this breach of obedience to God and rebellion against His
majesty . . . God forthwith, by laws given unto mankind, repaired
again the rule and order of obedience thus by rebellion over-
thrown; and, besides the obedience due unto His majesty, He not
only ordained that in families and households the wife should be
obedient unto her husband, the children unto their parents, the
servants unto their masters, but also, when mankind increased and
spread itself more largely over the world, He by His holy word did
constitute and ordain in cities and countries several and special
governors and rulers unto whom the residue of His people should
be obedient. . . .

What shall subjects do then? Shall they obey valiant, stout, wise,
and good princes, and condemn, disobey, and rebel against children
being their princes, or against indiscreet and evil governors? God
forbid. For first, what a perilous thing were it to commit unto subjects the judgment which prince is wise and godly and his government good, and which is otherwise—as though the foot must judge
of the head, an enterprise very heinous and must needs breed rebellion. For who else be they that are most inclined to rebellion but
such haughty spirits? From whom springeth such foul ruin of
realms? Is not rebellion the greatest of all mischiefs? And who are

most ready to the greatest mischiefs but the worst men? Rebels, therefore, the worst of all subjects, are most ready to rebellion as being the worst of all vices and furthest from the duty of a good subject; as, on the contrary part, the best subjects are most firm and constant in obedience, as in the special and peculiar virtue of good subjects. What an unworthy matter were it then to make the naughtiest subjects, and most inclined to rebellion and all evil, judges over their princes, over their government, and over their counsellors. . . .

. . . If we will have an evil prince (when God shall send such a one) taken away, and a good in his place, let us take away our wickedness, which provoketh God to place such a one over us, and God will either displace him, or of an evil prince make him a good prince, so that we first will change our evil into good. . . .

"Against Disobedience and Wilful Rebellion, the First Part" (1571) in *Shakespeare's World, Background Readings in the English Renaissance*, eds. Gerald M. Pinciss and Roger Lockyer. New York: Continuum, 1989.

Document 7: The Structure of Elizabethan Society

Sir Thomas Smith was professor of civil law at Cambridge University at the close of King Henry VIII's reign, secretary of state during King Edward VI's reign, and both a member of the House of Commons and later secretary of state during Elizabeth's reign. His De Republica Anglorum (The Commonwealth of England), *an account of the English constitution, was printed in 1583. In it Smith explains the distinctions in classes during Elizabeth's reign by focusing on wealth, birth, and education.*

OF THE FIRST PART OF GENTLEMEN OF ENGLAND, CALLED "NOBILITAS MAJOR"

. . . In England no man is created a baron, except he may dispend of yearly revenue one thousand pounds, or one thousand marks at the least. . . .

OF THE SECOND SORT OF GENTLEMEN, WHICH MAY BE CALLED *Nobilitas Minor,* AND FIRST OF KNIGHTS

No man is a knight by succession, not the king or prince . . . knights therefore be not born but made. . . . In England whosoever may dispend of his free lands forty pounds sterling of yearly revenue . . . may be by the king compelled to take that order and honor, or to pay a fine. . . .

OF ESQUIRES

Esquires (which we commonly call squires) be all those which bear arms (as we call them) or armories . . . these be taken for no distinct order of the commonwealth, but do go with the residue of the gentlemen. . . .

OF GENTLEMEN

Gentlemen be those whom their blood and race doth make noble and known. . . . Ordinarily the king doth only make knights and create barons or higher degrees, for as for gentlemen they be made good cheap in England. For whosoever studieth the laws of the realm, who studieth in the universities, who professeth liberal sciences, and to be short, who can live idly and without manual labor, and will bear the port, charge, and countenance of a gentleman, he shall be called master, . . . and shall be taken for a gentleman. . . .

OF YEOMEN

Those whom we call yeomen, next unto the nobility, knights, and squires, have the greatest charge and doings in the commonwealth . . . I call him a yeoman whom our laws do call *legalem hominem* . . . which is a freeman born English, and may dispend of his own free land in yearly revenue to the sum of 40s. sterling . . . This sort of people confess themselves to be no gentlemen . . . and yet they have a certain preeminence and more estimation than laborers and artificers, and commonly live wealthily. . . . These be (for the most part) farmers unto gentlemen, . . . and by these means do come to such wealth, that they are able and daily do buy the lands of unthrifty gentlemen, and after setting their sons to the school at the universities, to the laws of the realm, or otherwise leaving them sufficient lands whereon they may live without labor, do make their said sons by those means gentlemen. . . .

OF THE FOURTH SORT OF MEN WHICH DO NOT RULE

The fourth sort or class amongst us, is of those which the old Romans called *capite censi* . . . day laborers, poor husbandmen, yea merchants or retailers which have no free land, copyholders and all artificers. . . . These have no voice nor authority in our commonwealth, and no account is made of them, but only to be ruled.

Sir Thomas Smith, "The Structure of Society," in *In Shakespeare's Day*, ed. J.V. Cunningham. Greenwich, CT: Fawcett Publications, 1970.

Document 8: Contemporary Comments on Elizabethan Fashions

In his 1587 book The Description of England, *William Harrison castigates "the fantastical folly of our nation" when it comes to dress, beards, and hair styles.*

The fantastical folly of our nation, even from the courtier to the carter, is such that no form of apparel liketh [pleases] us longer than the first garment is in the wearing. . . . And as these fashions are diverse, so likewise it is a world to see the costliness and the curiosity, the excess and the vanity, the pomp and the bravery [splendor], the change and the variety, and finally the fickleness and the folly, that is in all degrees, insomuch that nothing is more constant in England than inconstancy of attire. Oh, how much cost is bestowed nowadays upon our bodies, and how little upon our souls! How many suits of apparel hath the one, and how little furniture hath the other! How long time is asked in decking up of the first, and how little space left wherein to feed the latter! How curious [hard to satisfy], how nice [fastidious] also, are a number of men and women, and how hardly can the tailor please them in making it fit for their bodies! How many times must it be sent back again to him that made it! What chafing, what fretting, what reproachful language doth the poor workman bear away! And many times when he doth nothing to it at all, yet when it is brought home again, it is very fit and handsome; then must we put it on, then must the long seams of our hose be set by a plumb-line, then we puff, then we blow, and finally, sweat till we drop, that our clothes may stand well upon us.

I will say nothing of our heads, which sometimes are polled [cut short], sometimes curled, or suffered to grow at length like woman's locks, many times cut off above or under the ears round, as by [using] a wooden dish. Neither will I meddle with our variety of beards, of which some are shaven from the chin like those of Turks, not a few cut short like to the beard of Marquis Otto, some made round like a rubbing brush, other with a *pique de vant* [a short, pointed Vandyke beard] (oh, fine fashion!) or now and then suffered to grow long, the barbers being grown to be so cunning in this behalf as the tailors. And therefore, if a man have a lean and straight face, a Marquis Otto's cut will make it broad and large; if it be platterlike, a long slender beard will make it seem the narrower; if he be weasel-beaked, then much hair left on the cheeks will make the owner look big, like a bowdled [ruffled] hen, and so grim as a goose. . . . Many old men do wear no beards at all. Some lusty courtiers also and gentlemen of courage do wear either rings of gold, stones, or pearl in their ears, whereby they imagine the workmanship of God not to be a little amended. But herein they rather disgrace than adorn their persons, as by their niceness [luxuriousness] in apparel, for which I say most nations do not unjustly deride us, as also for that we do seem to imitate all nations round about us, wherein we be like to the *polypus* [octopus] or chameleon; and thereunto bestow most cost upon our asses, and much more than upon all the rest of our bodies, as women do likewise upon their heads and shoulders.

In women also it is most to be lamented that they do now far exceed the lightness [lasciviousness] of our men (who nevertheless are transformed from the cap even to the very shoe), and such staring attire as in time past was supposed meet for none but light hussies only, is now become an habit for chaste and sober matrons. What should I say of their doublets with pendant codpieces on the breast, full of jags and cuts, and sleeves of sundry colors? their galligaskins [loose breeches] to bear out their bums and make their attire to fit plum round (as they term it) about them? their farthingales and diversely colored nether stocks of silk, jersey, and such like, whereby their bodies are rather deformed than commended? I have met with some of these trulls [loose women] in London so disguised, that it hath passed my skill to discern whether they were men or women.

Thus it is now come to pass that women are become men and men transformed into monsters.

William Harrison, "From *The Description of England*" in *The Bedford Companion to Shakespeare, an Introduction with Documents*, ed. Russ McDonald. Boston and New York: Bedford Books of St. Martin's Press, 1996.

Document 9: Elizabeth's Commitment to the Rule of Law

Lawyer, parliamentarian, and judge, Sir Edward Coke believed that England's strength lay in its tradition of common law. In the following excerpt from the preface to Book I of his Reports, *Coke praises Elizabeth for her commitment to the rule of law.*

There is no jewel in the world comparable to learning; no learning so excellent both for Prince and subject as knowledge of laws; and no knowledge of any laws (I speak of human) so necessary for all estates and for all causes concerning goods, lands, or life as the common laws of England. If the beauty of other countries be faded and wasted with bloody wars, thank God for the admirable peace wherein this realm hath long flourished under the due administration of these laws. If thou readest of the tyranny of other nations, wherein powerful Will and Pleasure stands for Law and Reason, and where, upon conceit of mislike, men are suddenly poisoned or otherwise murdered and never called to answer, praise God for the justice of thy gracious sovereign, who (to the world's admiration) governeth her people by God's goodness in peace and prosperity by these laws, and punisheth not the greatest offender—no, though his offense be *Crimen Laesae Majestatis*, Treason against her Sacred Person—but by the just and equal proceedings of Law.

If in other kingdoms the Laws only seem to govern, but the judges had rather misconstrue Law, and do injustice, than displease the king's humor . . . bless God for Queen Elizabeth, whose continual charge to her justice, agreeable with her ancient laws, is that for no commitment under the great or privy seal, writs or letters,[1] common right be disturbed or delayed. And if any such commitment (upon untrue surmises) should come, that the justices of her laws should not therefore cease to do right in any point. And this agreeth with the ancient law of England, declared by the Great Charter and spoken in the person of the king: *Nulli vendemus, nulli negabimus aut differemus justitiam, vel Rectum.*[2]

1. Writs and letters authenticated by the great seal or the privy seal were used by the government to enforce its commands.
2. This is clause 40 of Magna Carta: "To no-one will we sell, to no-one will we deny or delay, justice or right."

Sir Edward Coke, *Reports*, vol. 1 (1600) in *Shakespeare's World, Background Readings in the English Renaissance*, eds. Gerald M. Pinciss and Roger Lockyer. New York: Continuum, 1989.

Document 10: The Rebels in Ireland

In response to the second Irish uprising (1598) led by Hugh O'Neill, earl of Tyrone, Elizabeth announced in this 1599 proclamation that she would send a sizable army, led by Robert Devereux, earl of Essex, to Ireland. In this excerpt, Elizabeth clarifies her policy toward and expectations of the Irish, her disappointment with the rebels' actions, and her determination to separate the leaders from those whom they have misled.

ALTHOUGH OUR ACTIONS and carriage in the whole course of our government, ever since it pleased God to call us to the succession of this Crowne (being truely considered) may as evidently manifest to all our Subjects, as our conscience doeth clearely witnesse it to ourselfe, how earnestly we have affected the peace and tranquilitie of the people of our Dominions, and how much we have preferred clemencie before any other respect, as a vertue both agreeable to our naturall disposition, the sinceritie of the Religion which we professe, and alwayes esteemed by us the greatest surety to our Royall State, when our Subjects' heartes are assured to us by the bond of love, rather then by forced obedience; Notwithstanding it hath fallen out to our great discontentation, that this our gracious intention in the whole scope of our government, hath not wrought in all men's mindes a like effect, nor brought forth every-where that fruit of obedience which we expected, and namely in our kingdome and people of Ireland, where (as oftentimes hereto-fore, so nowe especially of late yeeres) divers of our Subjects, both of the better sort and of the meaner (abusing our lenitie to their ad-vantage) have unnaturally and without all ground or cause offered by us, forgotten their allegeance, and (rebelliously taking Armes) have committed many bloody and violent outrages upon our loyall Subjects. And though their owne consciences can beare them wit-nesse that both by us, and by our ministers there, more wayes have bene attempted to reclaime them by clemencie (for avoyding of bloodshed) then is usuall with Princes that have so good meanes to reduce them by other meanes, yet have we not thereof reaped those fruites which so great a grace hath deserved, if there had bene in them any sense of Religion, duetie, or common humanitie. This is therefore the cause that after so long patience wee have bene com-pelled to take resolution, to reduce that Kingdome to obedience (which by the Lawes of God and Nature is due unto us) by using an extraordinary power and force against them; Assuring ourselves so much in the justice of our cause, as we shall finde the same suc-cess (whichever it is the pleasure of God to give to Prince's rights) against unnaturall rebellions: wherein notwithstanding because we doe conceive that all our people which are at this present Actors in this Rebellion are not of one kinde, nor carried into it with one minde, but some out of sense they have of hard measures hereto-fore offered them by some of our ministers, some for feare of power and might which their adversse Sects and Factions have growne unto, by advantage of this loose time, and some for want of protection and defence against the wicked and barbarous Rebels, and many inveygled with superstitious impressions, wrought in them by the cunning of seditious Priestes and Seminaries (crept into them from forreine parts, suborned by those that are our ene-mies) and a great part out of a strong opinion put into them by the heades of this Rebellion, that we intended an utter extirpation and rooting out of that Nation, and conquest of the Countrey.

We have therefore thought it good and answerable to that Jus-tice and clemencie which we professe to be with us in accompt, above all other Royall vertues, to accompanie our Armie, which we send thither with this signification to our Subjects, that we are not ignorant of the divers causes that have misse-led them into these unnaturall actions, and that we both can and will make distinction of their offences.

Queen Elizabeth, "The Queene's Majestie's Proclamation declaring her princely resolution in sending over of her Army into the Realme of Ireland" in *Elizabethan Backgrounds, Historical Documents of the Age of Elizabeth I*, ed. Arthur F. Kinney. Hamden, CT: Archon Books, 1990.

Document 11: The Trial of Robert Devereux, Earl of Essex

Following his failure to defeat Hugh O'Neill in Ireland and his formation of a truce with the Irish rebel, Robert Devereux, earl of Essex returned to London, where he was rebuked by the queen and placed under house arrest. Angry and perhaps unstable, he staged an unsuccessful rebellion against the queen in 1601. The following excerpt from his trial for treason clarifies the charges against him and records his response.

Then Sergeant Yelverton opened the evidence . . . and said as followeth: "May it please your grace" (speaking to the High Steward), "about the 8th of February last, my lord of Essex (there prisoner at the bar) went about with armed men very rebelliously to disinherit the Queen of her crown and dignity; which when it came to Her Majesty's ear, she, of her abounding mercy, sent to see if it were possible to stop rebellion. And who did she send? She sent (my lord) no worse persons than my Lord Keeper, my Lord Chief Justice of England, the Earl of Worcester, and Sir William Knollys, all which went in Her Majesty's name and commanded the earls and their adherents very strictly to dissolve their assemblies and to lay down their arms. But he knowing it, very treacherously imprisoned the said lords and Councillors by Her Majesty so sent, and altogether refused Her Majesty's authority. And divers of their confederates cried out, 'Kill them! Kill them!,' thereby putting Her Majesty's Council in fear of their lives. . . .

"Good my lord, I beseech your grace, and you my lords that are the peers, to understand that if any man do but intend the death of the king, it is death by the law; for he is the head of the commonwealth, and all his subjects, as members, ought to obey and stand with him. But as for this rebellion, being duly considered it contains in it many branches of treason, which are and will be directly proved; which being found to be so, my lords who are their peers are to find them guilty. Hereof need to be made no doubt, for it is more manifest than the sedition of Catiline to the city of Rome, and consequently England is in no less danger; for as Catiline entertained the most seditious persons about all Rome to join with him in his conspiracy, so the Earl of Essex had none but papists, recusants, and atheists for his adjutors and abettors in their capital rebellion against the whole estate of England.

"My lord, I much wonder that his heart could forget all the

princely advancements given him by Her Majesty, and be so suddenly beflinted as to turn them all to rebellious ends. But it seems this overweighing a man's conceit, and an aspiring mind to wished honor, is like the crocodile, which is ever growing as long as he liveth. Your lordships know in what sort they went into the City, with armor and weapons, and how they returned to Essex House again . . . which makes me wonder they do not blush to be so forward to stand upon their trials without confession, when their intended treasons are in all men's judgments palpable. . . . My hope is that God, of His mercy, that hath revealed their treasons, will not suffer the rest of his or any others to the hurt of the state or prejudice to Her Majesty's most royal person, whom I pray God long to preserve from the hands of her enemies.". . .

Then the Clerk of the Crown, speaking first to the Earl of Essex, said "Robert, Earl of Essex, you have been arraigned and indicted of high treason. . . . The peers here, who have heard the evidence and your answer in your defense, have found you Guilty. Now what can you say for yourself why you should not have judgment of death?"

ESSEX: "I only say this. That since I have committed that which hath brought me within the compass of the law, I may be counted the law's traitor in offending the law, for which I am willing to die, and will as willingly go thereto as ever did any. But I beseech your lordship and the rest of the lords here to have consideration of what I have formerly spoken, and do me the right as to think me a Christian, and that I have a soul to save, and that I know it is no time to jest. Lying and counterfeiting my soul abhorreth, for I am not desperate nor void of grace now to speak falsely. I do not speak to save my life, for that I see were vain. I owe God a death, which shall be welcome, how soon soever it pleaseth Her Majesty. And to satisfy the opinion of the world that my conscience is free from atheism and popery, howsoever I have been in this action misled to transgress the points of the law in the course and defense of private matters . . . yet I will live and die in the faith and true religion which here I have professed."

"The Trial of Robert, Earl of Essex, and Henry, Earl of Southampton, before the Lords at Westminster, for High Treason: 43 Eliz. Feb. 19, A.D. 1601" in *Shakespeare's World, Background Readings in the English Renaissance*, eds. Gerald M. Pinciss and Roger Lockyer. New York: Continuum, 1989.

Document 12: Strained Relations with Spain

In 1568 Elizabeth issued an official proclamation explaining her seizure of a Spanish ship that was carrying newly minted money from Philip II of Spain to the duke of Alba's army in the Netherlands. Although the Spanish considered the action piracy, Elizabeth couched the decision in terms which reveal Spanish malice and English goodwill.

The Spanishe ambassadour came to her majestie about the xxix. of December, bryngyng with hym from the Duke of Alva a short letter, only of credence, and therupon required, that the vessels and money stayed in the portes might be put to libertie, as belonging to the kyng his maister. To whom her majestie aunswered, that she had in her doynges (if it were the kynge's) shewed hym great pleasure to save it from the Frenche, shewing hym therin some particularities of the diligence of her officers, but she was infourmed that it belonged to marchauntes, and herein within foure or five dayes she shoulde understande/more therof, and assured hym on her honor, that nothyng shoulde be herein done, that in reason shoulde miscontent the kyng her good brother, as he shoulde also knowe within foure or five dayes at his next commyng. And so he departed, not seemyng but to alowe of the aunswere. And her majestie in the meanetyme havyng accordyng to her expectation aunswere from the west countrey, whereupon she intended to have satisfied the ambassadour at his commyng (which she loked for accordyng to her appoyntment) not only for the delivery of the sayde shippes and treasure, for such portion as myght appeare to belong to the sayde kyng: but also to have perfourmed her first offer to have geven conduct for the same by lande or by sea. The first intelligence brought to her majestie (without any returne of the ambassadour) was, that all her subjectes, goodes, marchaundizes, and shippes, were arrested, taken, and kept at Andwerpe as prysoners, the very same present xxix. day that the ambassadour was with her meajestie, so as it falleth out to every man's understandyng, that howsoever her majestie had then satisfied the ambassadour the same xxix. day, all her subjectes and their goodes had ben neverthelesse arrested, as they were at Andwerpe the same day. Whereupon her majestie nowe leaveth it to the judgement of all the worlde, to consider not only whether such a pretence was sufficient to cause so sodaine, so violent, and so generall arrest to be made with force, in such maner, and at the tyme it was: but also in whom any default shalbe founde, whatsoever may folowe hereof, her majestie havyng had no intention to miscontent the kyng of Spayne, nor to possesse anythyng belongyng to his subjectes, otherwise then with their good wyll, upon juste, reasonable, and usuall conditions. And thus muche her majestic hath thought convenient to notifie to all persons, for testimonie of her sinceritie, and for maintenaunce of her actions, whatsoever they shalbe, wherunto she may by this meanes be provoked.

"Proclamation against the Traffic in Spanish Countries (1568)," in *Elizabethan Backgrounds, Historical Documents of the Age of Elizabeth I*, ed. Arthur F. Kinney. Hamden, CT: Archon Books, 1990.

Document 13: The Defeat of the Spanish Armada

Richard Hakluyt translated the Dutch Emanuel van Meteren's report on the defeat of the Spanish Armada in 1598 and included it in the third edition of his The Principal Navigations, Voyages, Traffiques and discoveries of the English Nation. *This excerpt focuses on the events of July 29, 1588.*

Upon the 29 of July in the morning, the Spanish Fleet after the foresayd tumult, having arranged themselves againe into order, were, within sight of *Greveling*, most bravely and furiously encountered by the English; where they once againe got the winde of the Spaniards: who suffered themselves to be deprived of the commodity of the place in *Caleis* rode, and of the advantage of the winde neere unto *Dunkerk*, rather then they would change their array or separate their forces now conjoyned and united together, standing onely upon their defence.

And albeit there were many excellent and warlike ships in the English fleet, yet scarse were there 22 or 23 among them all which matched 90 of the Spanish ships in bignesse, or could conveniently assault them. Wherefore the English shippes using their prerogative of nimble stirrage, whereby they could turne and wield themselves with the winde which way they listed, came oftentimes very neere upon the Spaniards, and charged them so sore, that now and then they were but a pike's length asunder: and so continually giving them one broadside after another, they discharged all their shot both great and small upon them, spending one whole day from morning till night in that violent kinde of conflict, untill such time as powder and bullets failed them. In regard of which want they thought it convenient not to pursue the Spaniards any longer, because they had many great vantages of the English, namely for the extraordinary bignesse of their ships, and also for that they were so neerely conjoyned, and kept together in so good array, that they could by no meanes be fought withall one to one. The English thought therefore, that they had right well acquited themselves, in chasing the Spaniards first from *Caleis*, and then from *Dunkerk*, and by that meanes to have hindered them from joyning with the Duke of *Parma* his forces, and getting the winde of them, to have driven them from their owne coasts.

The Spaniards that day sustained great losse and damage having many of their shippes shot thorow and thorow, and they discharged likewise great store of ordinance against the English; who indeed sustained some hinderance, but not comparable to the Spaniards' losse: for they lost not any one shippe or person of account. For very diligent inquisition being made, the Englishmen all that time wherein the Spanish Navy sayled upon their seas, are not found to have wanted above one hundreth of their people: albeit Sir *Francis Drake's* shippe was pierced with shot above forty times, and his very cabben was twise shot thorow, and about the conclusion of the fight, the bedde of a certaine gentleman lying weary thereupon, was taken quite from under him with the force of a bullet. Likewise, as the Earle of *Northumberland* and Sir *Charles Blunt* were at dinner upon a time, the bullet of a demi-culvering brake thorow the middest of their cabbin, touched their feet, and strooke downe two of the standers-by, with many such accidents befalling the English shippes, which it were tedious to rehearse. Whereupon it is most apparant, that God miraculously preserved the English nation. For the Lord Admirall wrote unto her Majestie that in all humane reason, and according to the judgement of all men (every circumstance being duly considered) the Englishmen were not of any such force, whereby they might, without a miracle, dare once to approch within sight of the Spanish Fleet: insomuch that they freely ascribed all the honour of their victory unto God, who had confounded the enemy, and had brought his counsels to none effect.

The same day the Spanish ships were so battered with English shot, that that very night and the day following, two or three of them suncke right downe: and among the rest a certaine great ship of *Biscay*, which Captaine *Crosse* assaulted, which perished even in the time of the conflict, so that very few therein escaped drowning; who reported that the governours of the same shippe slew one another upon the occasion following: one of them which would have yeelded the shippe was suddenly slaine; the brother of the slaine party in revenge of his death slew the murtherer, and in the meanewhile the ship suncke.

Emanuel van Meteren, "The miraculous victory achieved by the English Fleete," trans. Richard Hakluyt in *Elizabethan Backgrounds, Historical Documents of the Age of Elizabeth I*, ed. Arthur F. Kinney. Hamden, CT: Archon Books, 1990.

Document 14: The Players' Relationship to Their Patron

Professional entertainers, including acrobats, jugglers, circus performers, and actors, could be arrested as vagabonds if they were not formally protected by a patron. In the 1572 letter that follows, six actors request that Robert Dudley, earl of Leicester, name them legal retainers or household servants to protect them from arrest.

THE PLAYERS' RELATIONSHIP TO THEIR PATRON

To the Right Honorable Earl of Leicester, their good lord and master. May it please Your Honor to understand that forasmuch as there is a certain proclamation out for reviving of a statute as touching retainers, as Your Lordship knoweth better than we can inform you thereof, we therefore, your humble servants and daily orators, your players, for avoiding all inconvenients that may grow by reason of the said statute, are bold to trouble Your Lordship with this our suit, humbly desiring Your Honor that (as you have been always our good lord and master) you will now vouchsafe to retain us at this present as your household servants and daily waiters, not that we mean to crave any further stipend or benefit at Your Lordship's hands but our liveries as we have had and also Your Honor's license to certify that we are your household servants when we shall have occasion to travel amongst our friends, as we do usually once a year and as other noblemen's players do and have done in time past, whereby we may enjoy our faculty in Your Lordship's name as we have done heretofore. Thus being bound and ready to be always at Your Lordship's commandment, we commit Your Honor to the tuition of the Almighty.

Long may your Lordship live in peace,
 A peer of noblest peers,
In health, wealth and prosperity
 Redoubling Nestor's years.

Your Lordship's servants most bounden,
James Burbage
John Perkin
John Laneham
William Johnson
Robert Wilson
Thomas Clarke

—Leicester's Men (1572).

"The Players' Relationship to Their Patron" in *Shakespeare's Day*, ed. J.V. Cunningham. Greenwich, CT: Fawcett Publications, 1970.

Document 15: Puritan Attack on the Theater

Philip Stubbes was one of the most vocal of the Puritan social and religious critics. In this excerpt from The Anatomy of Abuses *(1583), Stubbs attacks the public theaters as the seats of immorality. He accuses the actors of sexual and social crimes, and he argues that plays teach and promote all manner of immoral behavior.*

Do they not maintain bawdry, insinuate foolery, and renew and remembrance of heathen idolatry? Do they not induce whoredom and uncleanness and nay, are they not rather plain devourers of maidenly virginity and chastity? For proof whereof, but mark the flocking and running to theaters and curtains, daily and hourly, night and day, time and tide, to see plays and interludes, where such wanton gestures, such bawdy speeches, such laughing and fleering [ridiculing], such kissing and bussing, such clipping and culling, such winking and glancing of wanton eyes and the like is used, as is wonderful to behold. Then the godly pageants being done, every mate sorts to his mate, every one brings another homeward of their way very friendly, and in their secret conclaves (covertly) they play the Sodomites, or worse. And these be the fruits of plays and interludes, for the most part. And whereas, you say, there are good examples to be learned in them.

Truly, so there are. If you will learn falsehood, if you will learn cozenage; if you will learn to play the hypocrite; to cog, lie, and falsify, if you will learn to jest, laugh, and fleer, to grin, to nod, and mow [jest]; if you will learn to play the vice, to swear, tear, and blaspheme both heaven and earth. If you will learn to become a bawd, unclean, and to devirginate maids, to deflower honest wives; if you will learn to murder, slay, kill, pick, steal, rob, and rove; if you will learn to rebel against princes, to commit treasons, to consume treasures, to practice idleness, to sing and talk of bawdy love and venery; if you will learn to deride, scoff, mock, and flout, to flatter and smooth; if you will learn to play the whoremaster, the glutton, drunkard, or incestuous person; if you will learn to become proud, haughty, and arrogant; and finally, if you will learn to condemn God and all his laws, to care neither for heaven nor hell, and to commit all kind of sin and mischief, you need to go to no other school, for all these good examples may you see painted before your eyes in interludes and plays. . . .

Therefore I beseech all players and founders of plays and interludes, in the bowels of Jesus Christ, as they tender the salvation of their souls, and others, to leave off that cursed kind of life and give themselves to such honest exercises and godly mysteries as God hath commanded them, in his word to get their livings withal. For who will call him a wise man that playeth the part of a fool and a vice? Who can call him a Christian who playeth the part of a devil, the sworn enemy of Christ? Who can call him a just man that playeth the part of a dissembling hypocrite? And to be brief, who can call him a straight-dealing man, who playeth a cozener's trick? And so of all the rest. Away therefore with this so infamous an art, for go they never so brave [no matter how splendid they appear], yet are they counted and taken but for beggars. And is it not true? Live they not upon beggings of every one that comes? Are they not taken by the laws of the realm for rogues and vagabonds? I speak of such as travel the countries with plays and interludes, making an occupation of it, and ought to be punished, if they had their deserts.

Philip Stubbes, *The Anatomy of Abuses*, in *The Bedford Companion to Shakespeare, An Introduction with Documents*, ed. Russ McDonald. Boston and New York: Bedford Books of St. Martin's Press, 1996.

Document 16: The Virtues of the Theater

In 1592 playwright Thomas Nashe responded to attacks on the immorality of the theater by arguing for its positive benefits: cleansing the language, celebrating virtue and punishing vice, and coaxing audience members away from worse vices like gaming, drinking, and visiting prostitutes.

To them that demand what fruits the poets of our time bring forth, or wherein they are able to prove themselves necessary to the state, thus I answer: first and foremost, they have cleansed our language from barbarism and made the vulgar sort here in London (which is the fountain whose rivers flow round about England) to aspire to a richer purity of speech than is communicated with the commonality of any nation under heaven. The virtuous by their praises they encourage to be more virtuous; to vicious men they are as infernal hags to haunt their ghosts with eternal infamy after death. The soldier, in hope to have his high deeds celebrated by their pens, despiseth a whole army of perils, and acteth wonders exceeding all human conjecture. Those that care neither for God nor the devil, by their quills are kept in awe.

That state of kingdom that is in league with all the world, and hath no foreign sword to vex it, is not half so strong or confirmed to endure as that which lives every hour in fear of invasion. There is a certain waste of the people for whom there is no use but war; and these men must have some employment still to cut them off;

Nam si foras hostem non habent, domi invenient. If they have no service abroad, they will make mutinies at home. Or if the affairs of the state be such as cannot exhale all these corrupt excrements, it is very expedient they have some light toys to busy their heads withal, cast before them as bones to gnaw upon, which may keep them from having leisure to intermeddle with higher matters.

To this effect, the policy of plays is very necessary, howsoever some shallow-brained censurers (not the deepest searches into the secrets of government) mightily oppugn them. For whereas the afternoon being idlest time of the day, wherein men that are their own masters (as gentlemen of the court, the Inns of the Court, and the number of captains and soldiers about London) do wholly bestow themselves upon pleasure, and that pleasure they divide (how virtuously, it skills not) either into gaming, following of harlots, drinking, or seeing a play; is it not then better (since of four extremes all the world cannot keep them but they will choose one) that they should betake them to the least, which is plays?

In plays, all cozenages, all cunning drifts overgilded with outward holiness, all strategems of war, all the cankerworms that breed on the rust of peace, are most lively anatomized; they show the ill success of treason, the fall of hasty climbers, the wretched end of usurpers, the misery of civil dissension, and how just God is evermore in punishing of murder. And to prove every one of these allegations could I propound the circumstances of this play and that play, if I meant to handle this theme otherwise than *obiter.*

Thomas Nashe, *Peirce Penniless* (1592) in *In Shakespeare's Day*, ed. J.V. Cunningham. Greenwich, CT: Fawcett Publications, 1970.

Document 17: Sir Philip Sidney's Poem of Praise

Sidney addressed only one poem specifically to Queen Elizabeth. "Most Gracious Sovereign" was presented to the queen in May of 1578 by one of the actors performing in Sidney's early play, The Lady of May. *The play was offered to flatter and entertain the queen, and the poem both flatters the queen and expresses Sidney's desire for recognition.*

Most Gracious Sovereign

To one whose state is raised over all,
Whose face doth oft the bravest sort enchant,
Whose mind is such, as wisest minds appall,*
Who in one self these diverse gifts can plant;
  How dare I (wretch) seek there my woes to rest,

*make pale by comparison

Where ears be burnt, eyes dazzled, heart oppres'd?

Your state is great, your greatness is your shield,
Your face hurts oft, but still it doth delight,
Your mind is wise, your wisdom makes you mild;
Such planted gifts enrich ev'n beggars' sight.
So dare I (wretch) my bashful fear subdue,
And feed mine eyes, mine ears, my heart on you.

"Most Gracious Sovereign" in *Sir Philip Sidney, Selected Prose and Poetry*, ed. Robert Kimbrough. New York: Holt, Rinehart and Winston, 1969.

Document 18: Spenser's *The Faerie Queene*

Sir Edmund Spenser dedicated his epic poem, The Faerie Queene, *to Queen Elizabeth. In the first four stanzas of Book I, Canto I, Spenser invokes the muse of heroic poetry, asks aid from Cupid and Mars, and in stanza 4 deifies Elizabeth as a "goddesse heavenly bright," "mirrour of grace," and sun-like focus of life-giving inspiration.*

The First Booke of The
Faerie Queene

    Contayning, the Legende of the Knight of the Red Crosse, or
    Of Holinesse

1 Lo I the man, whose Muse whilome> did maske,   *formerly*
    As time her taught, in lowly Shepheards weeds,>   *clothes*
    Am now enforst a far unfitter taske,
    For trumpets sterne to chaunge mine Oaten reeds,°
    And sing of Knights and Ladies gentle> deeds;   *noble*
    Whose prayses having slept in silence long,°
    Me, all too meane, the sacred Muse areeds>   *counsels*
    To blazon broad emongst her learned throng:
Fierce warres and faithfull loves shall moralize my song.

2 Helpe then, O holy Virgin chiefe of nine,°
    Thy weaker> Novice to performe thy will,   *too weak*
    Lay forth out of thine everlasting scryne>   *record chest*
    The antique rolles, which there lye hidden still,
    Of Faerie knights and fairest *Tanaquill,*>   *Gloriana*
    Whom that most noble Briton Prince° so long
    Sought through the world, and suffered so much ill,

That I must rue his undeserved wrong:
O helpe thou my weake wit, and sharpen my dull tong.

3 And thou most dreaded impe° of highest *Jove*,   *child*
   Faire *Venus* sonne,° that with thy cruell dart
   At that good knight so cunningly didst rove,°   *shoot*
   That glorious fire it kindled in his hart,
   Lay now thy deadly Heben° bow apart,   *ebony*
   And with thy mother milde, come to mine ayde:
   Come both, and with you bring triumphant *Mart*,°
   In loves and gentle jollities arrayd,
   After his murdrous spoiles and bloudy rage allayd.°   *calmed*

4 And with them eke,° O Goddesse heavenly bright,°   *also*
   Mirrour of grace and Majestie divine,
   Great Lady of the greatest Isle, whose light
   Like *Phœbus* lampe° throughout the world doth shine,
   Shed thy faire beames into my feeble eyne°,   *eyes*
   And raise my thoughts too humble and too vile,
   To thinke of that true glorious type° of thine,
   The argument of mine afflicted stile:
   The which to heare, vouchsafe, O dearest dred° a-while.

For trumpets . . . reeds He changes from the shepherd's pipe of pastoral to the trumpets of heroic poetry. This first stanza imitates the poem to Virgil's *Aeneid*. On Virgil's model it became prescriptive for an epic poet to prepare himself with pastoral.
And sing . . . long imitating the opening of Ariosto's *Orlando Furioso*
O holy . . . nine Calliope, chief of the Muses, presided over eloquence and heroic poetry; represented in art with a trumpet in the right hand, a book in the left.
most . . . Prince Arthur
sonne Cupid
Mart Mars, god of war and lover of Venus
Goddesse . . . bright Queen Elizabeth
Phoebus lamps the sun
true . . . type Gloriana, symbol of Queen Elizabeth
dearest dred object of greatest awe

Edmund Spenser, *The Faerie Queene*, in *The Literature of Renaissance England*, eds. John Hollander and Frank Kermode. New York and London: Oxford University Press, 1973.

Document 19: Marlowe's Mighty Lines

In Christopher Marlowe's most famous play, Doctor Faustus, *an old man encourages Faustus to repent of his pact with the devil, but Mephistophilis threatens Faustus with dismemberment, so Faustus reconfirms his deal with Satan. In one of the most memorable passages of the play, Faustus asks Mephistophilis to conjure Helen of Troy. When Faustus kisses the conjured Helen, he confirms the loss of his soul.*

   Old Man. Oh, stay, good Faustus, stay thy desperate steps!
I see an angel hover o'er thy head,

And, with a vial full of precious grace,
Offers to pour the same into thy soul:
Then call for mercy, and avoid despair.

    Faust. O friend, I feel
Thy words to comfort my distressed soul!
Leave me a while to ponder on my sins.

    Old Man. Faustus, I leave thee; but with grief of heart,
Fearing the enemy of thy hapless soul.   [*Exit.*

    Faust. Accursed Faustus, where is mercy now?
I do repent; and yet I do despair:
Hell strives with grace for conquest in my breast:
What shall I do to shun the snares of death?

    Meph. Thou traitor, Faustus, I arrest thy soul
For disobedience to my sovereign lord:
Revolt, or I'll in piecemeal tear thy flesh.

    Faust. I do repent I e'er offended him.
Sweet Mephistophilis, entreat thy lord
To pardon my unjust presumption,
And with my blood again I will confirm
The former vow I made to Lucifer.

    Meph. Do it, then, Faustus, with unfeigned heart,
Lest greater dangers do attend thy drift.

[FAUSTUS *stabs his arm, and writes on a paper with his blood.*

    Faust. Torment, sweet friend, that base and aged man.
That durst dissuade me from thy Lucifer,
With greatest torments that our hell affords.

    Meph. His faith is great; I cannot touch his soul;
But what I may afflict his body with
I will attempt, which is but little worth.

    Faust. One thing, good servant, let me crave of thee,
To glut the longing of my heart's desire,—
That I may have unto my paramour
That heavenly Helen which I saw of late,
Whose sweet embraces may extinguish clean
Those thoughts that do dissuade me from my vow,
And keep my oath I made to Lucifer.

    Meph. This, or what else, my Faustus shall desire,
Shall be perform'd in twinkling of an eye.

Enter HELEN *again, passing over the stage between two* Cupids.

    Faust. Was this the face that launch'd a thousand ships,
And burnt the topless towers of Ilium?—

Sweet Helen, make me immortal with a kiss.—

[She kisses him.

Her lips suck forth my soul: see where it flies!—
Come, Helen, come, give me my soul again.
Here will I dwell, for heaven is in these lips,
And all is dross that is not Helena.   *[Enter* Old Man.
I will be Paris, and for love of thee,
Instead of Troy, shall Wittenberg be sack'd;
And I will combat with weak Menelaus,
And wear thy colours on my plumed crest:
Yea, I will wound Achilles in the heel,
And then return to Helen for a kiss.
O, thou art fairer than the evening's air
Clad in the beauty of a thousand stars;
Brighter art thou than flaming Jupiter
When he appear'd to hapless Semele;
More lovely than the monarch of the sky
In wanton Arethusa's azured arms;
And none but thou shalt be my paramour!

[Exeunt FAUSTUS, HELEN *and* Cupids.

   Old Man. Accursed Faustus, miserable man,
That from thy soul exclud'st the grace of Heaven,
And fliest the throne of his tribunal-seat!

Christopher Marlowe, *Doctor Faustus* in *Christopher Marlowe, Five Plays*, ed. Havelock Ellis.
New York: Hill and Wang, 1956.

Document 20: Prologue to *Romeo and Juliet*

Shakespeare's Romeo and Juliet *was immediately popular and is justly famous for its lyrical quality. The prologue to the play, spoken by the Chorus, is written in the form of a sonnet. These fourteen line poems were exceptionally popular throughout the 1590s.*

[THE PROLOGUE]

[Enter *Chorus.*]

   Chor. Two households, both alike in dignity,
In fair Verona, where we lay our scene,
From ancient grudge break to new mutiny,
Where civil blood makes civil hands unclean.
From forth the fatal loins of these two foes
A pair of star-crossed lovers take their life,
Whose misadventured piteous overthrows

Doth with their death bury their parents' strife.
The fearful passage of their death-marked love,
And the continuance of their parents' rage,
Which, but their children's end, naught could remove,
Is now the two hours' traffic of our stage,
The which if you with patient ears attend,
What here shall miss, our toil shall strive to mend.

William Shakespeare, *Romeo and Juliet* (1594–95), Folger Shakespeare Library edition. Eds. Louis B. Wright and Virginia A. LaMar. New York: Washington Square Press, 1959.

Document 21: Ben Jonson's Praise for Shakespeare

The following poem was written by Shakespeare's friend and rival, Ben Jonson. It was prefixed to the First Folio, the earliest published collection of Shakespeare's plays. Shakespeare's fellow actors Henry Condell and John Hemings prepared the collection in 1623, seven years after Shakespeare's death.

To the Memory of My Beloved,
the Author Mr. William Shakespeare:°

  and What He Hath Left Us

To draw no envy (Shakespeare) on thy name,
  Am I thus ample° to thy book, and fame,
While I confess thy writings to be such
  As neither Man nor Muse can praise too much.
'Tis true, and all men's suffrage.° But these ways
  Were not the paths I meant unto thy praise:
For seeliest° ignorance on these may light,
  Which, when it sounds at best, but echoes right;
Or blind affection, which doth ne'er advance
  The truth, but gropes, and urgeth all by chance;
Or crafty malice might pretend this praise,
  And think to ruin, where it seemed to raise.
These are, as some infamous bawd or whore,
  Should praise a matron. What could hurt her more?
But thou art proof against them, and indeed
  Above the ill fortune of them, or the need,
I, therefore will begin. Soul of the age!
  The applause! delight! the wonder of our stage!

To the Memory . . . Shakespeare prefixed to
the Shakespeare First Folio of 1623
ample liberal

suffrage consent (as by vote)
seeliest silliest

My Shakespeare, rise; I will not lodge thee by
 Chaucer or Spenser, or bid Beaumont lie
A little further, to make thee a room:°
 Thou art a monument without a tomb,
And art alive still, while thy book doth live,
 And we have wits to read, and praise to give.
That I not mix thee so, my brain excuses,
 I mean with great, but disproportioned muses;
For, if I thought my judgment were of years,
 I should commit thee surely with thy peers,
And tell, how far thou didst our Lyly° outshine,
 Or sporting Kyd,° or Marlowe's mighty line.
And though thou hadst small Latin and less Greek,°
 From thence to honour thee, I would not seek
For names; but call forth thundering Aeschylus,
 Euripides and Sophocles° to us,
Paccuvius, Accius,° him° of Cordova dead,
 To life again, to hear thy buskin° tread,
And shake a stage: Or, when thy socks° were on,
 Leave thee alone, for the comparison
Of all that insolent Greece or haughty Rome
 Sent forth, or since did from their ashes come.
Triumph, My Britain, thou hast one to show,
 To whom all scenes of Europe homage owe.
He was not of an age, but for all time!
 And all the muses still were in their prime,
When like Apollo he came forth to warm
 Our ears, or like a Mercury to charm!
Nature herself was proud of his designs,
 And joyed to wear the dressing of his lines!
Which were so richly spun and woven so fit,
 As,° since, she will vouchsafe no other wit:
The merry Greek, tart Aristophanes,°

make thee a room in Westminster Abbey, where all these poets are ceremoniously entombed

Lyly See Headnote on John Lyly.

Kyd Thomas Kyd (1558–94), author of heavy melodrama; "sporting" is a sarcastic pun on "kidding"

small Latin and less Greek as compared with Jonson's own massive classical learning; as compared with our own, he had a good knowledge of Latin

Aeschylus, Euripides and Sophocles the three great Greek tragedians

Paccuvius, Accius Roman tragedians

him Seneca, Roman tragic poet and philosopher who strongly influenced Elizabethan dramatists; he was born, and died, at Corduba

buskin emblematic high boot of tragedy, worn by actors in the classical drama

socks the low shoes or slippers of comedy

As that

Aristophanes great Greek comic playwright

Neat Terence,° witty Plautus, now not please,
But antiquated, and deserted lie
    As they were not of nature's family.
Yet must I not give nature all: thy art,
    My gentle Shakespeare, must enjoy a part,
For though the poet's matter nature be,
    His art doth give the fashion; and that he
Who casts° to write a living line, must sweat
    (Such as thine are), and strike the second heat
Upon the muses' anvil, turn the same
    (And himself with it), that he thinks to frame,
Or for the laurel, he may gain a scorn;
    For a good poet's made, as well as born.
And such wert thou. Look how the father's face
    Lives in his issue; even so, the race
Of Shakespeare's mind, and manners brightly shines
    In his well turne'd, and true-filèd lines:
In each of which, he seems to shake a lance,°
    As brandished at the eyes of ignorance.
Sweet Swan of Avon!° what a sight it were
    To see thee in our waters yet appear,
And make those flights upon the banks of Thames,
    That so did take Eliza° and our James!
But stay, I see thee in the hemisphere
    Advanced and made a constellation there!
Shine forth, thou star of poets, and with rage°
    Or influence,° chide, or cheer the drooping stage;
Which, since thy flight from hence, hath mourned like night,
    And déspairs day, but for thy volume's light.

Terence with Plautus, greatest and most influential Roman comedians
casts sets out
shake a lance shake a spear (an old gag)
Swan of Avon He makes Shakespeare a swan
because that most noble and serene of birds,
"fair, upward and direct" as Jonson puts it
elsewhere, in flight, was reputed to sing mag-
nificently at its death; this poem celebrates a
posthumous volume of Shakespeare's works,
and its metamorphic image is that of the con-
stellations Cygnus (as the lyre of Orpheus, in
classical tradition, became Lyra).
Eliza Queen Elizabeth
rage rapture or enthusiasm
influence the way stars affected human lives

Ben Jonson, "To the Memory of My Beloved, the Author Mr. William Shakespeare" in *The Literature of Renaissance England*, eds. John Hollander and Frank Kermode. New York and London: Oxford University Press, 1973.

Chronology

1509–1547
Henry VIII, Elizabeth's father, reigns as the king of England.

1533
Elizabeth is born on September 7.

1534
The Act of Supremacy officially proclaims Henry VIII the supreme head of the Church of England.

1547
Henry VIII dies; his son, Edward VI, becomes king of England.

1553
Edward VI dies; his half sister Mary is crowned Mary I of England.

1558
Mary dies; her half sister, Elizabeth I, ascends the throne.

1559
Parliament approves Elizabeth's title, the supreme governor of the Church of England; the Protestant Prayer Book is adopted; Elizabeth refuses an offer of marriage from Philip II of Spain.

1560
Elizabeth is dissuaded from marrying Lord Robert Dudley; Parliament acts to reform debased coinage.

1561
Shane O'Neill leads a rebellion in Ireland.

1562
Foreign debt is paid off and England's credit is restored; Elizabeth is ill with smallpox.

1563
Parliament adopts the Thirty-nine Articles, formally establishing the Anglican Church; plague rages in London.

1564
William Shakespeare and Christopher Marlowe are born.

1565
Charles, Grand Duke of Austria, offers marriage; Elizabeth refuses in 1566.

1567
Mary Stuart, Queen of Scots, abdicates her throne and flees to England; Mary's thirteen-month-old son is crowned King James VI of Scotland; O'Neill rebellion in Ireland ends; Shane O'Neill is defeated and killed.

1568
War with Spain is averted.

1569
The rebellion of the Northern Earls, who supported Mary, Queen of Scots, for queen, fails; eight hundred peasants are executed.

1570
Papal bull excommunicates Elizabeth.

1571
Marriage with the duke of Anjou, later Henry III of France, is proposed and dropped; marriage with the duke of Alencon, Anjou's younger brother, is proposed; Roberto Ridolfi's plot to depose Elizabeth and place Mary, Queen of Scots, on the throne is exposed.

1572
Robert Dudley, Earl of Leicester, defines the company of actors under his patronage as "Leicester's Men"; marriage negotiations with the duke of Alencon continue; Francis Drake undertakes the first piratical success against the Spanish in Panama.

1573
The attempt to colonize Ulster, the northern province of Ireland, is unsuccessful.

1576
The first public theater, simply called the Theatre, is built by James Burbage.

1577–1580
Francis Drake circumnavigates the globe and is knighted upon his return.

1580

Sir Philip Sidney initiates the English Literary Renaissance and writes *Defense of Poesie, Arcadia,* and *Atrophel and Stella;* John Lyly writes *Euphues.*

1582

The plague in London continues; William Gilbert proclaims English sovereignty over St. John's Island, Newfoundland, but dies on the return journey, so no English colony is actually established.

1584

Sir Walter Raleigh sends an exploratory expedition to the New World and claims the land from present-day Florida to Newfoundland for England; it is called Virginia in honor of the virgin queen, Elizabeth; John Lyly writes *Campaspe.*

1585

Elizabeth sends military aid to Dutch Protestants who are fighting for their independence from the Spanish Netherlands; Richard Grenville, Sir Walter Raleigh's cousin, leads the first Virginia voyage and establishes a colony of 107 men on Roanoke Island (it survives for a year); William Parry is implicated in a plot to assassinate Elizabeth and place Mary, Queen of Scots, on the throne.

1586

Elizabeth establishes a colony in Munster, the southern province of Ireland; Sir Philip Sidney dies after being wounded in the Battle of Zutphen in the Netherlands; Anthony Babington is implicated in a plot to assassinate Elizabeth and place Mary, Queen of Scots, on the throne.

1587

Mary Stuart, formerly Queen of Scots, is executed because of her supposed complicity in plots to assassinate Elizabeth; Thomas Kyd writes *The Spanish Tragedy;* Christopher Marlowe writes *Tamburlaine;* Sir Walter Raleigh launches a second colony at Roanoke Island under the leadership of Sir John White.

1588

The English defeat the Spanish Armada; the War with Spain will last until 1603; John Lyly writes *Endymion.*

1589

Lyly writes *Midas* and *Mother Bombie;* Marlowe writes *The Jew of Malta;* Robert Greene writes *Friar Bacon and Friar Bungay.*

1590

Sir John White returns to Roanoke Island with supplies and finds no trace of the settlers; Sir Edmund Spenser completes the first three books of *The Faerie Queene*.

1590–1603

Shakespeare emerges as the greatest literary figure in London; he completes his sonnet cycle, two long poems, two tetralogies of history plays, and the early tragedies and comedies, including *Romeo and Juliet*, *The Taming of the Shrew*, *A Midsummer Night's Dream*, *The Merchant of Venice*, *Much Ado About Nothing*, *As You Like It*, and *Hamlet*.

1592–1593

Christopher Marlowe writes *Doctor Faustus* and *Massacre at Paris*; plague in London closes the theaters; Marlowe is killed in Deptford.

1594

Poor harvests lead to hoarding and riots; Hugh O'Neill, Earl of Tyrone, leads an uprising in Ireland.

1595

Harvest failures continue to plague England; the Swan Theater is built.

1596

Harvest failures continue; Sir Francis Drake sails on a voyage to the West Indies and dies on the expedition; Sir Edmund Spenser revises the first three books and adds three more books to *The Faerie Queene*; Hugh O'Neill leads another uprising in Ireland that will last until 1603.

1598

Ben Jonson writes *Everyman in His Humor*.

1599

The Globe Theater is built; Thomas Dekker writes *Old Fortunatus* and *The Shoemaker's Holiday*; Ben Jonson writes *Everyman Out of His Humor*; Robert Devereux, Earl of Essex, is sent to Ireland to battle Hugh O'Neill, but his efforts fail; plague continues in London.

1600

The Fortune Theater is built; Thomas Heywood writes *The Four Prentices of London*; John Marston writes *Antonio's Revenge*.

1601
The 1601 Poor Law establishes a tax to finance relief for the "deserving poor," specifies punishment for beggars, and authorizes work plans for the unemployed; the earl of Essex leads an unsuccessful rebellion against the queen and is executed.

1603
Queen Elizabeth dies on March 24; James VI of Scotland becomes James I of England; the English defeat the Irish and Spanish forces in Ireland; James I negotiates a peace treaty with Spain, which ends the War with Spain in 1604.

1608–1617
William Camden writes his history of Elizabeth's reign; three parts of the *Annales Rerum Anglicarum et Hibernicarum Regnante Elizabetha* are published in Latin in 1615 and in English in 1625; the fourth part is published in Latin in 1625 and in English in 1629.

For Further Research

About Queen Elizabeth I

Susan Bassnett, *Elizabeth I: A Feminist Perspective*. New York: St. Martin's, 1988.

Christopher Haigh, *Elizabeth I*. London and New York: Longman, 1988.

Paul Johnson, *Elizabeth I: A Study in Power and Intellect*. London: Weidenfeld and Nicolson, 1974.

John E. Neale, *Queen Elizabeth*. New York: Harcourt, Brace, 1934.

Maria Perry, *The Word of a Prince: A Life of Elizabeth I from Contemporary Documents*. Rochester, NE: Boydell, 1990.

Lacey Baldwin Smith, *Elizabeth Tudor: Biography of a Queen*. Boston: Little, Brown, 1975.

Anne Somerset, *Elizabeth I*. London: Weidenfeld and Nicolson, 1991.

About Elizabethan England

Philippa Berry, *Of Chastity and Power: Elizabethan Literature and the Unmarried Queen*. New York: Routledge, 1989.

Patrick Collinson, *The Religion of Protestants: The Church in English Society, 1559–1625*. Oxford, England: Clarendon, 1982.

Robert D. Edwards, *Ireland in the Age of the Tudors*. New York: Barnes & Noble Books, 1977.

Richard L. Greaves, *Society and Religion in Elizabethan England*. Minneapolis: University of Minnesota Press, 1981.

Norman Jones, *The Birth of the Elizabethan Age*. Cambridge, MA: Blackwell, 1993.

Hugh Kearney, *Science and Change, 1500–1700*. New York: McGraw-Hill, 1971.

Arthur F. Kinney, ed., *Elizabethan Backgrounds: Historical Documents of the Age of Elizabeth I*. Hamden, CT: Archon Books, 1975.

Peter Lake and Maria Dowling, *Protestantism and the National Church in Sixteenth-Century England*. London and New York: Croom Helm, 1987.

Wallace T. MacCaffrey, *Elizabeth I: War and Politics, 1588–1603.* Princeton, NJ: Princeton University Press, 1992.

———, *Queen Elizabeth and the Making of Policy, 1572–1588.* Princeton, NJ: Princeton University Press, 1981.

———, *The Shaping of the Elizabethan Regime.* Princeton, NJ: Princeton University Press, 1968.

Garrett Mattingly, *The Armada.* Boston: Houghton Mifflin, 1959.

Eric Mercer, *English Art, 1553–1625.* Oxford, England: Clarendon, 1962.

Arnold O. Meyer, *England and the Catholic Church Under Queen Elizabeth.* Trans. J.R. McKee. New York: Barnes & Noble Books, 1967.

John E. Neale, *Elizabeth I and Her Parliaments.* 2 vols. New York: St. Martin's, 1957.

D.M. Palliser, *The Age of Elizabeth: England Under the Later Tudors, 1547–1603.* 2nd ed. London: Longman Group, 1992.

Gerald M. Pinciss and Roger Lockyer, eds., *Shakespeare's World: Background Readings in the English Renaissance.* New York: Continuum, 1989.

Mary Beth Rose, ed., *Women in the Middle Ages and the Renaissance: Literary and Historical Perspectives.* Syracuse, NY: Syracuse University Press, 1986.

J.A. Sharpe, *Early Modern England: A Social History, 1550–1760.* London: Edward Arnold, 1987.

Arthur J. Slavin, *The Tudor Age and Beyond: England from the Black Death to the End of the Age of Elizabeth.* Malabar, FL: R.E. Krieger, 1987.

Roy C. Strong, *The Cult of Elizabeth: Elizabethan Portraiture and Pageantry.* London: Thames and Hudson, 1977.

Robert Weimann, *Shakespeare and the Popular Tradition in the Theater.* Baltimore, MD: Johns Hopkins University Press, 1978.

Richard B. Wernham, *The Making of Elizabethan Foreign Policy, 1558–1603.* Berkeley and Los Angeles: University of California Press, 1980.

Louis B. Wright, *Middle-Class Culture in Elizabethan England.* New York: Octagon Books, 1980.

Works Consulted

Kenneth R. Andrews, *Trade, Plunder, and Settlement: Maritime Enterprise and the Genesis of the British Empire, 1480–1630*. Cambridge, England: Cambridge University Press, 1984.

Charles Boyce, *Shakespeare A to Z*. New York: Roundtable, 1990.

Robert Cowley, *What If?* New York: Berkley Books, 1999.

Susan Doran, *Monarchy and Matrimony: The Courtships of Elizabeth I*. London and New York: Routledge, 1996.

Charles M. Gray, *Renaissance and Reformation England, 1509–1714*. New York: Harcourt Brace Jovanovich, 1973.

John Guy, *Tudor England*. Oxford, England: Oxford University Press, 1988.

Christopher Haigh, ed., *The Reign of Elizabeth I*. Athens: University of Georgia Press, 1985.

Ben Jonson, "To the Memory of My Beloved, the Author Mr. William Shakespeare." Prefatory poem to the first folio of Shakespeare's plays, 1623.

Arien Mack, ed., *In Time of Plague*. New York: New York University Press, 1991

Jo McMurtry, *Understanding Shakespeare's England: A Companion for the American Reader*. Hamden, CT: Archon Books, 1989.

Sara Mendelson and Patricia Crawford, *Women in Early Modern England, 1550–1720*. Oxford, England: Clarendon, 1998.

Allardyce Nicoll, *The Elizabethans*. London: Cambridge University Press, 1957.

J.W. Robinson, *British Writers and Their Work: No. 8*. Lincoln: University of Nebraska Press, 1965.

Lacey Baldwin Smith, *This Realm of England, 1399–1688*, 7th ed. Lexington, MA: D.C. Heath, 1996.

Gary Waller, *English Poetry of the Sixteenth Century*. London and New York: Longman Group, 1986.

Alison Weir, *The Life of Elizabeth I*. New York: Ballantine, 1998.

Glynne Wickham, Herbert Berry, William Ingram, eds., *English Professional Theatre, 1530–1660*. Cambridge, England: Cambridge University Press, 2000.

Frederic A. Youngs Jr. et al., *The English Heritage*. Wheeling, IL: Harlan Davidson, 1999.

Index